OFF THE BEATEN PATH®
OHIO ➡

Help Us Keep This Guide Up to Date

We would love to hear from you concerning your experiences with this guide and how you feel it could be improved and kept up to date. Please send your comments and suggestions to:

editorial@GlobePequot.com

Thanks for your input, and happy travels!

THIRTEENTH EDITION

OFF THE BEATEN PATH® OHIO →

A GUIDE TO UNIQUE PLACES

GEORGE AND CAROL ZIMMERMANN
Revised and updated by Jackie Sheckler Finch

gpp®
travel

Guilford, Connecticut

All the information in this guidebook is subject to change. We recommend that you call ahead to obtain current information before traveling.

To buy books in quantity for corporate use
or incentives, call **(800) 962-0973**
or e-mail **premiums@GlobePequot.com.**

Project Editor: Lynn Zelem, Staci Zacharski
Layout: Joanna Beyer
Text design: Linda R. Loiewski
Maps: Equator Graphics © Morris Book Publishing, LLC

ISSN 1539-8196
ISBN 978-0-7627-9206-1

Printed in the United States of America
10 9 8 7 6 5 4 3 2 1

To my parents, Jack and Margaret Poynter, for instilling in me
the desire to travel. And to my first traveling buddies: my sisters,
Elaine Emmich, Jennifer Boyer, Juliette Maples, and Jeanine
Clifford; and my brothers, Jim Poynter and Joe Poynter.

My gratitude to my family for their encouragement:
Kelly Rose; Sean, Devin, Dylan, and Emma Rose; Stefanie,
Will, Trey, and Arianna Scott; and Logan, Olivia, and Grayson
Peters. And a special remembrance to my husband, Bill Finch,
who taught me how to value every day on this earth.

—Jackie Sheckler Finch

Contents

About the Authors

George Zimmermann is a vice president for travel marketing at the Michigan Economic Development Corporation. Having lived in Ohio for more than 20 years, he served as the chairman of the Ohio Bicentennial Commission. For seven years, George was the tourism director for the state of Ohio. Prior to his appointment in October 1991, he was bureau chief for the Ohio Public Radio/Public Television Statehouse Bureau. He worked in broadcasting for 20 years, primarily for public television stations in Texas and Ohio. He spent two years in Los Angeles editing situation comedies, including *The Jeffersons*.

Carol and George met when she, too, worked as a statehouse reporter. After producing public television programs and producing, reporting, and anchoring in commercial television, Carol Rapp Zimmermann was appointed to the post of assistant director of the Ohio Department of Youth Services in 1992. Carol earned her PhD in 2006 and has joined the faculty at Saginaw Valley State University. She and George married in 1989.

An inveterate traveler, George Zimmermann has authored two other travel guidebooks: *The Complete Guide to Cabins and Lodges in America's State and National Parks* and *Travel Writers Recommend America's Best Resorts*. He was prompted to write this guide when he moved to Ohio in 1979 and wanted information about Ohio's attractions. He roamed Ohio's back roads for two years researching the points of interest included in the first edition. Together George and Carol add their latest discoveries in subsequent editions.

About the Revisor

An award-winning journalist and photographer, Jackie Sheckler Finch has covered a wide array of topics, from birth to death, with all the joy and sorrow in between. She has written more than a dozen travel guidebooks and had articles published in numerous magazines and newspapers. She has been named the Mark Twain Travel Writer of the Year by Midwest Travel Writers a record five times— in 1998, 2001, 2003, 2007, and 2012—and is a member of the Society of American Travel Writers.

Jackie shares her home with Pepper, resident guard dog and entertainer. One of her greatest joys is taking to the road to find the fascinating people and places that wait over the hill and around the next bend.

Acknowledgments

Thanks to the Ohio Division of Travel and Tourism, the Ohio Department of Natural Resources, and the Ohio Historical Society for providing supplemental information and materials about many of the places described in this book. Their cooperation made researching *Ohio Off the Beaten Path* a productive and enjoyable endeavor.

I'm grateful to Tracee Williams, Amy Lyons, Staci Zacharski, and the friendly and professional staff at Globe Pequot Press for allowing me the pleasure of revising this book. Sincere thanks to my Globe Pequot Press project editor Lynn Zelem for her kindness and consideration.

Introduction

When I was a child, my parents loved to pile all of us kids in the station wagon and take off for a weekend drive. Usually Mom did the driving and she didn't have any particular destination in mind. We would just drive through the countryside and along the rivers, stopping at little roadside stands and mom-and-pop stores to pick up pickled bologna, crackers, cheese, and other goodies for lunch at a roadside park. That was my first introduction to my birth state, probably a big part of why I became a travel writer and why I keep Ohio so close to my heart. I hope you'll come along on a trip off the beaten path with me to see some of the wealth that Ohio has to offer.

Ohio is an excellent state to explore—it has breathtaking natural beauty, a rich historical heritage, countless fine restaurants, and varied and unique overnight lodging. *Ohio Off the Beaten Path* exposes the reader to Ohio's best—from rolling pastoral farmland to rugged wooded cliffs and gorges, from restored canal towns and gristmills to country inns and working historical farms. After years of researching and traveling the state, I can only conclude that Ohio offers a wealth of opportunities for recreation, for appreciating the history that shaped its present and future, and for pleasurable excursions to suit any tastes or interests.

Most of the destinations described in this book, be they historical, culinary, or recreational, are located away from interstate highways and major metropolitan areas—an indication of our preference for scenic roads and picturesque towns and villages (traveling by interstate highway just does not provide the enjoyment of winding through forests and cresting hills on a narrow, two-lane country road). To take full advantage of *Ohio Off the Beaten Path,* you might find it handy to have an Ohio highway map. The Ohio Division of Travel and Tourism will mail you a map at no charge if you call (800) BUCKEYE (282-5393). The Division of Travel and Tourism can also provide another valuable service—confirmation of specific information on thousands of sites and attractions around the state.

Although every effort has been made to ensure that addresses, phone numbers, rates, hours, and seasons of the places described in this book are accurate at the time of publication, establishments do change owners or hours of operation, relocate, and even close. For this reason, I advise taking advantage of the state's toll-free service to verify important information before making that two- or three-hour drive. Another excellent resource is the Division of Travel and Tourism's website, discoverohio.com, which includes links to hundreds of other Ohio tourism websites.

Whether spending a week, a weekend, or just an afternoon traveling to a new destination, you will probably find, as I did, that Ohio's friendly people and splendid countryside make any trip that much more rewarding. And if you have yet to experience the state's historic and recreational opportunities, I believe you will be impressed and amazed by all Ohio has to offer.

Ohio Facts

- **Nickname:** Buckeye State

- **Capital:** Columbus

- **Population:** 11,544,225

- **Admitted to Union:** Ohio became the 17th state when it was admitted on February 19, 1803.

- **Major Cities and Populations:** Columbus, 797,434; Cleveland, 393,806; Cincinnati, 296,223; Toledo, 286,038; Akron, 198,402 Dayton, 142,148

- **Famous Residents:** William Henry Harrison, Ulysses S. Grant, Rutherford B. Hayes, James Garfield, Benjamin Harrison, William McKinley, William Howard Taft, Warren G. Harding, Harriet Beecher Stowe, James Thurber, George A. Custer, Johnny Appleseed, Wilbur and Orville Wright, Neil Armstrong, John Glenn, Charles Goodyear, John D. Rockefeller, Thomas Edison, Clark Gable, Bob Hope, Langston Hughes, Woody Harrelson, Rob Lowe, Paul Newman, Annie Oakley, Roy Rogers, Martin Sheen, Dean Martin, Drew Carey

- **Travel Information:** Contact the Ohio Division of Travel and Tourism at (800) BUCKEYE (282-5393) or discoverohio.com.

- **State Parks:** Contact Ohio State Parks at (614) 265-6561, (800) AT-A-PARK, or ohiodnr.com.

- **State Song:** "Beautiful Ohio"

- **State Rock Song:** "Hang On Sloopy"

- **State Wildflower:** White trillium

- **State Flower:** Red carnation

- **State Bird:** The cardinal

- **State Tree:** The buckeye

- **State Animal:** White-tailed deer

- **State Motto:** "With God All Things Are Possible"

Cuyahoga Valley

Tranquil, stream-fed Chippewa Lake provides the setting for an outstanding country dining establishment, the **Oaks Lakeside.** Eight acres of tall trees surround this rambling former estate, which rests a stone's throw from the water. Railroad industrialist J. F. Townsend remodeled this former farmhouse in 1914, using it to entertain such captains of industry as J. Pierpont Morgan. Townsend dubbed the place Five Oaks for the semicircle of oak trees that graced the front of the home at the time.

Don Casper and Al Hitchins purchased the Medina County property in 1961 and earned a reputation for an innovative menu and an impressive kitchen. In the summer of 2004, Johnny and Audrey Pollizi joined with Don's family to maintain the family's tradition of gracious elegance and outstanding cuisine. Each of the 6 dining areas has its own distinct character, and the large windows allow a view of the spacious patio—a perfect spot for a cocktail or after-dinner drink—and the gazebo at water's edge.

NORTHEAST OHIO

Dinner at the Oaks Lakeside includes dishes such as rack of lamb, pork Provençal, shrimp verde chicken, grilled filet mignon, lavender strip steak, and pistachio-crusted lamb, which is pan-seared lamb rib chops and rosemary-pistachio pesto wrapped in prosciutto with lemon scallion oil. Seafood fans can choose from wild-caught grilled salmon, sautéed walleye, and poached scampi.

A fine dinner salad distinguishes a quality restaurant from an ordinary one, and an Oaks Classic salad comes brimming with mixed greens, toasted pecans, dried cranberries, citrus vanilla vinaigrette, and Danish blue cheese. A nice variety of small plates includes the tasty sea scallops with gratin creamed spinach and crispy prosciutto. The lodge's luxurious desserts include tiramisu, chocolate mint torte, fallen chocolate soufflé and bread pudding with whiskey sauce. From the fresh flowers and stylish decor (the

BEST ATTRACTIONS

Oaks Lakeside

Hickories Museum

Allen Memorial Art Museum

Crawford Auto Aviation Museum

Cleveland Rock and Roll Hall of Fame and Museum

Hale Farm and Village

Blossom Music Center

Akron Art Museum

Stan Hywet Hall

Perkins Stone Mansion

John Brown House

Portage House

Kent State University Museum

Youngstown Historical Center of Industry and Labor

Butler Institute of American Art/ Arms Family Museum of Local History

Mill Creek MetroParks

The Welshfield Inn

Middlefield Cheese House

Burton Sugar Camp

Century Village

Richards Maple Products

Alpine Valley Ski Area

Holden Arboretum

Lake Metroparks Farmpark

Debonne Vineyards

Grand River Cellars

lodge has won several awards for interior design) to the culinary expertise, the Oaks Lakeside rates high marks.

The Oaks Lakeside is at 5878 Longacre Ln., Chippewa Lake; (330) 769-2601, (800) 922-5736; theoakslodge.com. Open Wed through Sat from 5 p.m. to closing, Sun from 2 p.m. to closing. Live entertainment is offered Thur and Fri evening June through Aug.

Medina County is also the location of a unique annual occurrence—Ohio's equivalent of the swallows returning to Capistrano. Each year on March 15, 75 turkey vultures come home to roost in trees by the cliffs and caverns of Whipp's Ledges near Hinckley. With clocklike regularity, the buzzards have returned to this summer home for more than 150 years. Hinckley townspeople mark the occasion with celebrations on the first Sunday after March 15, when a "buzzard breakfast" is served.

birthplace of aluminum

We have Charles M. Hall to thank for a world full of aluminum siding and aluminum everything else. Born in Thompson on December 6, 1863, Hall moved with his family to Oberlin. Along with a country full of scientists, he had been trying to find a cheap way to make aluminum; Hall did his experiments in an old woodshed while still in high school.

Hall attended Oberlin College, where he continued to experiment. Eight months after graduating, the 22-year-old discovered the process he and the others had been seeking. After a patent dispute with a French scientist claiming the same invention, Hall secured capital from Andrew Mellon and built what became the American Aluminum Company. Hall died in 1914, leaving a substantial bequest to Oberlin College.

The architect was Arthur Oviatt; the owner, Arthur Lovett Garford. The result of their vision: one of the finest residences in northeast Ohio, now the *Hickories Museum.*

Construction on this massive 19-room stone-and-shingle home began in 1894 and cost Garford $100,000. On the large corner lot stand many of the original shagbark hickory trees from which came the name Hickories.

Within its walls are Tiffany-style windows, 6 fireplaces, 12 built-in seats, and approximately 60 carved faces. Features are the grand staircase, pier mirrors, a Gothic chapel, and a bull moose head given to Garford by Teddy Roosevelt. An opulent Victorian bathroom as well as a restored master bedroom and guest room can be seen on the second floor.

Garford was a young banker when he hopped on a newfangled high-wheeled vehicle, the bicycle. A rough ride on the bike's hard seat launched a new career for A. L.—he invented a padded bicycle seat, which made him a millionaire. His interests would grow to include such diverse items as golf balls, telephone parts, lighting fixtures, and steel; he also became involved in car and truck manufacturing, mining, and publishing.

The Hickories Museum is at 509 Washington Ave., Elyria; (440) 322-3341; lchs.org. Open for tours Tues through Fri, 1 to 4 p.m.; Sat, 1 to 3 p.m. Admission: adults $5, children (ages 13 to 18) $3; children (ages 6 to 12) $2.

Founded in 1917, the *Allen Memorial Art Museum* at Oberlin College is ranked as one of the finest college or university collections in the nation. Cass Gilbert designed the original building; he also designed four other buildings for Oberlin College between 1907 and 1931. The museum's contemporary addition, designed by Robert Venturi, opened in 1977.

The museum's collection consists of some 11,000 objects from ancient Egypt to contemporary America. Collection highlights include Dutch and Flemish paintings of the 17th century, European art of the late 19th and 20th centuries, and contemporary American art. Of particular note are the Mary A. Ainsworth collection of Japanese woodblock prints, the Charles Martin Hall collection of Islamic carpets, the Joseph and Enid Bissett collection of modern European paintings, and a comprehensive collection of Old Master prints, including Rembrandt and Dürer. The museum also has a growing collection of African and African-American art. In addition to the galleries, a number of sculptures can be found on the museum's well-manicured grounds. Be sure to tour the Frank Lloyd Wright home on the grounds—built in 1950, this is an example of the compact Usonian houses he created for middle-class families.

The Allen Memorial Art Museum is at 87 N. Main St., Oberlin; (440) 775-8665; oberlin.edu/allenart. Open Tues through Sat, 10 a.m. to 5 p.m.; Sun, 1 to 5 p.m. No admission charge. Tours of the Frank Lloyd Wright Usonian House are offered the first and third Sunday of each month, noon to 5 p.m. Admission is $5 for adults.

Take the high road or take the low road, but those wishing for a wee bit of Scotland in Ohio should take to the road in late June to celebrate the *Ohio Scottish Game Weekend* in Oberlin. Visitors can enjoy the colorful Scottish games and the traditional dress in the parade of clan tartans. In addition there is a competition among the pipe and drum corps. The event is held in late June in Oberlin. Visit ohioscottishgames.com for information.

One of the best car collections you'll find is the ***Crawford Auto Aviation Museum*** in Cleveland. The collection tells the history of technological as well as stylistic changes and developments in the auto industry. With some 150 cars in the collection, the vehicles range from the famous to the obscure, from a Model T to a modern Jaguar. For example, the visitor can admire a rare 1897 Panhard et Lavassor, which was the first automobile to enclose the passenger area and protect the occupants from the elements. The car enthusiast can also view the 1982 Indy car driven by Ohio's own Bobby Rahal.

Since car manufacturing is now centered on a few dominant companies, many people may not know just how many small automotive manufacturers existed in the early 1900s. The Crawford Auto Aviation Museum highlights the remarkable number of carmakers that were located in the Cleveland area.

Between 1898 and 1931 more than 80 makes of cars were produced here, including the Winton Bullet. Alexander Winton was the leading automotive pioneer in Cleveland, selling his first car in 1898. The Winton Bullet held the land-speed record in 1902 and is on display in the museum.

Along with the car collection, the museum also features bikes, motorcycles, and aircraft. The centerpiece of the aviation collection is a 1912 Curtiss Hydroaeroplane, which was once piloted by Cleveland aviator Al Engel.

This museum is part of a larger complex, the Western Reserve Historical Society's University Circle. This campus-like setting also houses a history museum in a turn-of-the-20th-century mansion. A visitor to this museum can go on a mansion tour and view a costume collection and various special displays. Also nearby is the renowned Cleveland Museum of Art. The Western Reserve Historical Society's library is one of the best genealogical resources in the nation.

The Crawford Auto Aviation Museum is located at 10825 East Blvd., Cleveland; (216) 721-5722; wrhs.org. Open Tues through Sat, 10 a.m. to 5 p.m., Sun, noon to 5 p.m. Admission: adults $10; seniors $9; children (ages 3 to 12) $5. Parking in the museum lot costs $5.

The ***Dittrick Museum of Medical History*** presents the medical history of Cleveland and the Western Reserve. Exhibits trace advances in diagnostic technology from the stethoscope to the X-ray machine.

Visitors inspect an array of early surgical instruments, bloodletting tools, and the museum's collection of microscopes. Also featured are two complete and furnished doctors' offices, one from 1880 and the other from 1930.

The Dittrick Museum of Medical History is on the third floor of the Allen Memorial Medical Library at 11000 Euclid Ave., Cleveland; (216) 368-3648; cwru.edu/artsci/dittrick/museum. Open Mon through Fri, 9 a.m. to 4:30 p.m. No admission charge.

Critics have and will continue to debate the location of the birthplace of rock 'n' roll, but there's no debate that Cleveland has provided a home for rock for the ages with the outstanding *Rock and Roll Hall of Fame and Museum.* The spectacular $92 million facility overlooks Lake Erie. Designed by renowned architect I. M. Pei, the 150,000-square-foot building consists of bold geometric forms and dramatic spaces anchored by a 162-foot tower.

Rock fans of all ages will discover memorabilia from all phases of rock 'n' roll, from its birth in the 1950s to its explosion in the 1960s and its evolution to the present. Among the highlights of this most extensive collection are John Lennon's Sgt. Pepper uniform and the Rickenbacker guitar he used at the Shea Stadium concert, the black leather stage outfit Elvis wore during his 1968 "comeback" TV special, Tina Turner's "Acid Queen" costume from the movie *Tommy,* Jim Morrison's Cub Scout uniform, and Jimi Hendrix's handwritten lyrics to "Purple Haze." The original recording equipment from Sam Phillips's Memphis Recording Service is on display, along with Janis Joplin's psychedelic Porsche convertible.

Music plays throughout the museum, except in the actual top-floor Hall of Fame. Film and video presentations trace the history of rock

northolmstedto andfrom

Talk about "necessity being the mother of invention"! The mayor of North Olmsted was given one week's notice that the railway connecting his community with Cleveland was calling it quits. Mayor Charles Seltzer had until midnight February 28, 1931, to find a way to get 150 of his constituents to work.

His solution: that North Olmsted start a municipal bus line, the first in Ohio. The city council concurred, and they all scrambled to purchase two used buses and two sets of license plates and hire two drivers. At 5 a.m. March 1, two freshly painted red-and-white coaches hit the road, changing Ohio transportation history.

and offer snapshots of its various incarnations and tangents. If you are or ever have been a fan of rock 'n' roll, this is a must-see.

The Rock and Roll Hall of Fame and Museum is at 1100 Rock and Roll Blvd., Cleveland; (216) 781-7625; rockhall.com. Open daily, 10 a.m. to 5:30 p.m. (until 9 p.m. on Wed). Admission: adults $22; children (ages 9 to 12) $13.

Looking for an unusual tour or for a unique setting for lunch or dinner? Then be ready to board the ***Goodtime III.*** This 1,000-passenger boat offers two-hour sightseeing tours Tuesday through Sunday and has provided a great way to see Cleveland since 1958. As you cruise by, your guide will help you learn more about the area. The boat offers indoor and outdoor seating so you can tour even if the weather is not perfect. Along with sightseeing you can also enjoy a box or buffet lunch. Dance cruises sail on Friday and Saturday evenings, dinner cruises on Saturday, and Rush Hour Cruises on Friday nights. A Sunday brunch cruise is a popular option.

Goodtime III is at 825 E. 9th St. Pier, Cleveland; (216) 861-5110; goodtimeiii.com. The summer sailing schedule runs from June 15 through Labor Day; limited sailings in May and Sept. Tours are available Tues through Sat at noon and 3 p.m.; Sun, 1 and 3:30 p.m. Dinner and dance cruises are offered Fri and Sat. Tour rates: adults $17; children (ages 5 to 12) $9; luncheon cruise: adults $29.95, children (ages 2 to 12) $22.95; dinner and dance cruise: adults $49.95; Sunday brunch: adults $32, children (ages 2 to 12) $22.95. For the luncheon or dinner and dance cruise, be sure to call ahead for reservations. Ask about departure times for the evening cruise.

For more cruising and dining, board the ***Nautica Queen.*** Buffet lunches, brunches, and dinners are part of the sightseeing experience aboard this pleasure cruise. You glide by the "Flats" and parks, and view the Cleveland skyline while munching on a wide variety of salads, entrees, and desserts. There are outdoor observation decks so you can enjoy the sun or stars during your approximately two-hour voyage. The dining areas are enclosed so that a bit of foul weather won't put a damper on the dining experience. When you call for information you might want to ask about the *Nautica's* special events. You might enjoy one of their theme cruises, or have the staff plan something special for a birthday or anniversary.

The *Nautica Queen* is located at 1153 Main Ave. (on the West Bank of the Flats), Cleveland; (216) 696-8888, (800) 837-0604; nauticaqueen.com.

ALSO WORTH SEEING

Great Lakes Science Center,
Cleveland

Cleveland Museum of Art

Cleveland MetroPark Zoo

Cleveland Children's Museum

Sails Apr through Dec. Lunch cruises: Mon through Fri, noon; Sat, 11 a.m.; Sun, 1 p.m. Dinner cruises: Mon through Thurs, 7 p.m.; Fri and Sat, 7:30 p.m. Lunch cruise prices: adults $28.12; children (age11 and under) $18.73. Dinner cruise prices: Mon through Thurs, adults $35.16, children (age 11 and under) $22.25; Fri and Sat, adults $45, children (age 11 and under) $26.94. Sunday brunch prices: adults $35.16; children (age 11 and under) $22.25. All cruises include unlimited buffet, coffee, tea, or iced tea, and musical entertainment.

The North Union Colony of Shakers was established here in 1822 and thrived for 67 years. This unique religious group of more than 200 people stressed social justice, freedom, and equality of men and women. They built their own school and cared for orphans. They farmed and sold their apple products, herbs, and high-quality, simple handmade furniture. When the community declined, the Shakers' property was sold to a real estate company and developed to become Shaker Heights.

The *Shaker Historical Museum* occupies a Tudor-style mansion facing Horseshoe Lake. The Shaker Historical Society presents exhibits about the Shakers, the development of Shaker Heights by the Van Sweringen brothers, as well as seasonal displays, programs, and events. The museum shop offers books, herbs, candles, cards, and Shaker-style boxes and carriers.

The Shaker Historical Museum is located at 16740 S. Park Blvd., Shaker Heights; (216) 921-1201, (800) 860-6078; ohiohistory.org/places/shaker. Open Tues through Fri, 11 a.m. to 5 p.m., and Sun, 2 to 5 p.m. Admission: adults $4; children (ages 6 to 18) $2.

Pigs, ponies, and a gaggle of geese are likely to greet visitors to the *Stearns Homestead.* The Parma Area Historical Society, mostly with a lot of volunteer labor, has saved a little chunk of rural Ohio and preserved the Stearns Homestead in the midst of urban growth. The Stearns family built

Twins Day Festival

You'll be seeing double, but that's to be expected if you visit Twinsburg for the annual Twins Day Festival. What better place than Twinsburg to host a national gathering of those special siblings we call twins?

Matched sets of brothers and sisters come from all over the nation to gather for this celebration of duality. Infants and oldsters and in-betweeners all attend. Some are so close in looks and dress, down to the hat, the socks, or the tie tack, that you have to wonder how even their mothers and fathers tell them apart.

Triplets, quadruplets, and beyond are also welcome. To add to the fun of celebrating these look-alikes, there's a parade, a fireworks display, arts and crafts, food, of course, and even a golf tournament (with identical twins on the course, keeping the scoring straight could be a challenge).

The Twins Day Festival is held first weekend in August in Twinsburg. For more information call (330) 425-3652 (or get your twin to call) or visit twinsday.org.

the farmhouse in 1855. When the Gibbs family bought the farm, they added a second house in 1919. A barn, which is tilting a little to the west, is home to an unlikely vehicle collection: a 1948 fire engine and a horse carriage once used by President William McKinley. The collection of farm animals delights visiting children, and volunteers sell feed so you can offer a treat to one of these four-legged inhabitants. There are also a variety of special events at the farm throughout the summer months, such as ice-cream socials and antiques markets.

Check out the Stearns County Store, where you can buy gifts, homemade crafts, old-fashioned candy, ice cream, and beverages. Items from the past are displayed on store shelves, giving the store a museum feel.

The Stearns Homestead is at 6975 Ridge Rd., Parma; (440) 845-9770; stearnshomestead.com. Open mid-May to mid-Oct, Sat and Sun, noon to 4 p.m. Admission and parking are free but donations are welcomed.

The Western Reserve region of Ohio was "reserved" for settlers moving west from Connecticut after the American Revolution. One of those settlers, Jonathan Hale, relocated his family in 1810, establishing a farm in the rolling acreage of what is today northern Summit County. The Hale property remained in the family until the death of Miss Clara Belle Ritchie, great-granddaughter of Jonathan, in 1956. She willed the farm to the Western Reserve Historical Society, stipulating that it be opened to the public so that as many people as possible could "be informed about the history and culture of the Western Reserve."

The history and culture of the region are faithfully preserved at the working *Hale Farm and Village.* Guides in period clothing help transport the visitor back to 1848. You will meet Jacob and Hannah Meredith, who will tell you about their prosperous dairy farm and life at their household in the mid-1800s. You will also have the opportunity to chat with the village founder and the town gossip to learn even more about the flavor of the place and the time. The color and scents of the mid-19th century are reflected in the gardens and in the arts on display around the village. You can watch glassblowing, spinning, weaving, candle and basket making, and even try your hand at making bricks.

Hale Farm and Village is in the 32,000-acre Cuyahoga Valley National Park at 2686 Oak Hill Rd., Bath; (330) 666-3711, (800) 589-9703; wrhs.org. Open May through Oct, Wed through Sun, 10 a.m. to 5 p.m. (shorter hours in the fall). Admission: adults $10; children (ages 3 to 12) $5.

Cuyahoga Valley National Park follows the Cuyahoga River for 22 miles between Akron and Cleveland. The park offers numerous hiking, nature, and bicycle trails, scenic overlooks, and picnic areas.

The Towpath Trail follows the historic route of the Ohio & Erie Canal, which was built between 1825 and 1832. This canal provided a transportation link between Cleveland, on Lake Erie, and Portsmouth, on the Ohio River, and opened Ohio to the eastern US. Prior to the canal, Ohio was a sparsely populated wilderness, where travel was difficult and the shipping of crops was nearly impossible.

Today hikers, joggers, and cyclists follow the same route once used by "canawlers." Locks and related structures are still visible, as you travel through forests, fields, and wetlands brimming with wildlife.

Information about all of the recreational opportunities and programs at this vast park are available at the 6 visitor centers: Canal Visitor Center, Boston Store, Hunt Farm Visitor Information Center, Happy Days Visitor Center, the Frazer House, and the Peninsula Depot. Or you can call (216) 524-1497 or visit the website at nps.gov/cuva. For information on the Cuyahoga Valley Scenic Railroad, call (800) 468-4070 or go to cvsr.com.

TOP ANNUAL EVENTS

Medina Ice Festival,
Medina, Feb;
(330) 952-0910

Burton Pancake Breakfast,
Burton, Mar;
(440) 834-4204;
burtonchamberofcommerce.org

Geauga County Maple Festival,
Chardon, Apr;
(440) 286-3007;
maplefestival.com

Blossom Time Festival,
Chagrin Falls, May;
(440) 247-6607;
cvcc.org/blossomtime.htm

Great American Rib Cook-off,
Cleveland, May;
(440) 247-2722;
cleveland.com/rib

Strawberry Festival and Craft Bazaar,
Jefferson, June;
(440) 576-0133;
jeffersonchamber.com

Ohio Scottish Games,
Oberlin, June;
(440) 942-6362;
ohioscottishgames.com

Lorain International Festival,
Lorain, June;
loraininternational.com

Rock and Soul Festival,
Cleveland, June;
(216) 781-7625;
rockhall.com

Festival of the Fish,
Vermilion, June;
(440) 967-4477;
vermilionchamber.net

Winter sports in the park include sledding, ice-skating, and cross-country skiing. Two complete ski centers, **Brandywine** in Sagamore Hills and **Boston Mills** in nearby Peninsula (both at 800-875-4241), serve downhill skiers with complete ski shops, lifts, instruction, and equipment rentals.

Nestled in 800 acres of rolling hills between Akron and Cleveland is one of America's premier outdoor cultural and entertainment complexes, **Blossom Music Center.** The summer home for the renowned Cleveland Orchestra, Blossom also attracts audiences for performances that range from jazz to rock 'n' roll.

The nation's top artists take the stage in the innovative pavilion, a fan-shaped open-air structure seating 5,281. Its enormous roof rises 94 feet

Shakespeare at Stan Hywet,
Akron, July/Aug;
(330) 673-8761;
ohioshakespeare.com

Port Fest,
Lorain, July;
(440) 204-2269;
lorainportauthority.com/calendar/
portfest.shtml

Civil War Encampment,
Bath, Aug;
(330) 666-3711, (800) 589-9703;
wrhs.org

Twins Festival,
Twinsburg, Aug;
(330) 425-3652;
twinsday.org

North Ridgeville Corn Festival,
North Ridgeville, Aug;
(440) 218-9802;
nrcornfest.org

Vintage Ohio Wine Festival,
Kirtland, Aug;
(800) 227-6972;
visitvintageohio.com

Woollybear Festival,
Vermilion, Sept;
(440) 967-4477;
vermilionchamber.net

Mantua Potato Festival,
Mantua, Sept;
(330) 274-0770,
mantuapotatofestival.com

Grape Jamboree,
Geneva, Sept;
grapejamboree.com

Ashtabula County Covered Bridge Festival,
Jefferson, Oct;
(440) 576-3769;
coveredbridgefestival.org

above the stage level (it's the largest shingled area in the country), creating a sound chamber requiring little or no electronic amplification for those seated in the pavilion.

Four acres of lawn on the gentle hillside provide outdoor seating for an additional 13,500 patrons. A unique computerized sound system has a delay feature that transmits the sound from speakers at precisely the moment the sound from the stage reaches the lawn audience, creating near-perfect listening conditions.

Artists perform almost every evening during the June-through-September season. A full-service restaurant is open on all concert nights. For information and a schedule of coming attractions, April through September you can phone the center at (330) 920-8040 or visit livenation.com.

The **Akron Art Museum** originally was housed in an 1899 Italian Renaissance-style structure that once served as the Akron post office. In 2007 the museum opened its new, magnificent Coop Himmelb(l)au–designed building just south of the original. This ultramodern structure provides a compelling contrast with the original museum. The permanent collection boasts more than 3,000 works from the mid-1800s to the present. Much of the collection is dedicated to contemporary painting and photography. Works by photographers Robert Frank, Margaret Bourke-White, and Harry Callahan are featured, along with the contemporary art of Andy Warhol, Frank Stella, and Carrie Mae Weems. The Myers Sculpture Court is an outdoor venue for large-scale sculpture as well as concerts during the spring and summer months. The museum also hosts traveling exhibitions throughout the year.

The Akron Art Museum is at One S. High St., Akron; (330) 376-9185; akronartmuseum.org. Open Wed through Sun, 11 a.m. to 5 p.m.; open until 9 p.m. on Thurs. Admission: adults $7; seniors $5; students $5. Free admission is offered on the third Thursday of every month. Constructed at an estimated cost of $2 million, Frank A. and Gertrude Seiberling's **Stan Hywet Hall** in Akron took four years to build and was completed in 1915. Frank Seiberling founded the Goodyear and Seiberling rubber companies, and this lavish 65-room mansion gives testimony to the personal wealth amassed by industrialists in that era.

Considered to be one of the finest examples of American Tudor revival architecture, Stan Hywet is patterned after three Tudor estates in England, with elements of each incorporated in the design of the structure. As is typical of Tudor buildings, windows, doors, chimneys, and roof peaks are asymmetrical and appear randomly placed. The name Stan Hywet means "stone quarry" in Anglo-Saxon, a reference to the sandstone quarry once located on the original 3,000-acre estate.

Molded plaster ceilings and hand-carved oak walls, both commonly used in English Tudor residences, can be found throughout the Seiberling home. The Seiberlings went to considerable trouble to make Stan Hywet as faithful as possible to the Tudor style; they concealed telephones behind wall coverings and installed 23 working fireplaces, even though the building is equipped with central heating. They also built in a rope elevator for hauling firewood from the basement to the upper floors.

Formal balls and other social functions were held in the large music room, which has 3 massive crystal chandeliers, 16 wall sconces, and a second-floor balcony for a small orchestra. The formal dining room seats 40, and an oil-on-canvas mural above the oak walls depicts Chaucer's *Canterbury Tales*. Rare American chestnut, a type of wood that's no longer available because of devastating blight, lines the walls of the billiard room.

The Seiberlings removed the paneling and fireplace from a room in an English manor house scheduled for demolition and installed these materials in the second-floor master bedroom. Also in their bedroom is an original Tudor canopy bed, ca. 1575. Throughout the tour, guides point out many of the outstanding pieces in the Seiberlings' priceless collection of antiques.

Formal gardens, woodlands crisscrossed with paths and trails, and splendid shrubbery surround Stan Hywet Hall. Clear stream water pours over a stone waterfall in a cool pond in the tall trees just behind the Seiberling mansion.

Stan Hywet Hall and Gardens is at 714 N. Portage Path, Akron; (330) 836-5533, (888) 836-5533; stanhywet .org. Open Apr through Dec, Tues through Sun, 10 a.m. to 6 p.m. Admission for self-guided manor house tour: adults $14; children (ages 6 to 17) $6; children (ages 5 and under) free. Admission closes at 4:30 p.m.

stanhywet/ shakespeare

The owners of the impressive Stan Hywet Hall were well known for their love of music and the performing arts. That love continues as the estate hosts Shakespeare at Stan Hywet each July.

Outdoor performances are held in the early evenings on the grounds of the great hall. Generally the performances are held on two consecutive weekends in July. The grand mansion and grounds also are the setting for other special activities, including art shows and teas on the terrace featuring period music and entertainment. For information on Shakespeare and other special events at Stan Hywet, call (330) 836-5533.

From Stan Hywet Hall, take Portage Path south for a drive past many fine old Akron homes and estates. If you continue south to the intersection of Copley Road and South Portage Path, you will find two museums.

The mansion of Colonel Simon Perkins was constructed adjacent to the historic Portage Path at Akron between the years 1835 and 1837. The home is an example of the Greek revival style, which had great influence on architecture during the early settlement of the Western Reserve. Built of native sandstone on the brow of a hill, the *Perkins Stone Mansion,* with its two-story portico, overlooks the city of Akron. Through the years, it has become recognized as one of the most imposing homes of northern Ohio.

Colonel Perkins was born to General and Mrs. Simon Perkins at Warren, Ohio, in 1805. His father organized the Western Reserve Bank in 1813, and, in connection with Paul Williams, founded the village of Akron in 1825.

Colonel Perkins, who served in the Ohio legislature and was an active promoter of the Cleveland, Zanesville & Cincinnati Railroad, purchased 115 acres of land on this site in 1832 for $1,300. Perkins and his wife, sister of the future governor of Ohio, David Tod, resided in Warren before moving to Akron in 1835. While the mansion was under construction, they lived in a small frame house, now known as the *John Brown House.*

allfiredup inbarberton

The unusually named Ohio Columbus Barber was a premier matchmaker, but he was not one involved in pairing couples for romance. No, Barber and his company, Diamond Match Company, made fire-starting matches, a quarter billion a day during the company's heyday.

Barber came from a family of match makers: His father made them, too, and peddled them. The younger Barber founded Diamond Match in 1880, and his success resulted in the creation of a new town, Barberton, which he conceived and promoted. He was known during his day as the "Match King."

Surrounded by more than 10 acres of beautiful grounds, the mansion today contains some of its original furnishings, as well as items connected with the early history of Summit County. Situated on the grounds are the original carriage house, a combination summer kitchen and laundry built in 1890, the original well—dug through 40 feet of sandstone—and a visitor center, previously the Perkins' woodshed.

Across the street is the John Brown House, so named to commemorate the residency of that abolitionist leader from 1844 to 1854. At the time, Brown was associated with Colonel Simon Perkins in the sheep and wool business. The original frame structure, to which several additions have been made, is believed to have been built around 1830. Inside is an exhibit that explains the importance of the canal to the development of Akron, as well as a replica of a canal boat captain's cabin.

Both museums are operated by the Summit County Historical Society, 550 Copley Rd., Akron; (330) 535-1120; summithistory.org. Tours are available by appointment Wed through Fri, at 1 and 3 p.m. Apr through Dec. Admission (to both museums): adults $6; children (ages 17 and under) and senior citizens $4.

Just up the street from the museums, Carol Pinnick offers bed-and-breakfast accommodations in her 1918 *Portage House.* Founded as a bed-and-breakfast by her parents in 1982, this three-story Tudor home provides a pleasant stop in a quiet, parklike setting for weary travelers.

Carol lives on the third floor; the second-floor bedrooms are available for guests. Downstairs, the large living room is a quiet place to relax or read the evening paper.

Depending on the number of guests in the house, Carol serves a full breakfast either at an island in the center of the kitchen or in the formal dining room. Breakfasts include eggs, bacon, a variety of fresh-from-the-oven breads, frittatas, and pancakes with homemade fruit syrup. Friendly people like Carol Pinnick and modest prices are why bed-and-breakfasts are increasingly popular throughout Ohio.

The Portage House is at 601 Copley Rd., Akron; (330) 535-1952; home.rr .com/portagehouse. Rates: $50 to $70 per night. Personal checks accepted.

Kay and Donna Vaughan have been farming in the Hartville area since the 1960s, and both quit their teaching jobs in the '70s to farm full-time. By 2000 their children had joined the operation, they purchased a 140-year-old barn and refurbished it, and the Maize Valley Farm Market opened for business. In 2005 the next expansion created what is now known as the *Maize Valley Winery.*

Today the Vaughan family farms 750 acres, including 200 acres of fruits and vegetables. Super-sweet corn and juicy tomatoes grow alongside cantaloupes, watermelons, peppers, green beans, squash, strawberries, raspberries, and blueberries.

The winery produces a crisp, dry, fruity Riesling, and a medium-bodied Chambourcin, a spicy dry red with hints of black cherries and raspberries balanced by soft tannins and toasted oak. The Maize Valley cabernet sauvignon is aged in American oak barrels and features rich currant and black-cherry flavors. The winery has come up with some unusual names, such as Hanky Panky Pink, a slightly sweetened wine made from the Catawba grape with a citrus finish. Among other selections, try the red table wine known as Red Neck Red or one of the many fun fruit wines produced here. The wines are already winning regional awards.

The Vaughans often stage special events at the winery, everything from a performance by an Elvis-tribute artist to hot-air balloons. The winery has live music every Friday and Saturday from 7:30 to 9:30 p.m. Fall harvest time means corn mazes and that the Pumpkin Cannon is locked and loaded—be sure not to park down range, or plan on a trip to the nearest car wash. Wagon rides around the property are popular with visitors, as is the petting pasture for younger guests.

The Maize Valley Winery is at 6193 Edison St. NE (OH 619), Hartville; (330) 877-8344; maizevalleywinery.com. Open Mon through Wed, 9 a.m. to 7 p.m.; Thurs until 9 p.m.; Fri and Sat until 10 p.m. Sun hours for the market are 10 a.m. to 4 p.m., but there are no wine sales. Shorter hours Nov through Apr.

Heritage Hills

Founded with an initial gift from Jerry Silverman and Shannon Rodgers, the **Kent State University Museum** opened its doors in 1985. Silverman and Rodgers, New York dress manufacturers, donated 4,000 costumes and accessories, almost 1,000 pieces of decorative art, and a 5,000-volume reference library. Today the collection consists of more than 20,000 pieces representing the major world cultures.

Highlights of the collection include the black velvet evening cape, trimmed with a band of crystals, worn by Joan Crawford at Truman Capote's Black and White Ball. Another favorite is the 18th-century English silk dress, in a style typical of the Spitalfields silk-weaving district in London. There's a magnificent uniform of the Chinese Imperial Palace Guard worn at the end of the Manchu dynasty around 1900 and a fancy blue silk ball gown from the French couture house of Balenciaga, ca. 1958.

A second gift to the museum was the Tarter/Miller collection of more than 200,000 pieces of collectible glass. A distinctive part of this collection is the Vaseline glass, so called because of its unusual yellow-green color. The recent acquisition of the Paige Palmer Collection of Ohio art pottery includes exquisite examples of Roseville, Weller, and Rookwood pieces.

The Kent State University Museum is in Rockwell Hall on the corner of East Main and South Lincoln Streets on the Kent State University campus, Kent; (330) 672-3450; kent.edu/museum. Open Wed, Fri, and Sat, 10 a.m. to 4:45 p.m.; Thurs, 10 a.m. to 8:45 p.m.; Sun, noon to 4:45 p.m. Admission: adults $5; seniors $4; students $3.

The history of the Mahoning Valley is the history of the iron and steel industries. Deposits of black coal suitable for blast furnaces were discovered near Youngstown in 1845, and by the 1850s the Valley was one of the nation's centers of iron production. As technology advanced, the Valley switched to steel production; the Ohio Steel Company, the area's first steel company, was organized in 1892.

Steel mill jobs attracted immigrants from eastern and southern Europe, as well as African Americans from the South. Working conditions for these laborers were appalling: typically 12-hour days, six or even seven days a week, in an environment of heavy machinery, poisonous gases, and open vats of molten steel. These conditions eventually led to the formation of the United Steelworkers of America in 1936.

Youngstown's steel production and employment soared during the middle of the 20th century, peaking in 1973. But just four years later, "Black Monday" hit the area on September 19, 1977, with the closing of Youngstown's Sheet and Tube's Campbell Works. Global changes in the steel market, labor-management disputes, and a depletion of high-grade ores all contributed to the death of the Valley's steel industry.

The ups and downs of this pivotal industry are presented at the **Youngstown Historical Center of Industry and Labor.** The museum's permanent exhibit, *By the Sweat of Their Brow: Forging the Steel Valley,* uses videos, artifacts, photographs, and reconstructed scenes to tell the story of steel in the valley.

The Youngstown Historical Center of Industry and Labor is at 151 W. Wood St., Youngstown; (330) 941-1314, (800) 262-6137; ohiohistory.org/places/youngst. Open Wed through Fri, 10 a.m. to 4 p.m.; Sat, noon to 4 p.m. Admission: adults $7; children (ages 6 to 12) $3.

In a city best known for steel and other heavy industry, Youngstown's **Butler Institute of American Art** houses an outstanding permanent collection of more than 10,000 works. From the earliest Limner painters of the colonial period through contemporary masters, the Butler Institute features representative works by Benjamin West, John Singleton Copley, Winslow Homer, Thomas Eakins, Martin Johnson Heade, and Mary Cassatt.

Specialty collections include western art by the likes of Albert Bierstadt, Frederic Remington, and Victor Higgins, and an expansive group of marine paintings featuring the works of Fitz Hugh Lane, Edward Moran, William Bradford, and Alfred Bricher. The Lester F. Donnell Gallery of American Sports Art features paintings, sculpture, drawings, and prints of all things sporting, including works by George Bellows, John Steuart Curry, Red Grooms, Robert Riggs, and Roy Lichtenstein.

Founded in 1919 by industrialist Joseph G. Butler Jr., the Butler Institute is housed in a classic building, the first structure built in the US specifically to house a collection of American art. Additions to this historic edifice in the 1930s and 1960s preceded the impressive West Wing addition in 1987 and the Beecher Center for Art and Technology in 2000. These postmodern structures, awash in marble and partially lit by soaring skylights, brings to 20 the number of galleries at the Butler Institute.

The Butler Institute of American Art is at 524 Wick Ave., Youngstown; (330) 743-1107; butlerart.com. Open Tues through Sat, 11 a.m. to 4 p.m.; Sun, noon to 4 p.m. No admission charge.

Just down the road from the Butler Institute is another Youngstown treasure: the early 20th -century mansion of Wilford and Olive Arms, Greystone, now the ***Arms Family Museum of Local History.*** The 3 main rooms on the first floor of this elegant mansion preserve the Arms' way of life; their family portraits, furniture, china, glassware, silver, linens, Oriental rugs, and objets d'art are still in place.

On the lower level, a large exhibition room depicts pioneer life in the region, with a collection of farm and household tools, implements and utensils, antique toys, and Native American relics. Second-floor exhibits explore the more recent history of the Mahoning Valley through photographs, costumes, and artifacts.

Period gowns adorn mannequins throughout the museum, and the table setting in the dining room changes periodically to rotate the display of china, crystal, and silver. Special exhibits here include toys and dolls, costumes and accessories, political memorabilia, and works of art.

The Arms Family Museum of Local History is at 648 Wick Ave., Youngstown; (330) 743-2589; mahoninghistory.org/arms-family-museum. Open Tues through Sun, 1 to 5 p.m. Admission: adults $4; senior citizens $3; children (3 to 18) $2.

One of Ohio's greatest regional parks offers visitors more than 4,400 acres of streams, lakes, gardens, woods, meadows, and wildlife. It's Mahoning County's *Mill Creek MetroParks,* and it features 21 miles of roads and 15 miles of foot trails through truly spectacular scenery. Hiking, picnicking, and boating are popular pastimes on Lake Newport and Lake Glacier.

The central feature of the park is picturesque Mill Creek. Many pioneer industries developed along the creek, and relics still remain to be discovered by visitors. Lanterman's Mill operates today as it did in the early 1800s, grinding corn, wheat, and buckwheat via power driven by a 14-foot oak waterwheel. The mill had ceased operation in 1888, only to reopen a century later. A covered bridge stands just south of the mill and is one of the scenic highlights of the park.

Downstream from the mill is the start of the Gorge Trail. Mill Creek borders one side of this 2-mile trail; a massive wall of sandstone forms the other boundary. The trail takes hikers past a stunning waterfall.

More than 40,000 flowering bulbs announce the arrival of spring each year at the Fellows Riverside Garden. As summer arrives, a spectacle of colorful annuals takes over. The wooded setting of the shade garden is a showcase for ornamental plants that thrive in low light. Other park highlights include a golf course, tennis courts, miniature golf, an ice-skating rink, ball fields, and basketball courts.

Mill Creek Park is at 810 Glenwood Ave., Youngstown; (330) 702-3000; millcreekmetroparks.com. Open during daylight hours.

The collectibles at the *Hummel Gift Shop* may be diminutive, but the shop that houses them is anything but. With 30,000 square feet of display space, this may be the largest gift shop in the state. Hummel collectors will be instantly attracted by the shop name, but the Hummel Gift Shop also carries a wide range of other gifts and collectibles. There are also year-round displays of ancient artifacts and a Christmas wonderland.

The Hummel Gift Shop is located at 1656 Garfield Rd., New Springfield; (330) 549-3728 or (800) 354-5438; hummelgiftshop.com. Open Mon through

Sat from 10 a.m. to 5 p.m.; from June 1 through December 24, it's also open Sun from 1 to 5 p.m.

The Packard automobile may be a thing of America's past, but its history is preserved at the *National Packard Museum.* The museum is located in the community of Warren, and its mission is to document and tell the story of the Packard family, the Packard Electric Company, the Packard Motor Car Company, and the innovations they created. The museum has several wonderfully restored Packards, and plenty of displays and Packard memorabilia, as well as changing exhibits. Bring your camera. Photography is not only allowed, it is encouraged.

The National Packard Museum is at 1899 Mahoning Ave. NW, Warren; (330) 394-1899; packardmuseum.org. Open Tues through Sat, noon to 5 p.m.; Sun, 1 to 5 p.m. Admission: adults $8; senior citizens $5; children (ages 7 to 12) $5.

Jacob Welsh and his daughter traveled from Boston, Massachusetts, in 1811 to the Western Reserve area of northeast Ohio. Mr. Welsh donated 50 acres of his land on which to build a church, parsonage, and cemetery. In addition, he agreed to provide the nails and glass for the church if his neighbors would call the area Welshfield, in honor of his family.

Built in the 1840s by Alden J. Nash and originally called the Nash Hotel, the *Welshfield Inn* served as an Underground Railway station for slaves escaping from the South to Canada. Stagecoaches traveling between Cleveland and Pittsburgh also frequently stopped here for food and overnight accommodations.

In 2007 the inn was purchased by the proprietors of the Gamekeepers Taverne in Chagrin Falls, Bass Lake Taverne and Inn in Chardon, and the Allegheny Grille in Foxburg, Pennsylvania. After extensive renovation and restoration, the Welshfield Inn reopened in November 2007.

Although lodging is no longer offered here, the tradition of serving old-fashioned country cooking has been maintained by the new owners. The menu at the Welshfield Inn features unpretentious comfort food—pastas, steaks, chops, and fresh seafood. Every Friday the inn offers the popular beer-battered fish fry with all-you-can-eat cod, french fries, and coleslaw for $12.99.

The large dining room with a fireplace contains an eclectic mix of bentwood chairs and wooden tables; browns, greens, and other earth tones predominate, and fresh flowers dress up each table. One of the smaller dining rooms, called Peddlers Parlor, has Early American decor with antiques, Quaker lace tablecloths, and seasonal flowers. On the front porch, lawn furniture creates a friendly, informal atmosphere under the tall columns. Also under the porch roof is a huge wooden sled named Snowbird capable of carrying 20 to 30 people.

The Welshfield Inn is on OH 422, 14001 Main Market Rd., Burton; (440) 834-0190. Open Mon through Thurs, 11:30 a.m. to 9 p.m.; Fri and Sat, 11:30 a.m. to 10 p.m.; and Sun, 10 a.m. to 9 p.m.

Approximately 16,000 Amish live in Geauga County, making it one of the largest Amish communities in the country. Wearing the traditional dark, solid-colored clothing and rejecting modern conveniences such as electricity and automobiles, the "plain people" strive for a simple farming life. Merchants in Middlefield, Ohio, provide hitching posts for their Amish customers.

The Schaden family has a most unique and charming business. They are the owners of the ***End of the Commons General Store*** in picturesque Mesopotamia.

Ken Schaden, once a frequent customer, gave up a corporate position with extensive international travel requirements to purchase the store in 1982 and spend more time with his wife, Margaret, and their 11 children. The Schadens sell more than 800 products in bulk to area Amish families, most arriving at the store in horse-drawn buggies. As its name indicates, the store sits at the end of a parklike commons, surrounded by 30 historic homes, the oldest of which was built in 1816.

When they purchased the store and began to clean out the old storage areas, they found hundreds of items related to the store's and the town's history. Today visitors find on display old clothes, shoes, a barber chair, a post office, a player piano, and many things of bygone days. Penny candy still lines shelves by the checkout counter (yes, it is still just a penny), where slots and boxes of the old post office remain. In summer, hand-dipped ice cream is dispensed from a window where stamps once were sold. Amish families who host church services in their homes buy pounds and pounds of bologna and cheese here and also bake lots of bread and goodies with the unusual flours they find here in suitable quantities. The Commons Cafe serves lunch and dinner daily.

The family also operates a truck route that calls on 375 Amish families in the surrounding countryside. It is equipped with a cooler and freezers so they can bring them ice cream and milk along with other essentials. It is a grocery store on wheels.

The End of the Commons General Store is at 8719 OH 534, Mesopotamia; (440) 693-4295; endofthecommons.com. Open Mon through Fri, 8:30 a.m. to 8:30 p.m.; Sat, 8:30 a.m. to 6 p.m.

Mid-February through mid-April is a special time in Geauga County—maple syrup season. Those first February thaws start the sap flowing, and farmers throughout the county use special taps and buckets to drain the sap from their sugar maple trees. Once collected it is boiled and evaporated, with 30 to 60 gallons of sap needed to make one gallon of maple syrup. Smoke rising from area sugarhouses means syrup production is underway.

The **Burton Sugar Camp** is the only municipally owned sugar camp in the country. In a 10-acre park in the center of Burton at 14590 E. Park St., sap from the park's 1,500 sugar maples is boiled into syrup in a rustic log cabin. The cabin is open daily from late Feb through Apr, and maple syrup products are sold on weekends from May through the middle of Dec. Call (800) 526-5630.

At the south end of Burton's town square is *Century Village*—18 restored buildings that provide a glimpse of the Western Reserve in the 1800s. The Blacksmith Shop, built in 1822, has an impressive complement of smithy tools and equipment. For a look at upper-middle-class life in the region, the Boughton House is furnished with pieces typical of the 1840s. The B&O Railroad built the Aultman station after the Civil War, and next to it sits a 20-ton B&O caboose. Guides from the Geauga County Historical Society conduct one-and-a-half-hour tours of the village.

Century Village is on the town square in Burton at 14653 E. Park St.; (440) 834-1492; centuryvillagemuseum.org. Open mid-Apr through mid-Nov, Sat and Sun, with tours at 1 and 3 p.m. Admission: adults $7; children (ages 6 to 12) $5.

The annual *Geauga County Maple Festival,* held on the last full weekend in April, takes place in Chardon, 10 miles north of Burton. Parades, maple syrup contests, a quilt and afghan show, competitions in pancake flipping and eating, wood chopping, rooster crowing, and beard shaving with an ax are just some of the activities at this yearly celebration. For more information, check the website at maplefestival.com.

Many of the Amish operate dairy farms, and they bring their milk to the **Middlefield Cheese House** to be manufactured into swiss cheese. The cheese plant, founded as a cooperative in 1956 by 25 area farmers, is one of the largest producers of quality swiss in the US, with an output of more than 20 million pounds annually.

Visitors are invited to view a film, *Middlefield Cheese...Better Than Ever,* which carefully describes each step in the cheese-making process. A tour of the cheese house museum features Old World carvings from Switzerland, antique cheese-making equipment, Amish artifacts, and historical photos. Be sure to stop in the Cheese Chalet Shop, where fresh sausages, homemade breads and pastries, Geauga County maple syrup, plus a wide selection of fine cheeses are available for purchase. A light lunch of soup, sandwiches, muffins, pie, and ice cream is served.

Middlefield Cheese House is on OH 608 at 15815 Nauvoo Rd., Middlefield; (440) 632-5228, (800) 327-9477; middlefieldcheese.com. Open Mon through Sat, 8 a.m. to 5:30 p.m. No admission charge.

The king of maple products in Geauga County has to be Paul Richards, of **Richards Maple Products**—his family has been in the business since 1910.

Paul purchases tens of thousands of gallons of syrup annually from area farmers, syrup that he transforms into pure maple spread (similar to honey butter), maple sugar, maple cream (a fudgelike concoction available with or without black walnuts), maple candy, and of course, three grades of maple syrup. All of these are produced without the use of preservatives.

Richards Maple Products also sells a wide selection of gift boxes containing endless combinations of their various products. Catalogs of gift box selections are available by mail.

Richards Maple Products is at 545 Water St. (US 6, west of the central business district), Chardon; (800) 352-4052; richardsmapleproducts.com. Open Mon through Fri, 9 a.m. to 6 p.m.; Sat, 9 a.m. to 4:30 p.m.; Sun, 10 a.m. to 4:30 p.m. From May 15 through July 15, Richards closes at 5:30 p.m. daily and all day Wed.

You can return home from your visit to **Fowler's Milling Company** with a taste of the 1800s. The mill was established in 1834 by Milo and

Hiram Fowler and has been operating for almost all of the years since. Currently the millstones grind corn and wheat. You can purchase their stone-ground flours in traditional cloth bags and do some scratch baking. The mill also offers a variety of baking mixes, pastas, and gift items.

Fowler's Mill is at 12500 Fowlers Mill Rd., Chardon; (440) 286-2024, (800) 321-2024; fowlermill.com. Open Mon through Sat, 10 a.m. to 5 p.m.

From late November to the middle of March, skiers hit the powder at the **Alpine Valley Ski Area.** This complete ski resort has 6 slopes and a backwoods trail, high-powered lighting towers for night skiing, and a 10,000-square-foot rental shop with 1,400 pairs of skis. Their Professional Ski Instructors of America (PSIA) ski school offers both private and group lessons. After a strenuous day on the slopes, a blazing fire in the lodge's fireplace lures skiers there to unwind. The lodge offers a great view of the slopes, as well as a full-service cafeteria, a pizza shop, and a pub called Chaser's.

The Alpine Valley Ski Area is on US 322, 4 miles east of Chesterland at 10620 Mayfield Rd.; (440) 285-2211, (440) 729-9775 (ski reports); alpinevalley ohio.com.

Eastern Lakefront

The **Holden Arboretum,** one of the world's largest arboreta, encompasses 3,600 acres of wooded trails, ponds full of ducks and geese, fields, and deep ravines. Dedicated to increasing knowledge of the plant world, Holden has 5 primary nature trails, which take visitors past the maple collection, renowned for its beauty when the leaves change color in the fall; the conifer collection of pines, firs, spruces, and junipers; and the wildflower garden, where a showcase of Ohio's flora can be enjoyed.

The lilac and rhododendron gardens and crabapple and shrub collections are other examples of the many and varied exhibits in this vast nature preserve. Nature walks and frequent lectures are offered at the arboretum, as are memberships. Membership entitles you to free admission to the grounds, cross-country skiing privileges, and discounts on courses, lectures, and gift shop purchases. Bird-watching and wildflower walks are popular at Holden, and the arboretum has summertime nature discovery sessions as well as special programs for children on subjects such as animal communication.

The Holden Arboretum is at 9500 Sperry Rd., Kirtland; (440) 946-4400; holdenarb.org. Open daily, 9 a.m. to 5 p.m. Admission: adults $6; senior citizens $5 (free on Tues); children (ages 6 to 12) $3.

Picture, if you will, a giant tomato plant with vines as thick as your waist, fruit 6 feet across, and leaves up to 12 feet long. The stuff of science fiction? No, science, not science fiction. These are features of the creative Great Tomato Works at *Lake Metroparks Farmpark.* The Farmpark is an outdoor museum where city folks can learn about and learn to appreciate agriculture—the source of our food supply. The number of farmers among us has declined from more than 90 percent in 1800 to less than 3 percent today. Relatively few Americans have ever met a farmer, let alone understand what he or she does.

Try your hand milking a cow, or just enjoy the 235 acres of fields and forests. Two miles of easy walking roads cross the property, and wagon rides are also offered. You'll discover more than 50 breeds of livestock including cattle, sheep, goats, pigs, and poultry, plus orchards, gardens, and vineyards. You'll leave knowing the difference between strip cropping and contour plowing, and perhaps having seen the planting, cultivating, or harvesting of fields of hay, oats, rye, wheat, corn, and barley.

Lake Metroparks Farmpark is at 8800 Euclid Chardon Rd. (US 6), Kirtland; (440) 256-2122, (800) 366-3276; lakemetroparks.com./select-park/farmpark.shtml. Open daily, 9 a.m. to 5 p.m. (Closed on Mon, Jan through Mar.) Admission: adults (ages 12 and up) $6; senior citizens $5; children $4.

After a day exploring the Lake Metroparks Farmpark or the Holden Arboretum, you might want to relax with a night's stay at *Rider's Inn.* Rider's Inn has offered hospitality to Ohio visitors since 1812, when Joseph Rider opened it as a stagecoach stop for those heading to the Western Reserve and beyond. The inn provided a different kind of hospitality prior to the Civil War, as it served as a stop on the Underground Railroad, offering safe haven to fleeing slaves. The inn also was briefly a hot springs spa and was reputed to offer yet another kind of hospitality to thirsty drinkers during Prohibition.

The new owners purchased the inn in 1988 and refurbished the 11 guest rooms. Some of the guest rooms have private baths, but others share facilities so if you have a preference, be sure and ask when you are making reservations. The Innkeeper's Suite and Suzanne's Suite (named after Joseph

Rider's third wife) have some of the Rider's original furnishings. Guests have a gathering room to enjoy and are served a continental breakfast in bed.

Along with the accommodations, the inn also houses Mistress Suzanne's Dining Room, featuring fish and game recipes from the colonial period as well as more traditional dishes. You also can enjoy a game of darts in the English-style pub or just sit and sip your favorite beverage by the old stone fireplace. The pub has live music every Tues, Fri, and Sat. The innkeepers enjoy outdoor activities, including boating and sailing, and are happy to introduce their guests to the many sporting and cultural activities in the area.

Rider's Inn is located at 792 Mentor Ave., Painesville; (440) 354-8200; ridersinn.com. Rates: $79 to $105 per night. The restaurant is open for lunch Mon through Sat, 11:30 a.m. to 4 p.m.; dinner Sun through Thurs, 4:30 to 9 p.m.; until 11 p.m. on Fri and Sat; Sun brunch, 10 a.m. to 3 p.m.

The Debevcs have made wine for family and friends for three generations, but it wasn't until 1970 that Tony Sr. and Tony Jr. decided to convert some of their farm acreage into a commercial vineyard. **Debonne Vineyards** produced its first bottle for sale in 1972, and near-constant expansion has taken place ever since. Winemaker Tony Jr. oversees production from 100 acres of vineyard.

Guests at Debonne sample the 24 varieties of Debevc wine—12 white wines, 8 reds, and 4 blush wines—in a Swiss-style A-frame chalet with a large fireplace, burgundy tablecloths, and weathered barn-board siding on the inside walls. Visitors may also sit under the covered patio during warm weather, and snacks such as cheese and sausage and homemade bread are served. Regional bands perform on Wednesday and Friday evenings and Saturday afternoons.

Tours of the winery take place hourly, or as needed, with members of the Debevc family explaining the various steps in winemaking, from grape crushing and filtering to aging and bottling. Debonne holds 100,000 gallons of wine in various stages of fermentation in the cellar and bottled for sale.

Debonne Vineyards is off OH 528 and Griswold Road at 7840 Doty Rd., Madison; (440) 466-3485, (800) 424-WINE; debonne.com. Open Mon and Tues, noon to 6 p.m.; Wed noon to 10:30 p.m.; Thurs and Sat, noon to 8 p.m.; Fri, noon to 11 p.m. Open Sun, Apr through Oct, 1 to 6 p.m. Shorter hours in Jan.

Acres of vineyards can be seen throughout eastern Lake County, and 5 minutes from Debonne is another winery invested in by the Debevc family and two other area families, **Grand River Cellars.** After driving past the rows of grapevines, you reach a modern building at the edge of a cool forest. Its Riesling, Chardonnay, Cabernet franc, and pinot grigio all benefit from the care taken in the vineyard to produce a quality Ohio wine. A second label was created, Stonewood Vineyards, to represent the sweeter side of wine tasting. Stonewood labels market to the palates of those who enjoy sweeter blends as well as distinct Concord wine found in the Wine Hound Red and Niagara wine found in the White Fox. The winery also offers a large range of appetizers, grilled sandwiches, and a diverse dinner menu.

Grand River Cellars is at 5750 S. Madison Rd. (OH 528), Madison; (440) 298-9838; grandrivercellars.com. Open Wed and Thurs, noon to 8 p.m.; Fri and Sat, noon to 11 p.m.; Sun, 1 to 8 p.m. Shorter hours Jan through Apr.

His Majesty's Bed and Breakfast has 3 guest rooms located in a historic home in Madison. The Queen's Cottage is a charming home, built in 1861, and located on the village square. The 3 rooms in the Queen's Cottage are ornate with a Victorian theme, and one room features a whirlpool tub. All 3 rooms have private baths.

A full-course breakfast is included with your stay. In addition, the proprietors will be happy to create a package for you, steer you to local wine tastings, or make reservations for that perfect night of dinner and dancing.

The Queen's Cottage is located at 25 Park St., Madison; (440) 221-1758; hismajestys.com. Rates: $109 to $149 per night.

Two years of extensive renovation of this distinctive French Tudor home, built in 1937, earned the **Fitzgerald's Irish Bed and Breakfast** a "Best Interior Design and Decor" designation, one of 15 North American bed-and-breakfasts to be so honored in *Arrington's 2005 Book of Lists*. The innkeepers, Tom and Debra Fitzgerald, bought the castle-like home from the original owners and opened it as a bed-and-breakfast in 1998.

The common areas of the home are graced with grand architectural features, such as a majestic staircase, a turret, and a huge fireplace. The 3 guest rooms have private baths; one—the Bushmills Room—has a whirlpool tub. Continental breakfasts are served to guests on weekdays and full breakfasts on the weekends. If you would like a traditional Irish breakfast, please request it when you make your reservations. For lunch and dinner, restaurants are within walking distance.

Fitzgerald's Irish Bed and Breakfast is located at 47 Mentor Ave., Painesville; (440) 639-0845; fitzgeraldsbnb.com. Rates: $95 to $130 weeknights and $110 to $150 on weekends.

The ***Victorian Perambulator Museum of Jefferson*** has to be a little girl's or an antique-lover's dream come true. The museum has the largest collection of early wicker baby and doll carriages anywhere—more than 200. The handiwork and shapes are fascinating. One carriage is shaped like a Model T Ford, and another like an Italian gondola. The most recent acquisition is a pram used by Queen Elizabeth and Princess Margaret as children—it was pulled by miniature horses. There are also charming and unusual toys, many from the 1800s. Along with rare dolls, there are rocking horses, sleighs, books, and games. For those who can't resist taking a little bit of the past home, there is a museum store brimming with collectibles and craft items.

The Victorian Perambulator Museum of Jefferson is at 26 E. Cedar St., Jefferson; (440) 576-9588; victorianperambulatormuseum.com. Open Sat, May and Sept through Dec, from 11 a.m. to 5 p.m.; Wed and Sat, June through Aug, 11 a.m. to 5 p.m.; and by appointment. Admission: adults $5; children $4.

Places to Stay in Northeast Ohio

AKRON

O'Neil House Bed & Breakfast
1290 W. Exchange St.
(330) 867-2650
oneilhouse.com

Portage House
601 Copley Rd.
(330) 535-1952

Quaker Square Inn at the University of Akron
135 S. Broadway
(330) 253-5970
quakersquareakron.com

CLEVELAND

Clifford House Bed & Breakfast
1810 W. 28th St.
(216) 589-0121
cliffordhouse.com

Stone Gables Bed & Breakfast
3806 Franklin Blvd.
(877) 215-4326
stonegables.net

MADISON

His Majesty's Bed and Breakfast
25 Park St.
(440) 221-1758
hismajestys.com

HELPFUL WEBSITES

Ohio Division of Travel and Tourism:
discoverohio.com

Cleveland Convention and Visitors Bureau:
positivelycleveland.com

Cleveland Plain Dealer:
cleveland.com/plaindealer

Youngstown Convention and Visitors Bureau:
youngstownlive.com

PAINESVILLE

Fitzgerald's Irish Bed and Breakfast
47 Mentor Ave.
(440) 639-0845
fitzgeraldsbnb.com

Quail Hollow Resort and Country Club
11080 Concord-Hambden Rd.
(440) 497-1100
quailhollowresort.com

Rider's Inn
792 Mentor Ave.
(440) 354-8200
ridersinn.com

Places to Eat in Northeast Ohio

AKRON

Ken Stewart's Lodge
1911 N. Cleveland Massillon Rd.
(330) 666-8881
kenstewarts.com

Old Harbor Inn
562 Portage Lakes Dr.
(330) 644-1664
theoldharborinn.com

BURTON

Welshfield Inn
14001 Main Market Rd.
(440) 834-0190
welshfielddining.com

CLEVELAND

Balaton Restaurant
13133 Shaker Sq.
(216) 921-9691
balaton-restaurant.com

Table 45
9801 Carnegie Ave.
(216) 707-4045
tbl45.com

LAKE AT CHIPPEWA

Oaks Lakeside
5878 Longacre Lane
(330) 769-2601 or
(800) 922-5736
theoakslakeside.com

MADISON

Vault Steak House & Wine Room
63 W. Main St.
(440) 417-0220
vaultsteakhouse.com

Legacy Trail

Stunning natural beauty and re-created pioneer history blend in a state park in the foothills of the Appalachians, **Beaver Creek State Park.** Wide, swift Little Beaver Creek rushes through deep gorges and past pine and fir forests, the locks of the old Sandy and Beaver Canal, and a restored pioneer village.

Private entrepreneurs constructed the canal between 1834 and 1848, connecting the Ohio River with the Ohio and Erie Canal. Though they spent $3 million on the project by its completion, the canal carried paying traffic only until 1852, when competition from the railroad doomed the canal era in this part of the state. Ironically, the directors of the Sandy and Beaver kept the Pennsylvania Railroad out of the county to avoid competition between the railroad and their canal—a move that had dire consequences for the canal towns in Columbiana County after the Sandy and Beaver failed.

Fifteen miles of hiking trails and numerous bridle trails follow Little Beaver Creek and wind through the woods up

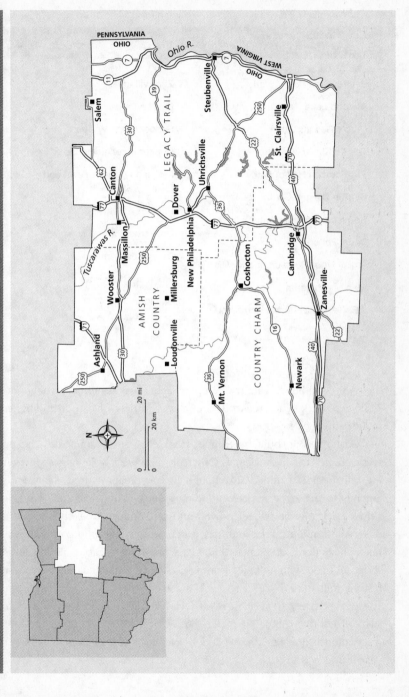

EAST CENTRAL OHIO

BEST ATTRACTIONS

Beaver Creek State Park	Zoar Village
Atwood Lake Resort	Fort Laurens
Cibo's Restaurant	Schoenbrunn Village
The McKinley Museum	Quaker Meeting House
Pro Football Hall of Fame	Lehman's/Kidron Town and Country Store
Canton Classic Car Museum	
Hoover Historical Center	Pine Tree Barn
Canal Fulton	Quailcrest Farm
Amish Door Restaurant and Village	Delagrange Antiques
Warther Museum	Mohican State Park
J.E. Reeves Victorian Home and Museum	Blackfork Inn

the steep foothills. Primitive camping areas are scattered throughout the 3,000-acre park. The creek offers anglers a variety of fish, including smallmouth and rock bass.

Gaston's Mill, built by Samuel Conkle in 1830, dominates the park's reconstructed pioneer village. Originally powered by a large waterwheel, the mill operated until 1920, though in later years it used steam and gas engines to drive the massive grinding stones. When restored, it was converted back to waterwheel power, and on summer weekends visitors can observe the mill at work and may purchase stone-ground corn, wheat, and buckwheat flour. A pioneer church, schoolhouse, cabin, and blacksmith shop, all filled with antiques from Ohio's early settlement era, surround the historic mill.

Beaver Creek State Park is off OH 7 at 12021 Echo Dell Rd., 15 miles east of Lisbon; (330) 385-3091, (866) 644-6727 for camping and rental reservations; dnr.state.oh.us/parks/beaverck/tabid/714/Default.aspx. Open year-round.

Perched on a hilltop overlooking 8,000 acres of rolling hills and water is a great getaway destination, ***Atwood Lake Resort.*** This complete resort complex features a rustic yet modern lodge with 103 guest rooms, the Vista dining room, and the View Lounge.

Atwood Lake is 1,540 acres of boating, swimming, and fishing, with sailboat and powerboat rentals available. Golfers will enjoy the 6,007-yard, par 70 course, which features challenging doglegs, rolling fairways, and gorgeous greens, as well as the lighted 9-hole par 3. Other amenities include

Beaver Creek Ghost

Visitors to Beaver Creek State Park will want to bring a camera to get some pictures of the restored mill and locks, but be prepared to miss at least one of those shots if one of the park's ghosts is in residence. At Beaver Creek one of the men who was a lock keeper is said to continue to work shifts along the water's edge. If you visit "Jake's Lock," you may become part of his legend. In life, he sometimes worked the day shift; sometimes at night. At night he would light a lantern and keep watch for boats needing his services to transverse the lock. But one night, it is said, a bolt of lightning shot from the sky and hit poor Jake, killing him and propelling his body into the lock.

Visitors say that to this day they occasionally see the light from Jake's lantern bobbing along the side of the canal or even under the water where Jake fell that night. If you try to take a picture near the lock, the legend says that your camera may malfunction if Jake is working his shift. Be careful that your flash doesn't remind Jake of the fateful flash of lightning!

One of the 1830s locks is nicknamed "Gretchen's Lock." Tales say that Gretchen was the daughter of Gill Hans, an engineer who came from Holland to build the lock. His daughter never adjusted to the move to America and eventually grew sick and died in 1838.

Her family made plans to return to Holland to bury their daughter. Until they could, the coffin was temporarily placed in the stone sides of the lock. The arrangements were made and the family set sail with the coffin containing the remains of their homesick daughter.

But as fate would have it, their ship was sunk in a storm in the Atlantic. Legend says the girl, named Gretchen, has not found her rest, and instead she walks the lock that was her last, unhappy home.

5 lighted tennis courts, bike rentals, hiking trails, and indoor and outdoor swimming pools.

Atwood Lake Resort is at 2650 Lodge Rd., Sherrodsville; (330) 735-2211; atwoodlakeresort.com. Lodge rates: $109 to $189 per night, double occupancy, depending on season.

The family known as the Fighting McCooks did not earn that moniker in barroom brawls. Rather, the Ohio McCooks earned that distinction because of their incredible family commitment to the US military before and during the Civil War. In fact, Daniel McCook and his eight sons and the five sons of Daniel's brother John all served in the Union army. The Daniel McCook family included three major generals, two brigadier generals, one colonel, two majors, and one private. John McCook's sons served as a major general, two lieutenants, a commander, and a brigadier general.

About 1837 Daniel McCook erected the large brick home on the southwest corner of the public square in Carrollton. The **McCook House** was in the family until 1853, and it was acquired by the State of Ohio more than a century later. It is furnished with period pieces and relics from the McCook family.

The McCook House is on the square in Carrollton at 15 S. Lisbon St.; (330) 627-3345, (800) 600-7172; carrollcountyohio.com/history. Open Memorial Day to Labor Day, Fri and Sat, 10 a.m. to 5 p.m.; Sun, 1 to 5 p.m.; Labor Day to mid-Oct, Sat, 10 a.m. to 5 p.m.; Sun, 1 to 5 p.m. Admission: adults $3; children (ages 6 to 12) $1.

It's not usual to see cows and bulls in farm fields in Ohio, so you might do a double take when heading down Muskrat Road toward the **Dickinson Cattle Ranch.** During summer months, visitors can take bus tours through this working cattle ranch to see not only prize-winning cattle, but breeds that are not common in the Midwest. Perhaps the most striking of those is the Texas longhorn. These magnificent creatures have horns that are about 5 or 6 feet from tip to tip. Longhorns can be many colors: speckled, brown, black, blue, even an orange color. Rivaling the Texas longhorns for, well, long horns is the ranch's herd of Watusi cattle. The horns of Watusi bulls measure 6 feet or more from tip to tip, while the base of the horns can be more than 2 feet around. These cattle are tall, too. Looking out the bus window will put you right about at horn-level with these huge animals.

Another interesting breed at the ranch is the Blue Lingo. Unlike the multicolored and speckled longhorn, Blue Lingos look like dark cows wearing a white cummerbund. They are more docile animals, but the big white stripe around their middles certainly makes them striking.

This is not a tourist attraction, but a working cattle ranch. The owners breed animals for sale internationally. The ranch features the Longhorn Head to Tail Store, where you can purchase souvenirs and beef products. An example is the Barrel O' Beef, featuring longhorn jerky, longhorn beef sticks, and longhorn pepper stick summer sausage.

The Dickinson Cattle Ranch is at 35500 Muskrat Rd., Barnesville; (740) 758-5050; texaslonghorn.net. Open June through Aug, Mon through Sat, 10 a.m. to 5 p.m.; Sun, 1 to 6 p.m. Bus tour ticket: adults $10; children (ages 4 to 12) $4.

Cibo's Restaurant serves authentic Italian cooking in a very unusual setting—an old movie theater. The Mohawk Theater, built in the early 1940s, presented feature films for the people of Waynesburg

barnesville's "gay '90s mansion"

Founded in 1808 by James Barnes, a Quaker from Maryland, Barnesville prospered as a producer of tobacco and strawberries during the 19th century. As the town flourished, so did its banks. It was the Bradfields, the owners of the First National Bank, who built the town's most dramatic residence, what's known as the "Gay '90s Mansion."

This elegant 26-room, 11,000-square-foot structure, complete with dramatic turret, took five years to construct, and cost $60,000 when completed in 1893. In its prime, the mansion hosted Barnesville's most important dinners and parties, guests climbing the massive oak staircase to the third-floor ballroom. Today the mansion is a museum and the restored home of the local historical society. Located at 432 N. Chestnut St., the mansion offers guided tours May 1 through October 1 from 1 to 4:30 p.m. Wed through Sun. Tours are $5 for adults and $2 for children. Call (740) 425-2926; belmontcounty museum.com.

for decades. But since 1971 it has been spaghetti the pasta, not spaghetti the western, that attracts crowds at 134 W. Lisbon St.

At first, dining was limited to the Mohawk's old lobby, but now the entire theater has been remodeled and converted to a multilevel eating area, complete with ceiling fans and oak dividers. Italian favorites such as antipasto, pasta *e fagioli* (beans), *spezzato* (wedding) soup, and home-made chicken noodle soup constitute the list of appetizers. The reasonably priced entrees include spaghetti, rigatoni, cavatelli, lasagna, ravioli, and cannelloni, and for those who have trouble choosing from that list, a combination plate offers a sample of all the above. Cibo's offers American dishes as well—baked steak and chicken, plus family-style combinations of spaghetti, ravioli, chicken, lasagna, and baked steak. Pizza and sandwiches are also served.

Cibo's is at 134 W. Lisbon St., Waynesburg; (330) 866-3838; cibosrestaurant.com. Open Thurs and Sun, 11 a.m. to 8 p.m.; Fri and Sat, 11 a.m. to 9 p.m.

William McKinley was elected the 25th US president in 1896. Five years later he was assassinated at the Pan-American Exposition in Buffalo, New York. He died in office on September 14, 1901. The story of this Ohio native's life and public career is preserved at **The McKinley Museum,** a multifaceted complex that also includes the McKinley National Memorial, a hands-on science center for kids of all ages, a history museum, and a 65-seat planetarium.

Perhaps the most dramatic section of this vast museum is the Street of Shops. Visitors stroll down a 19th-century boulevard that is complete with a pioneer home; a general store; an early print shop; dentist's, physician's, and lawyer's offices; a photography studio; a hotel; a fire station; and a toy company and shop. There is also an 84-foot model train layout, including a Pennsylvania Railroad train station.

Included in this impressive complex is Discover World, an interactive scientific program geared for children and the young at heart. At the entrance to Discover World, you're greeted by the spine-tingling roar of a life-size allosaurus, with jaws that open and legs that move thanks to the magic of robotics. Ingenious inverted periscopes let you check out the plant and animal life in a series of ponds. Once aboard Space Station Earth, you find yourself in a scientific laboratory, where you can activate demonstrations on lasers and light waves, water in motion, and air under pressure.

The McKinley Museum is at 800 McKinley Monument Dr. NW, Canton; (330) 455-7043; mckinleymuseum.org. Open Mon through Sat, 9 a.m. to 4 p.m.; Sun, noon to 4 p.m. Admission: adults $8; senior citizens $7; children (ages 3 to 18) $6.

You might think that the likely home for the *First Ladies National Historic Site* would be somewhere in Washington, DC. You might think that, but you would be incorrect. It is actually in downtown Canton. The mission of the First Ladies National Historic Site is to create a central location where people can explore the lives of our nation's first ladies and their contributions to our nation's history. The site is both a primary research facility and an educational center that includes three major components: the National First Ladies' Library online bibliographic database, the library in the historically documented Saxton McKinley home, and an educational center adjacent to the Saxton McKinley home in the former City National Bank Building.

The Saxton McKinley house is a two- and three-story brick building of irregular massing. It was constructed in two segments in 1841 and ca. 1865. It is significant as the only remaining residence with direct historical ties to President William McKinley in his hometown of Canton. It was the family home of McKinley's wife, Ida, and he and his wife lived in the house between 1878 and 1891.

The Saxton McKinley House in Canton celebrated its national debut as the home of the National First Ladies' Library with a dedication ceremony and Victorian Gala in June 1998, with former First Lady Rosalynn Carter. The public rooms of the house have been restored to their original splendor, complete with ornate historical wallpapers and period furniture. Great care has been taken to ensure that all design elements, including patterns of wallpaper, carpets, and area rugs, are authentic.

kilnsaplenty

As early as 1806, small kilns were fired in East Liverpool to take advantage of the area's unique clay and produce the popular "yellow ware" pottery. James Bennett, a potter from England, walked into town in 1839 determined to build a pottery empire. Profits from his effort the first year were $250, a huge sum in those days and just the beginning of a dramatic expansion for East Liverpool's pottery industry. By the end of the century, more than one-third of all the kilns operating in the US were in East Liverpool—239 of them.

The renovated ballroom is, and always has been, located on the third floor of the house. Many parties were held in this ballroom, since the Saxtons were among the most prominent families in Canton. In President

McKinley's study, all of the wallpapers were custom-made by historic merchants to replicate wallpaper depicted in an early photograph of the study taken during his official residence. The photo revealed wallpaper that resembles an intricate quilt of Oriental scenes.

The library and parlor are decorated in the more opulent Italianate style that became popular after the Civil War. In this area there are 23 different wallpaper patterns in subtle shades of tan, grayish green, rose, and warm beige. The flow of the color and pattern creates an ambience that is feminine, but understated and elegant. Lace curtains, authentically reproduced from an 1876 pattern, are thrown over rods and pinned in place—just as the Victorians did it. The chrysanthemum-patterned Wilton carpet was loomed in the same mill that provided carpet for the White House at First Lady Dolly Madison's request.

The building housing the educational and research center was constructed in 1895 and has 7 floors with approximately 20,000 square feet of usable space. It had a large skylight over the main banking room on the first floor that has been fully restored, as well as an extensive glass block floor under the skylight. There is extensive use of marble on the first floor foyer/lobby and main banking room, as well as in the lobbies on the upper floors of the building.

There is a 91-seat Victorian theater on the lower level, where films and documentaries on first ladies are shown, and author presentations and live lectures take place. The center also houses a collection of books that replicates the first White House library created by First Lady Abigail Fillmore.

stateflower timestwo

President William McKinley wore a red carnation in his lapel every day for 29 years. After McKinley's assassination in 1901, Ohio legislators searched for a fitting tribute to the fallen president. In his honor, they made the red carnation Ohio's state flower in 1904. Their resolution read: "for its beauty, its fragrance and its fitness, let it be adopted as the state flower of Ohio; and let the action of its adoption be to the memory of William McKinley."

Not contented with a single state flower, Ohio lawmakers declared the *Trillium grandiflorum* the state wildflower in 1987. They noted that the large-flowered or white trillium is found in all 88 Ohio counties and is easy to identify.

The First Ladies National Historic Site is at 331 Market Ave. South, Canton; (330) 452-0876 x320; firstladies.org. Tours are given Tues through Sat at 9:30 and 10:30 a.m. and at 12:30, 1:30, and 2:30 p.m. (Sun tours are offered in the summer); reservations recommended. Admission: adults $7; senior citizens $5; children (under age 18), $5.

Canton was once home to the Canton Bulldogs, an early-day powerhouse in professional football. Today Canton, where the National Football League began in 1920, is the home of the national shrine of professional football, the **Pro Football Hall of Fame.** This 5-building complex delights every pigskin addict, with action films, displays, and gridiron history. Why wait to celebrate the Super Bowl just once a year? Football fans have been flocking to the Lamar Hunt Super Bowl Gallery since it opened in 2009 to relive every Super Bowl and watch their favorite gridiron heroes again. Game highlights can be enjoyed via interactive video kiosks. The Super Bowl Theater brings the magic of a Super Bowl to life with all the hoopla and thrilling moments that make the annual pageant of professional football an eagerly awaited event. Discover how football started and how the merger of the AFL and NFL helped make professional football into the successful passion of today.

A 7-foot bronze rendition of Jim Thorpe greets visitors to this comprehensive museum. A 1912 Olympic gold medal winner in the pentathlon and decathlon, Thorpe is considered one of the most versatile athletes of modern sports, playing professional football, basketball and baseball. Exhibits trace the history of the sport from the first game in 1892 to the latest teams. In the Pro Football Photo Art Gallery, you'll find the best of professional sports photography. The African-American Pioneers display tells the story of African Americans in the NFL. A favorite here are the twin Enshrinee Galleries, where the best of the best are honored. Each year a new class is enshrined, to join the ranks of pro football legends. After your tour, stop by the museum store for those can't-be-passed-up football souvenirs.

The Pro Football Hall of Fame is at 2121 George Halas Dr. NW, Canton; (330) 456-8207; profootballhof.com. Open daily, 9 a.m. to 5 p.m. (until 8 p.m. during the summer). Admission: adults $22; senior citizens $18; children (ages 6 to 12) $16.

For those who appreciate the rumble seats, wooden-spoke wheels, and V-16 engines of antique automobiles, a stop at the **Canton Classic**

Car Museum is a must. The museum, housed in one of Ohio's earliest Ford-Lincoln dealerships (1914–1929), comprises dozens of meticulously restored vehicles, from a blue 1906 Reo to a 1938 Cadillac convertible with a 452-cubic-inch, 185-horsepower engine.

Six Packard automobiles, from model years between 1920 and 1937, trace the evolution of that distinctive make. For elegant driving, the museum contains a Rolls-Royce—a red and white 1929 Phantom I convertible. The museum also has a rare Marmon Sixteen, which, according to an advertisement used at a 1931 automobile show, "looks and performs like no other car—16 cylinders, 200 horsepower and under $5,000."

The two-seat 1929 Kissel White Eagle Speedster (available with rumble seat) conjures up images of goggles, blowing scarves, and deserted country roads. The very rare 1914 Benham is the only survivor of the 19 cars produced by the short-lived automaker, which folded after only one year in business. Celebrity cars include Amelia Earhart's 1916 Pierce Arrow, Queen Elizabeth's 1939 Canadian tour car, and a movie car from *Those Daring Young Men in Their Jaunty Jalopies.* The museum also has an armor-plated, bulletproof 1937 Studebaker from the Canton Police Department.

In addition to the fine old cars, vintage gas and steam engines and other automotive paraphernalia are on display. In the restoration shop, future classics await rejuvenation.

The Canton Classic Car Museum is at 123 6th St. SW, Canton; (330) 455-3603; cantonclassiccar.org. Open daily, 10 a.m. to 5 p.m. Admission: adults $7.50; senior citizens $6; students $5.

Daniel and Mary Hoover arrived in 1852 on their 82-acre farm, where Daniel's father had established a leather tannery. At the turn of the 20th century, Daniel's son, W. H. Hoover, realized that the coming age of automobiles would drastically reduce the demand for leather goods such as harnesses and saddles. So W. H. Hoover searched for a new product for the Hoover Company, and bought the rights to inventor Murray Spangler's upright vacuum cleaner. In 1908 Hoover offered the public the first commercially viable upright vacuum cleaner, the Hoover Suction Sweeper Model O.

In less than a decade, the Hoover Company blossomed into an international concern. With its world headquarters in North Canton, the company has established the *Hoover Historical Center* on the family's original Stark

County farmstead. Hoover history unfolds in the Italianate-style farmhouse accented with elegant Victorian decor.

A six-minute video presentation details the history of the company, and guided tours begin in the tannery, which was the original family home, where many leather-working tools and artifacts from the late 1800s are displayed. The two-story white farmhouse contains what has to be the world's most complete collection of antique vacuums, ranging from the 1869 Whirlwind Cleaner, which was the first manual vacuum cleaner offered for sale that picked up dust with suction, to modern Hoover units.

The Kotten Suction Cleaner, built in 1910, required the operator to stand and rock on the bellows to create suction—it sold for $25. The 1905 Skinner electric vacuum was advertised as a portable but weighed more than 100 pounds! Murray Spangler's original 1907 upright stands next to the Hoover Model O, which launched this multinational corporation. Other Hoover exhibits include old photos of W. H. Hoover and various Hoover factories around the world, early advertisements for Hoover products, World War II memorabilia, and some furnishings used by the family in the farmhouse. Herb and flower gardens surround the museum, which hosts changing exhibits throughout the year.

The Hoover Historical Center is located at 1875 E. Maple St. NW, North Canton; (330) 499-0287; walsh.edu/hoover-historical-village. It's open Mar through mid-Dec, Wed through Sat, with tours conducted hourly from 1 to 4 p.m. No admission charge.

As the mules clip-clop down the towpath, for a moment you can imagine yourself back in the days of Ohio's canal era—people waving, men tossing horseshoes, barefoot boys fishing. The captain points out the sights, such as a dry dock where canal boats were built and repaired. In less than 30 minutes, you reach the Lock 4 turning basin. The captain describes how the lock works as the skillful crew poles the boat around for the scenic trip home. You float along in the *St. Helena III,* a 60-foot replica of the freight barges that slipped through the canal network crisscrossing the state more than 100 years ago.

Canal Fulton is a living canal town of 3,500 residents, where tourism and historical appreciation have replaced the commerce that once thrived on this section of the Ohio and Erie Canal. In addition to the authentic canal boat rides, Canal Fulton features an inviting 19th-century business district, listed on the National Register of Historic Places, with everything from antiques and gifts to candy and ice cream.

Other attractions include a Canal Days Museum and tours of a saltbox-style residence built in 1847. Biking along a section of the Cardinal Trail and canoeing on the Tuscarawas River are popular.

Canal Fulton is between Barberton and Massillon on OH 93; (330) 854-6835; discovercanalfulton.com. Canal boat rides are given daily except Mon at 1 and 2:30 p.m. in the summer, plus weekends in May, Sept, and early Oct. Adults, $8; senior citizens $7; children (ages 6 to 13) $5.

For charming accommodations in the area, try the ***Fulton House on Pleasant Hill***. This bed-and-breakfast at 451 E. Cherry St. was built in 1845 by dry-dock owner Michael Ruch. As a builder and repairer of canal boats, Ruch wanted to live where he could keep an eye on his business, so he built his home facing the canal instead of facing the street. When local builder and prominent businessman John Hammer bought the home in 1870, he added a library wing. For over 120 years, the home remained in the Hammer family. Today the house offers 2 bedrooms for guests and a full breakfast for $100. Call (330) 854-4645 or visit fultonhousebb.com.

If cooking is the way to your heart, you will find just what you're looking for at the ***Amish Door Restaurant & Village.*** The restaurant features family-style meals as well as a standard menu. This is Amish country, so fresh-baked breads and real mashed potatoes have got to be part of your meal, along with a country-fresh salad from the salad bar. Inside the restaurant is a bakery, so you can take some of those fresh baked goodies with you.

If you're spending some time in the area, the Amish Door Village offers two choices of accommodations. The Hasseman Bed and Breakfast has 4 guest rooms in an early 1900s Victorian home. The most unusual is the Attic room, which is the inn's honeymoon suite. A full breakfast is served at the B&B.

The Inn at Amish Door offers 52 Victorian-style rooms in a modern inn. Your stay includes a continental breakfast, and the inn offers such amenities as a heated indoor pool and a fitness room.

The Amish Door Restaurant & Village is located at 1210 Winesburg St., Wilmot; 888-264-7436; amishdoor.com. Rates: $79 to $215 per night.

Europe's foremost woodcarvers proclaimed Ernest Warther "the world's master carver," and the intricately crafted carvings displayed at the ***Warther***

Museum give credence to that proclamation. Born near Dover, Ohio, in 1885, Ernest started carving at age 5 when he found an old pocketknife while tending the family's cow. His formal education ended in the second grade, and at the age of 14 he went to work in the American Sheet and Tin Plate Company's mill. During his 20 years at the plant, he used his spare time to perfect his craft.

That steel-rolling mill is preserved today in a 3-by-5-foot working model carved by Warther—a model built with thousands of small, handmade walnut parts. Warther mechanized not only the model's steel-rolling equipment, but also many of the workers, including the foreman raising a sandwich to his mouth, a second worker nodding off on the job, and a third "drinking" his lunch by raising a tiny bottle to his lips. An intricate belt-drive system designed by Warther and a sewing-machine motor power the model's many moving parts.

Warther's most widely acclaimed carvings, however, are the series he created tracing the history of steam power, particularly his many steam locomotives and trains. Starting with working models of the simplest steam devices dating from 250 BC, Warther produced models of the various developmental stages of the steam era. By far the most impressive of these are the dozens of steam railroad locomotives on display at the museum, many with hundreds of moving parts.

Warther used walnut for the dark pieces of his models and, in the early part of his career, pieces of bone for the white pieces. In later years, he could afford ivory and carved entire trains, some with as many as 10,000 parts, from pure white ivory. Warther used arguto, an oil-bearing wood, for the moving parts of his carvings, some of which have run for 80 years without repair.

Of the steam locomotives displayed at the Warther Museum, perhaps the most intriguing is the 8-foot replica of Abraham Lincoln's funeral train. An avid admirer of Lincoln, Warther spent a year at age 80 carving the ebony and ivory locomotive, coal car, funeral car, and passenger cars. Thousands of miniature parts make up the magnificent carving. As an example of the extraordinary detail work done by Warther, outside the restroom in one of the passenger cars there is even a tiny ivory key hanging on a hook on the wall.

Warther's exacting craft demanded fine precision knives and blades, and, not satisfied with those commercially available, he created his own

TOP ANNUAL EVENTS

Maple Syrup Madness,
Newark, Feb, Mar;
(740) 323-2355, (800) 443-2937;
dawesarb.org

Utica Old Fashioned Ice Cream Festival,
Utica, May;
uticaoldfashionedicecreamfestival.com

Dennison Railroad Festival,
Dennison, June;
tusco.net/drrf

Dulcimer Days,
Coshocton, June;
(740) 545-6265;
coshoctondulcimerdays.com

Trumpet in the Land,
New Philadelphia, June to Aug;
(330) 339-1132;
trumpetintheland.com

The Living Word Outdoor Drama,
Cambridge, July through Sept;
(740) 439-2761;
livingworddrama.org

First Town Days Festival,
New Philadelphia, 4th of July weekend;
firsttowndays.com

Ohio Hills Folk Festival,
Quaker City, July;
(740) 679-2704;
ohiohillsfolkfestival.com

Jamboree in the Hills,
Morristown, July;
(800) 594-8499;
jamboreeinthehills.com

Pro Football Hall of Fame Festival,
Canton, late July to Aug;
(330) 456-7253, (800) 533-4302;
profootballhoffestival.com

custom cutlery. In fact, he supplemented his income by selling this cutlery, a business still operated by his family today. Ernest Warther died at the age of 87 in 1973, leaving his 64th carving incomplete. Footage of Warther working at his craft is shown in the Warther theater.

The small original museum behind the present one houses Mrs. Warther's button collection—more than 70,000 buttons, no two alike. Beautiful Swiss-style gardens surround the museums and the Warther home.

The Warther Museum is at 331 Karl Ave., Dover; (330) 343-7513; warthers.com. Open daily, 9 a.m. to 5 p.m. (last tour starts at 3:45 p.m.), except for major holidays. Admission: adults $13; children (ages 7 to 17) $5.

A new century was just beginning when Jeremiah E. Reeves moved his family into a newly remodeled home in 1901. Originally built as a stately

Coshocton Canal Festival,
Coshocton, Aug;
(740) 622-4877, (800) 338-4724
visitcoshocton.com

Tuscarawas County Italian-American Festival,
Dover, Aug;
(330) 602-2420;
tuscitalianamerican.org

Fredericktown Tomato Show,
Fredericktown, Sept;
tomatoshow.com

Ohio Swiss Festival,
Sugarcreek, late Sept, early Oct;
(330) 852-4113, (888) 609-7592;
villageofsugarcreek.com/ohioswissfest

Barnesville Pumpkin Festival,
Barnesville, Sept;
(740) 425-2593;
barnesvillepumpkinfestival.com

Holmes County Antique Festival,
Millersburg, Oct;
(330) 674-6781;
holmescountyantiquefestival.org

Algonquin Mill Fall Festival,
Carrollton, Oct;
(877) 727-0103;
carrollcountyohio.com/history/mill/
millfest.htm

Buckeye Book Fair,
Wooster, Nov;
(330) 627-5910;
buckeyebookfair.com

Holiday at the Orville Depot,
Orville, Nov and Dec;
(330) 683-2426;
orvillerailroad.com

Dalton Holidays Festival,
Dalton, Dec;
(330) 828-2323;
daltonfestival.org

eight-room farmhouse around 1870, the house was expanded into a magnificent 17-room mansion by Reeves, Dover's wealthiest citizen. Its gleaming white exterior is enhanced by dormers, bays, turrets, classical columns, and a porte cochere. To the rear of this Victorian mansion is a large turreted carriage house.

Today the Dover Historical Society invites you to tour the *J.E. Reeves Victorian Home and Museum* for a magnificent look at turn-of-the-20th-century elegance.

Lush drawing-room draperies, gleaming windows of stained and leaded glass, luxurious parquet floors, and artistic mementos of the Reeves family all greet the eye. Nearly all of the furnishings on display belong to the Reeves and are placed where they were when the family lived here. Other special features include a distinctive hand-carved oak grand stairway and a delightful third-floor ballroom.

Out in the carriage house, built in 1902, the first floor houses a marvelous 1892 two-horse carriage that belonged to the Reeves family, a one-horse sleigh, and a 1922 automobile. Upstairs, visitors find remnants of the old Dover post office, along with displays of early household tools and sports memorabilia, plus historic maps, photographs, and documents. Following the crooked stairs to the Tower Rooms rewards the visitor with collections of old-fashioned cameras and radios.

The J.E. Reeves Victorian Home and Museum is at 325 E. Iron Ave., Dover; (330) 343-7040, (800) 815-2794; doverhistory.org. Open June through Oct, Wed through Sun, noon to 4 p.m., plus special holiday tours in Nov and Dec. Admission: adults $8; senior citizens $7; children (ages 6 to 17) $3.

Seeking freedom from the new religious tenets in their native Kingdom of Wurttemburg in Germany, 300 men, women, and children known as Separatists, led by Joseph Baumeler, came to 5,500 acres they had purchased along the Tuscarawas River and established *Zoar Village* in 1817. Two years later, frustrated by their progress, the Zoarites abandoned personal property ownership to establish a communal system. Under the new system, all property in the village was owned by the Society of Separatists at Zoar, with men and women each given a vote in the election of a board of trustees. The board governed the day-to-day operations of the community, and under this system, with Baumeler remaining as leader of the group, Zoar flourished.

The community established its own farms for food products, a tin shop, a blacksmith shop, 2 blast furnaces, a bakery, a garden with greenhouse, and a wagon shop. Many of these enterprises produced more goods than needed by the village, with the surplus sold for profit at a store established by the villagers. The Zoarites even landed the contract to build a section of the Ohio and Erie Canal, which passed through their land.

In 1852, the assets of the society were more than $1 million, and the future appeared bright for this hardworking community. But a year later, Joseph Baumeler was dead, leaving a serious leadership void at Zoar. Baumeler had served as the inspiration of the village, as well as its financial administrator. After his death, Zoar began a gradual decline, which persisted for 40 years. Finally, in 1898, having lost its competitive edge both in agriculture and in industry, the community disbanded.

Many of the original Zoar buildings have been restored or reconstructed, allowing visitors to better understand the unique experiment that took place here. Inside the Number One House, an audiovisual presentation provides the history of the village. The rooms in this rambling two-story brick building, which once housed the aged and infirm, contain many original furnishings. In the music room, for example, is Peter Bimeler's magnificent hand-built pipe organ. Bimeler was the village miller, and he powered the organ with the mill's water turbine.

The second-floor windows provide a splendid view of the adjacent gardens and greenhouse. A guide at the greenhouse explains the religious significance of the formal gardens, with the large Norway spruce symbolizing Christ and the 12 slip junipers representing the apostles. The greenhouse, constructed in 1835, utilized a unique heating system—charcoal fires burned under the floor; vents funneled the warm air into the greenhouse—allowing the Zoarites to cultivate a wide variety of fruits and vegetables, including tropical fruits. In the Zoar bakery, huge wooden bins stored flour and meal, and the brick oven baked 80 loaves of bread per day.

Other buildings in the village include a tin shop, which has the tools, patterns, and products used and produced by the tinsmith, and the Bimeler House, with its outstanding collection of wool coverlets woven at the community's woolen mill. Knowledgeable guides provide information and answer questions in each building of the village.

Zoar Village is on OH 212, Zoar; (330) 874-3011, (800) 262-6195; historiczoarvillage.com. Open Apr through Oct, Fri and Sun, 11 a.m. to 4 p.m.; Sat, noon to 4 p.m. Admission: adults $8; children (ages 5 to 17) $4.

Named for Henry Laurens, then president of the Continental Congress, Fort Laurens, Ohio's only Revolutionary War fort, was constructed in 1778 as part of an ill-fated campaign to attack the British at Detroit. The 1,200 troops under the command of General Lachlan McIntosh, who built the fort, dubbed it "Fort Nonsense," since no attack on Detroit was ever executed. Supplying this wilderness outpost proved impossible, forcing the starving troops to survive on boiled moccasins while under siege from British-led Indians for a month. The fort was abandoned one year after it was built.

Today visitors to **Fort Laurens State Memorial** find the outline of the old fort, and a small museum that commemorates the conflict with both video and artifacts from the fort's excavation. The remains of soldiers who died defending Fort Laurens are buried in a crypt in the museum wall and at the Tomb of the Unknown Patriot of the American Revolution.

Fort Laurens State Memorial is at 11067 Fort Laurens Rd. NW, Bolivar; (330) 874-2059, (800) 283-8914; ohiohistory.org/places/ftlauren. Open May through Oct, Wed through Sat, 10 a.m. to 5 p.m.; Sun, noon to 5 p.m. Admission: adults $3; children (ages 6 to 12) $1.

Nestled on a wooded and secluded 6-acre site, ***Enchanted Pines Bed and Breakfast*** was constructed with the visitor in mind. Built in 1981 in Yankee Barn design, the home features post-and-beam openness throughout. A living room with 35-foot ceilings and impressive fireplace is the heart of this 5,000-square-foot home. There is plenty of room to get away on your own on the home's grounds, or to join hosts Linda and Earl Menges for traditional high tea. Other amenities include a swimming pool, hot tub, and screened porch.

The 3 rooms have second-floor views of the woods. The English Ivy Suite features separate sleeping and living areas, private porch with swing, and easy access to the pool.

Enchanted Pines Bed and Breakfast is at 1862 Old Trail Rd. NE, Bolivar; (330) 874-3197, (877) 536-7508; enchantedpines.com. Rates: $139 to $169 per night double occupancy including breakfast.

Mingo Junction

George Washington slept here—actually he camped here in the fall of 1770. He came via canoe to scout the land in the Ohio Valley, and he found rugged country and plenty of Indians. He was here to secure land for the officers and soldiers of the Virginia Regiment before the British tried to claim it.

Upon his arrival in poor weather, Washington and his party heard of a killing down river, the direction they were heading. It was unclear whether it was an Indian dispute or a simple homicide. After one night's rest, they left the spot that is known today as Mingo Junction and paddled downstream.

They arrived at Powhatan Point, from which Washington dispatched several in his party to uncover the truth about the alleged murder. They returned and told Washington that the rumors were untrue; the death had been an accidental drowning. On October 25, 1770, they departed, continuing their journey down the Ohio River.

Missionary David Zeisberger migrated to the US in 1737 to work with the American Moravian Church in Bethlehem, Pennsylvania. In 1772, accompanied by a band of Delaware Indians, Zeisberger traveled to the wilderness in Ohio to convert other Indians to Christianity, founding *Schoenbrunn Village.*

The efforts at Schoenbrunn were interrupted by the coming of the Revolutionary War. The village was on the trail between the American outpost at Fort Pitt and the British at Fort Detroit, and neither side trusted the Moravians or their Christian Indians. Harassment eventually forced Zeisberger to abandon Schoenbrunn Village in 1777 and to relocate to a new settlement at nearby Gnadenhutten. Even there, they were not safe. The British arrested Zeisberger and other village leaders and transported them to Detroit for trial on charges of treason. While the leaders were away, American troops, seeking revenge for the death of a settler's wife and children, massacred the Christian Indians at Gnadenhutten by striking them with heavy coopers' mallets.

Schoenbrunn Village today contains 18 reconstructed rustic log buildings, the original village cemetery, and 2.5 acres of planted fields. Log cots with stretched animal skins and a fire pit in the center of the floor (with a hole in the roof for smoke to escape) are the only conveniences in some of these cabins. Others feature modest pioneer furnishings such as rough rope-spring beds, wooden baby cradles, spinning and flax wheels, and butter churns. Schoenbrunn's settlers constructed Ohio's first schoolhouse, a one-room building completed in 1773. In addition to the log structures, a museum displays Schoenbrunn artifacts excavated from the site, including nails,

famouspeople fromlittlecadiz

The little town of Cadiz boasts an impressive roster of native sons. Clark Gable was from this town, as was Edward Stanton, President Lincoln's secretary of war during the Civil War, and John Bingham, who also has a Lincoln connection. Bingham, an attorney, worked in William Henry Harrison's presidential campaign and was elected to Congress in 1854.

During his tenure in Washington, he served as special-judge advocate in the trial of Lincoln's assassins. He also was minister to Japan from 1873 to 1885.

knives, horseshoes, and chips of cups, jars, and a kettle used at the village more than 200 years ago.

Schoenbrunn Village is on OH 259 on the southeast edge of New Philadelphia; (877) 278-8020; ohiosfirstvillage.com. Open Memorial Day to Labor Day, Tues through Sat, 9:30 a.m. to 5 p.m.; Sun, noon to 5 p.m., plus weekends in Sept and Oct. Admission: adults $7; children (ages 7 to 19) $4.

For a dramatic presentation of the story of David Zeisberger and the settlement of Schoenbrunn and Gnadenhutten, attend a performance of Paul Green's *Trumpet in the Land.* Staged in a lovely hilltop outdoor amphitheater, this spirited drama uses a mix of song and dance, humor, adventure, and ultimately tragedy to tell of Zeisberger's missionary work in frontier Ohio.

Trumpet in the Land is presented in repertoire with *The White Savage* at the Schoenbrunn Amphitheatre on University Drive, just off US 250, New Philadelphia; (330) 339-1132; trumpetintheland.com. Performances from June through Aug, Mon through Sat at 8:30 p.m. Admission: adults $20 at the door, $17 in advance; children (ages 12 and under) $10 at the door, $8 in advance. Reserved tickets available. Tickets are cheaper on Monday and Tuesday Bargain Nights.

The *Dennison Railroad Depot Museum* has been drawing people from all across the US since it opened in 1989. This fully restored railroad station gives the visitor a glimpse into the role that railroads played in America's past. At the turn of the 20th century this depot was a busy crossroads, hosting 22 arrivals daily. In the 1940s the station became an oasis of homegrown comfort for many World War II service men and women passing through on the National Defense Railroad Route. The depot grew famous as more and more military men and women were welcomed by scores of volunteers at the Salvation Army Servicemen's Canteen. This canteen was the third largest in the country and served free food and provided a little hometown warmth to thousands passing through on their way to and from the fronts.

Visitors can relive the early eras of railroad travel by visiting the museum and the various restored areas, including the women's lounge and the ticket booth. The large model N-scale train display will fascinate children, even the adult kind. You can also experience the flavor of the 1940s in the Pennsy Dining Company, which is filled with photos, hosts a documentary video, and serves pasta, seafood, and steaks.

The Dennison Railroad Depot Museum is at 400 Center St., Dennison; (740) 922-6776, (877) 278-8020; dennisondepot.org. Open Tues through Fri, 10 a.m. to 5 p.m.; Sat, 11 a.m. to 4 p.m.; Sun, 11 a.m. to 3 p.m. Admission: adults $8; senior citizens $6; children (ages 7 to 17) $4.

The *Quaker Meeting House,* set in a field in a hilly section of Jefferson County, housed the annual August meeting of 2,000 Ohio and Pennsylvania Quakers for nearly a century. Constructed in 1814, this impressive three-story brick structure measures 92 feet by 60 feet and has walls 2 feet thick.

The Society of Friends relocated an entire meeting from North Carolina to Jefferson County in 1813 and built the meetinghouse of brick fired right on the site. The interior of the building is one large room, with the

thehousethat jackbuilt

You might know that Bellaire is the site of the original "house that Jack built." But did you know that "Jack" was a mule? Englishman Jacob Heatherington immigrated to this area and worked his way up from a laborer hauling coal to an industrialist. His faithful mule, Jack, helped him move coal in those early years, and Jacob never forgot this. So, when he erected a mansion in 1870, he referred to it as the "house that Jack built" and even took the old mule on a tour of the home's interior, describing the features as they clip-clopped through the magnificent residence. Jack died shortly afterward, and Jacob, grief-stricken, buried him nearby under an apple tree.`

original floors, poplar benches, and a large balcony. A massive wooden center divider splits the room—four men in the attic raised and lowered this divider as needed. Men sat on one side of the room during the meetings, women on the other side, and young men and women sat in their respective balconies. The elders and overseers used the facing benches—benches resting on a small platform and facing the congregation. "Strict services" took place here until 1909, with no formal ceremony or music; the group simply meditated in silence until a member felt moved to speak out. The interior of the meetinghouse is exactly as it was 170 years ago, though it has been more than 70 years since the Quakers last gathered in Jefferson County.

The Quaker Meeting House is just off OH 150 in Mount Pleasant. Open by appointment Apr through Oct; call (740) 769-2893 or (800) 752-2631; ohiohistory.org. Admission: adults $3; children (ages 6 to 12) $1.50.

Amish Country

Ohio's largest Amish and Swiss Mennonite communities are in four east central Ohio counties: Holmes, Wayne, Tuscarawas, and Stark. The Amish espouse a simple agrarian lifestyle and reject the use of automobiles and electricity as potentially disruptive to that lifestyle. Living in the 20th century without electricity creates a demand for unusual products, such as kerosene-powered refrigerators, and one Wayne County business, *Lehman's,* has established itself as the nonelectric appliance and equipment supplier for the area's substantial Amish population.

Although Lehman's stocks the nails, wire, and garden tools found in every hardware store, the bulk of the floor space is dedicated to merchandise such as gas-powered washing machines, and gas and kerosene lamps. Wood- and coal-burning cooking and heating stoves fill one large showroom, with many of the cooking stoves ornately trimmed in chrome and costing from $700 to $3,000.

Other items in Lehman's inventory include hardwood fruit presses, an apple parer, a cherry stoner, and a bottle capper. How many other stores carry a variety of hand-crank butter churns and a hand-powered cream separator that produces 85 liters of milk per hour?

The store's crowded hitching posts, used by the Amish to secure their horse-drawn buggies, indicate the popularity of Lehman's with the local Amish population, but in recent years Lehman's has attracted another type of customer—people drawn to wood- and coal-burning appliances because of the increasing cost of utilities. Lehman's sells a 160-page catalog called *Lehman's Non-Electric Good Neighbor Heritage Catalog* for $3. It's full of major appliances, small gristmills, copper wash boilers, sausage stuffers, noodle makers, and carbide lamps. And city people have been known to purchase unique nonelectric devices, particularly the fancy chrome cooking stoves, simply for use as decorative pieces.

A recently opened Lehman's Outlet Store is located on the square across the parking lot from Lehman's at 13110 Emerson Rd., Apple Creek. The store offers great deals on closeout, overstock, and clearance items. The inventory changes daily, so you never know what you might find.

Lehman's is located at 4779 Kidron Rd., Kidron; (888) 438-5346; lehmans .com. Open Jan through May 26, Mon through Thurs, 9 a.m. to 5 p.m.; Fri and Sat, 9 a.m. to 6 p.m.; May 27 through Dec, Mon through Sat, 8 a.m. to 6 p.m.

Just down the street is the ***Kidron Town and Country Store,*** where you can purchase an array of Amish clothing—men's broadfall barn-door pants, black felt church hats, and wide-rimmed flat or mushroom-top straw hats.

Upstairs you'll find quilting supplies, and the store also offers fresh-cut meats, fresh fruits and vegetables, and other bulk food items. It has long been the custom of the Amish to come in from the fields at noon and enjoy *es midaugh*. They continue that tradition at the store, serving a hearty mid-day meal prepared by local Amish women in their restaurant. The restaurant opens at 7 a.m. for breakfast and serves lunch until 2:30 p.m.

The Kidron Town and Country Store is at 4959 Kidron Rd., Kidron; (330) 857-2131; kidrontownandcountry.com. Open Mon through Sat, 7 a.m. to 8 p.m.

After establishing their Christmas tree farm, Robert Dush and his son Roger's next challenge was to convert a barn built in the 1860s into a Christmas shop and country store, the ***Pine Tree Barn.*** This massive old barn has been designated a Wayne County Historic Landmark, and its original rough-hewn beams and floors create a rustic atmosphere.

What started as a gift shop in 1980 has evolved into a complete home furnishing and accessories center, featuring indoor and outdoor lighting, carpeting, floor coverings, and window treatments, plus gifts and accessories, all displayed on three floors in this marvelous historic structure. In fact, Roger Dush and his wife, Rita, offer a complete interior decorating and design service.

The gift shops at Pine Tree include a Colonial Williamsburg shop; a floral shop featuring silk and dried flowers, wreaths, and garlands; and a year-round Christmas shop. Christmas is a special time of year at Pine Tree; you'll find 30 or more fully decorated trees throughout the structure, along with hundreds of unique ornaments and baubles.

A similar transformation took place at The Granary, the Pine Tree's dining facility. In the early '80s, this former dairy barn's old grain bins were converted into a small kitchen, serving simple refreshments. Today The Granary presents gourmet lunches of crepes, quiches, soups, salads, pastas, pizza, fresh breads and muffins, and sandwiches. Top off your meal with a slice of one of the sour cream fruit pies, a Pine Tree Barn tradition for more than 20 years. The Granary also offers beer and wine, but not on Sunday.

Large windows along the back wall of the barn provide those eating lunch with a view down the hill to the private 40-acre lake and rows of young Christmas trees. Diners also see antique farm implements on the walls of the barn and the block and tackle that once hauled bales of hay up from the ground level to the second-floor loft.

The Pine Tree Barn is on OH 226, 4374 Shreve Rd., 4 miles south of Wooster; (330) 264-1014; pinetreebarn.com. Open Mon through Sat, 9 a.m. to 5 p.m.; Sun, 10 a.m. to 5 p.m.

Before Deanna and Andy Troutman converted their property into a vineyard, the previous owner used it to raise chickens and sell produce. The winery building formerly served as one of the chicken coops. The Troutmans moved in back in 1997 and began planting their vineyard the next year. By the fall of 2000, the first crop was harvested, and **Troutman Vineyards** unveiled their first three wines the following summer.

Deanna and Andy, who also serves as vineyard manager at Wolf Creek Vineyards, currently have 16 different wines ready to pour. During the holidays, try their Chambourcin Ice Wine, aged in French oak barrels with a hint of raisin and walnut. Another favorite is their White Menagerie Seyval blanc, an award-winning fruity yet dry German-style white. Visitors are encouraged to take a self-guided tour of the vineyard's operations. Free live music is offered every Saturday from 6 to 8 p.m.

Troutman Vineyards is at 4243 Columbus Rd., Wooster; (330) 263-4345; troutmanvineyards.com. Open Apr through Dec, Mon through Thurs, 11 a.m. to 6 p.m.; Fri and Sat, 11 a.m. to 9 p.m. Open Jan through March, Thurs, 11 a.m. to 6 p.m.; Fri and Sat, 11 a.m. to 8 p.m.

Set in rolling Wayne County farmland is charming **Quailcrest Farm.** More than 600 different herbs and perennial plants, both potted and field grown, are cultivated here, ready for transplanting to your backyard garden. Flowering shrubs and trees are also available. April through June is the peak season for plants at Quailcrest, but a good selection is available throughout the summer and into fall.

Avid gardeners will love browsing through the various shops. Under the Lattice contains pottery and several garden ornaments. A 12,000-square-foot greenhouse solarium displays a wide variety of perennials and herbs for sale. Another restored building, the 175-year-old Garden Barn, sells contemporary gift items, including books, jewelry, gourmet foods, linens, and pet and children's items.

Outside, even people without green thumbs can enjoy wandering through 5 acres of display gardens overlooking the Killbuck Valley. You can view herb gardens, perennial plantings, and water gardens, or just sit and relax in the gazebo.

Quailcrest Farm is just off OH 83 at 2810 Armstrong Rd., 5 miles north of Wooster; (330) 345-6722; quailcrest.com. Open late Mar through Dec, Tues through Sat, 9 a.m. to 5 p.m. (extended and Sun hours from the end of Apr through June and also after Thanksgiving).

Out-of-state antiques dealers have frequented Jeromesville, Ohio, for years, but most native Ohioans are unaware of the town's reputation as an antiques stop. George Delagrange owns one of Jeromesville's more intriguing shops, *Delagrange Antiques,* which is in an 1870s storefront that originally housed the town's drugstore.

Delagrange's business specializes in the poplar, cherry, and walnut pieces so in demand with East Coast buyers. Delagrange (whose name means "from the farm" in French) purchases four-poster rope-spring beds, cupboards, tables, and chests from area farms, selling scores of major pieces each year. In addition, George and his wife, Susan, always are delighted to chat with visitors about tidbits of local history that pertain to the pieces in the shop.

Delagrange Antiques is at 12 N. High St. (OH 89), Jeromesville; (419) 368-8371; ohioantiques.com. Open Sat and Sun, noon to 5 p.m.

stateflag/ pennant

Flying overhead at public buildings and parks in Ohio, visitors may be surprised to see what appears to be a pennant where they would expect a state flag to fly. That is Ohio's state flag. No other state flag has a pennant shape.

Cleveland designer John Eisenmann created this unusual design in the 1880s. At the wide end of the pennant is a blue triangle with a large circle and 17 stars. The 13 stars clustered closest to the circle represent the 13 colonies. The four stars at the apex of the triangle represent the next four states admitted to the union, since Ohio was the 17th state to join. The circle represents the Northwest Territory, but with a smaller red circle at its center; it also forms an O for "Ohio."

The natural beauty of the Mohican area, with its steep and rolling hills, swift rivers, and deep forests, once prompted author Louis Bromfield to remark, "I live on the edge of paradise." Visitors to the area quickly realize that statement was no exaggeration.

White pines flourish along the ridges of the **Mohican State Park,** while hemlock abounds in the hollows and gorges.

Cabins in Ohio's state parks typically are located in scenic surroundings, but the 25 two-bedroom Mohican State Park cabins, isolated from the rest of the park in woodlands along the bank of Clear Fork Creek, may just be in the most picturesque setting of any cabins in Ohio.

They come furnished with all linens, blankets, and kitchen equipment, and may be rented in the summer for full weeks only. (There are no restrictions on the length of stay the rest of the year.) Canoeing and rafting are favorite summertime activities on Clear Fork Creek, and hiking, fishing, and camping are also popular in the park.

Mohican State Park cabins are just north of OH 97 at 3116 OH 3, Loudonville; (866) 644-6727, (419) 994-5125; mohicanstatepark.org. Open year-round. Rates range from $115 to $125 per night; early reservations are a must.

Another lodging option in the lush Mohican State Park is the impressive stone-and-timber **Mohican Lodge and Conference Center,** perched on a bluff overlooking Pleasant Hill Lake. Each of the 96 rooms in the lodge has a private balcony or patio, many with views of either the lake or the woods surrounding the lodge. Facilities include indoor and outdoor pools, 2 tennis courts, shuffleboard, a sauna, an exercise room, and a game room. In addition to the meals served in the dining room, poolside barbecues are offered occasionally during summer months.

The Mohican Resort is on OH 97, 6 miles west of Loudonville; (800) 282-7275, (419) 938-5411; mohicanstateparklodge.com Open year-round. Rates: $169 to $199 per night, double occupancy.

The confluence of Black Fork River and Clear Fork Creek forms the scenic Mohican River, probably Ohio's most popular stream for canoeing, kayaking, and rafting. Canoe liveries rent hundreds of canoes and kayaks in the Loudonville area, from as early as April to as late as November. With prices of $15 and up per canoe and trips lasting from 2 hours to several days, the liveries provide access to these scenic waterways. One of the liveries, on OH

3 south of Loudonville and north of Route 97, is the **Mohican Adventures Camping, Canoe, and Fun Center,** which also has cabins, go-karts, horseback rides, waterslides, and miniature golf; (800) 662-2663, (888) 909-7400; canoemohican.com. Many other liveries operate in the area, and a complete list is available from the Loudonville Chamber of Commerce, 131 W. Main St., Loudonville 44842, (419) 994-4789; loudonville-mohican.com/chamber .html; or by calling (800) BUCKEYE or visiting discoverohio.com, Ohio's tourism information center.

It's a dream you may have had, too: Purchase one of those charming Victorian houses on a quiet street in a small Ohio town and restore it to create the perfect bed-and-breakfast. City people would flock to your new establishment, attracted by the charm of your stately residence, not to mention your gracious hospitality. You would earn extra income while enjoying the company of "new friends."

I'm sure that's what the couple who originally restored the **Blackfork Inn** believed when they acquired this 1865-vintage property on Water Street in Loudonville. Built by Philip J. Black, this delightful brick three-story home seemed destined to be a fine small inn. And the couple restoring it decided to "do it right" by importing antiques from Europe, installing a complete commercial kitchen, securing accurate reproductions of period wallpapers, and updating the 6 guest rooms with private baths, while retaining the high ceilings and natural woodwork that make such properties both distinctive and desirable. It's rumored they spent upward of a half million dollars on this project, and that may have been their undoing. Less than a year from their grand opening, the Blackfork Inn was closed down and boarded up— its brief resurrection snuffed out.

On Labor Day weekend in 1982, Al and Sue Gorisek arrived at the sheriff's auction at the Blackfork hoping to pick up some good deals on antiques, which they have collected for years. But they walked away as the proud new owners of the entire inn. Todd and Cheryl Brown later bought the beautiful landmark from the Goriseks and are continuing the hospitality.

The inn was originally the home of Philip Black, who built it from the profits he made during the Civil War selling groceries and such to federal troops. It's said he was instrumental in bringing the railroad to Loudonville, so it seems appropriate that railroad tracks are next door—it's the main line between New York and Chicago, so trains do rumble by!

Accommodations at the Blackfork Inn—6 rooms plus 2 large suites—include home-cooked breakfasts. The Blackfork Inn is at 303 N. Water St., Loudonville; (419) 994-3252; blackforkinn.com. Rates: $85 to $150 per night, including breakfast. Open year-round.

The fertile, rolling farmland of Holmes County is the center of Ohio's largest Amish community, with 20,000 of the 145,000 Amish in the US living in the area. Amish men and women can be seen in the markets, restaurants, and shops, or driving their black horse-drawn buggies through the pastoral countryside.

Amish restaurants in Holmes and surrounding counties serve simple country cooking at reasonable prices, and shops sell Amish goods, such as quilts.

This section of east central Ohio also contains a sizable Swiss Mennonite population, and there are many cheese houses producing swiss cheese from the milk brought in by Amish dairy farmers.

The Amish were the largest group of the 1694 Swiss Brethren split, following the leadership of Jacob Ammann, from whom the sect gets its name. Facing religious persecution in their native Germany and Switzerland, they began a migration to the US in the 1730s, settling in Pennsylvania. The move to Ohio took place in 1808, and Holmes County, Ohio, now is the world's largest community of Amish. The Amish continue the agricultural traditions of the past 200 years.

Artist Heinz Gaugel painted the history of the Amish-Mennonite-Hutterite people in a spectacular 10-foot-by-265-foot cyclorama called **Behalt,** which means "to remember." Completed in 1992 after four years' labor, *Behalt* spans the centuries from the time of Christ to the Amish migration to the New World to the present day. *Behalt* is permanently displayed at the Mennonite Information Center, where guides use the cyclorama to educate visitors about Amish history, culture, and lifestyle.

Behalt and the Mennonite Information Center are at 5798 CR 77, Berlin; (330) 893-3192, (877) 858-4634; behalt.com. Open Mon through Sat, 9 a.m. to 5 p.m.; extended hours until 8 p.m., Fri and Sat, June through Oct. Admission: adults $8.75; children (ages 6 to 12) $4.25.

Gloria and Eli **Yoder's Amish Home** is a 116-acre working farm that can be explored by visitors to Amish country. Children will enjoy the horses, rabbits, chickens, sheep, cows, pigs, and goats that fill the barn.

Adults will probably be more interested in the 2 farmhouses, both built more than 100 years ago. The first home on your tour contains furnishings typical of an Amish farmhouse in the late 1800s. Built in 1866, this home last served as a residence more than 30 years ago. Its wood floors, simple heavy furniture, wood-burning stove, and people-powered appliances (such as a pump sewing machine) give a glimpse of the lifestyle of Amish farm families.

The larger home, constructed in 1885 and occupied for 100 years, is similarly furnished but contains some unusual items such as gas floor lamps.

Religious services have been held here many times, as in most Amish homes and barns. These services take three full hours to complete.

The Amish bakery offers a large selection of jams, jellies, bread, cinnamon rolls, and cookies, made fresh daily at the bakery.

Walk down by the brook to visit the one-room schoolhouse and learn how the Amish parochial school system works. Be sure to open one of the textbooks, written mostly in English with a few German words scattered here and there. How can the Amish use a modern copy machine if they don't have electricity? An Amish teacher explains how it is done, for an interesting lesson in ingenuity.

Many who visit here enjoy buggy tours of the property, which even has a hilltop family cemetery. Inside the craft shop, you'll discover quilts, dolls, pottery, woodwork, and many other country favorites. And be sure to pick up a copy of the *Downhome Shoppers Guide*. This 100-page magazine-style publication is the guide to Ohio's Amish settlements. It's packed with information on Amish restaurants, tours, crafts, quilts, cheese, and the like, with hundreds of entries and very detailed maps.

Yoder's Amish Home between Trail and Walnut Creek at 6050 OH 515 in Millersburg; (330) 893-2541; yodersamishhome.com. Open mid-Apr through Oct, Mon through Sat, 10 a.m. to 5 p.m. Tours: adults $7.50; children (ages 2 through 12) $4.50. Buggy rides: adults $4.50; children $3.50.

If you admire fine handmade quilts, stop by the ***Helping Hands Quilt Shop.*** A nonprofit enterprise with all proceeds donated to charities and missions, the shop stocks hundreds of marvelous quilts in every conceivable pattern and color combination. Many of these are sewn in the large, sunlit quilting room in the back of the shop, where Helping Hands serves a social function in addition to its contributions to charity.

Helping Hands will quilt your quilt top, custom design a quilt for you, or even finish a quilt you have already started. The shop also sells quilted pillow covers, quilting books, embroidery kits and floss, quilting needles, thread, fabrics, stencils, and patterns—in short, everything a quilter could need. Also visit the Quilt Museum, with its many antique quilts.

The Helping Hands Quilt Shop is at 4818 OH 39, Berlin; (330) 893-2233; helpinghandsquilts.com. Open Mon through Sat, 9 a.m. to 5 p.m.

A variety of romantic options await guests of ***Donna's Premier Lodging*** in the heart of Amish country. Along with rooms in the main building, Donna's offers a variety of upscale log cabins, chalets, villas, and bridal suites. Honeymoon and anniversary chalets are two-level, brick, freestanding guest cottages located on a wooded hillside. Designed as luxurious retreats, they feature a main level with a king-size bed, a brick fireplace, and a heart-shaped Jacuzzi for two. The lower level is a recreation room with another fireplace and a billiard table. Throughout the chalets you will find elegant touches such as leaded glass windows, chandeliers, and homemade cookies for your late-night snack. Chalets are equipped with 2 televisions, stereo, CD player, microwave, coffeemaker, and a refrigerator. The log cabin is similarly equipped but has a queen-size bed tucked in a loft.

Whether summer or winter, the cabin, cottages, and chalets offer guests natural views and a good opportunity to wander just outside the door to visit with the birds or enjoy the woodland displays.

Donna's Premier Lodging is located ½ block off Main Street at 5523 East St., just behind the Helping Hands Quilt Shop, Berlin; (330) 893-3068, (800) 320-3338; donnasofberlin.com. Rates: $149 to $369 per night.

Opened for guests in 1996, ***Garden Gate Get-A-Way*** has a surprisingly long history. Many elements in the home are from a dismantled

ALSO WORTH SEEING

Salt Fork State Park,
Cambridge

Fort Steuben,
Steubenville

Steubenville Murals,
Steubenville

one-room schoolhouse. The original bell tower is now perched on the roof's south peak, and the original foundation stones now form many of the retaining walls and line the flowerbeds. Inside, lumber, oak flooring, tongue-and-groove ceiling, and wainscoting have found new uses in this modern facility.

Carol and Herb Steffey are your innkeepers, offering 6 very different guest rooms, each with a garden theme. The Potting Shed Room features a picket fence headboard, a cane chair, and a hickory rocker. A white iron bed is the centerpiece of the Rose Garden Room, flanked by an antique tapestry chair and chest. The Briar Patch Room features engraved head-boards and individual furnishings. The Magnolia Garden Room, renovated in 2011, has a cherry finish electric fireplace with a 32-inch flat-screen TV above it. The Summer Breeze Suite is the only guest room with a king bed and the only two-room suite. The Garden Gate Suite has a corner two-person jetted tub and a large oak fireplace. All five have private baths and coffeemakers.

Added in 2009, two cottages are popular lodging options. The Falls Kiss Cottage has a peninsula fireplace and an Amish-made bed. The Spring Desire Cottage features an Amish-made sleigh bed and a Roman-style jetted tub.

The beautiful gardens include a grape arbor, birdhouses, and porch swings. Previous owner Roger Steiner's design talent is on display with the fieldstone landscaping and winding brick paths through the lush gardens.

Garden Gate Get-A-Way is located just outside Berlin at 6041 Township Rd. 310; (330) 674-7608; garden-gate.com. Room rates: $105 to $185 per night; cottages are $185 to $189 per night.

When I first heard about a "modern" inn that opened outside Millers-burg, right in the heart of Amish country, I must admit I was skeptical. I envisioned a motel-like structure on a bulldozed and paved chunk of earth, and I wasn't thrilled by the prospect. *The Inn and Spa at Honey Run* does not fit that description in the least. As you motor up a winding county road, through dense vegetation, your curiosity can't help but be aroused. And when you reach the tasteful contemporary structure that is the Inn and Spa at Honey Run, it's difficult not to let out a sigh of approval. Care-fully blended into the surrounding trees—trees so close that I'm not sure how they managed to get the inn up without disturbing them—is a truly unique getaway. Lots of exposed wood, inside and out, creates a harmony between the inn and the peaceful forest. The inn's 25 guest rooms combine a potpourri of styles—everything from Shaker and Early American to very contemporary. Cherry, pine, oak, and walnut furnishings complete these rooms; some feature bi-level floor plans with skylights. All have living areas and tabletop space for work (if absolutely necessary), writing, card playing, or whatever.

Up a hill from the main inn are 12 additional guest rooms in a most unusual setting—dug into the hillside. Called the Honeycomb, this earth-sheltered building looks down onto a peaceful landscape.

Each room has a stone patio, gas log fireplace, and a bath with a whirl-pool tub. And breakfast is brought right to your door. The newest accom-modations are 2 cabins nestled in the woods. The Trillium is a one-bedroom unit with large Jacuzzi tub; the Cardinal features 2 bedrooms and 2 baths.

If you can't stay the night, then come by and enjoy an excellent meal in the Tarragon dining room, which has a wall of glass for viewing the trees and wildflowers. The inn prides itself on its from-scratch recipes, including some spectacular pastries and des-serts, and regional specialties like pan-fried trout. The dining room is open daily to all for breakfast, lunch, and dinner, by reservation.

The Inn and Spa at Honey Run is 3 miles northeast of Millersburg off OH 241 at 6920 CR 203; (330) 674-0011, (800) 468-6639; innathoneyrun .com. Lodging rates: $119 to $339 per night for two people, including conti-nental breakfast.

Charm is the state's only predom-inantly Amish town, and evidence of that fact includes the popularity of the local icehouse (since the Amish don't use electric refrigerators), the town's harness shop (for the horse-drawn

statebird/fish/ insect

The designation of the cardinal as Ohio's state bird was uncontrover-sial; the Ohio General Assembly unanimously made it official in 1933. Lawmakers deemed the choice appropriate because the cardinal is a permanent resident of the state, its song is pleasing to hear, and its coloring is impres-sive. But other species have not had it so easy. A debate in the 1980s between fans of the walleye and boosters of the smallmouth bass resulted in a legislative standoff; neither side could muster the votes to be declared Ohio's state fish. One species did make the cut: the ladybug. Legislators declared it the state insect in 1975.

buggies and field horses' leather needs), and the hitching posts behind *Grandma's Homestead Restaurant.*

This is not the largest Amish restaurant in the county, nor the fanciest, but it does serve authentic Amish cooking at reasonable prices. The menu features a variety of sandwiches, and the dinner entrees include country favorites such as fried chicken, pork tenderloin, fresh lake perch, beef tenderloin, ham, and fish. Family-style dinners of chicken, roast beef, and ham, or any combination of the three include potatoes, gravy, noodles, salad, and dressing. Fresh desserts are one of the trademarks of Amish restaurants, and Grandma's Homestead is no exception, offering very tasty peanut butter cream and pecan pies, plus date pudding, sundaes, and Amish cracker pudding. Homemade breads are also available to carry out.

For a total immersion into the life of Charm, spend the night in the accommodations offered in the cottage across the street at Grandma's Homestead Cottage Bed and Breakfast. The cottage was formerly a lock- and watch-repair shop. The cottage has a private bath with Jacuzzi tub, a sitting room, and a great fireplace, and rents for $99 per night. Lodging includes a breakfast buffet and dinner at the restaurant.

Grandma's Homestead Restaurant is at 4450 OH 557 in Charm; (330) 893-2717; grandmashomestead.com. Open Mon through Sat, 11 a.m. to 7 p.m.

Just up the road is the "home of Ohio Baby Swiss Cheese," the *Guggisberg Cheese Company,* owned and operated by Alfred and Margaret Guggisberg. Born in Switzerland, Alfred began work in a cheese factory more than 40 years ago at the age of 16.

Today their plant produces 1,000 five-pound wheels of baby swiss Monday through Friday between 8 a.m. and noon, cheese that is then shipped worldwide. Local Amish dairy farmers supply the milk, which arrives daily in horse-pulled wagons. Visitors to the plant can see the cheese forming in large stainless-steel vats by looking through the windows that connect the plant with the retail store. Guggisberg stocks a wide variety of cheeses in addition to Ohio baby swiss, and cuckoo clocks, books, gift items, and ice cream are also sold.

Guggisberg Cheese Company is at 5060 OH 557, north of Charm; (330) 893-2500, (800) 262-2505; babyswiss.com. Open Apr through Dec, Mon through Sat, 8 a.m. to 6 p.m.; Sun, 11 a.m. to 4 p.m. Open the rest of the year Mon through Sat, 8 a.m. to 5 p.m.

If you want to unwind after a day of touring Amish country, the *Guggisberg Swiss Inn* is waiting to welcome you with a comfortable room and a country-style breakfast. The inn is a modern structure set in Amish farming country. You can hike or picnic nearby or just take a walk around the inn pond to watch the swans. In the winter months sleigh rides take guests into the rolling countryside.

Rooms are air-conditioned and all have private baths and in-room coffee. Breakfast is included in the room rate and takes advantage of the wonderful, fresh goodies available in farm country. Dinner is also served. Reservations required.

The Guggisberg Swiss Inn is at 5025 OH 557, Charm; (330) 893-3600, (877) 467-9477; guggisbergswissinn.com. Rates: $89.95 to $210 per night.

One of Ashland's best-known landmark homes is now a delightful bed-and-breakfast, the *Winfield Bed & Breakfast.* Built in 1876 in the Victorian Italianate style, it's perched on 2 acres of well-manicured lawns and gardens surrounded by green pastures.

Visitors have a choice of 3 very different rooms, each with a private bath. Light pours into the Garden Suite, which features English country decor, a fireplace, and a private sitting room with French doors that open to a garden terrace. The East Room is more formal, with its magnificent 18th-century French armoire and wingback chairs. Tucked up high in the front of the house, the Crow's Nest features rich cocoa walls, fresh white moldings, a washed pine armoire, and a polished mahogany queen-size bed. All rooms have free Wi-Fi. You will be greeted with a fresh fruit and cheese plate, and each morning starts with a gourmet breakfast. Unlimited beverages, fresh popcorn, and other snacks are available. The nightly turndown service includes fine French chocolate mints.

Afternoon tea ($16.95) and lunch are served to groups only, Tues through Fri, noon to 2 p.m. Gather some friends to enjoy a Welsh Rarebit Flashback—smooth flavorful aged cheese served over thin toast points and garnished with toasted whole almonds. Cost is $12.50 for the entree, along with beverage, salad, and dessert. A tiny home accessories shop in the upper foyer carries vintage goods, antiques, and decorator accessories.

The Winfield Bed & Breakfast is at 1568 OH 60, Ashland; (419) 281-5587, (800) 269-7166; winfieldbb.com. Rates: $85 to $175 per night single or double occupancy.

Country Charm

The nearly 10,000 acres that constitute The **Wilds** have made a dramatic transformation—from an open strip mine to North America's largest preserve for endangered species. American Electric Power reclaimed the land and then gave it as a gift to the public to spur the creation of this unique facility. Animals from around the world are free to roam the rolling hills; visitors observe them from open-air safari buses, which take them past every species imaginable.

The preserve is divided in large sections where African, Asian, and North American wildlife live and thrive. During your visit, you might encounter camel, exotic deer, wild horses, or rhinos. Zebras and giraffes mingle with gazelles and antelopes in the preserve's African environment. During your visit, you'll learn the issues affecting the survival of each species.

The Wilds offers many adventures, including mountain biking, birding, fishing safari, horseback safari, zipline safari, and exploration of the butterfly habitat. The Wilds has a snack shop, grill, and Overlook Cafe and Restaurant. The restaurant menu includes specialty sandwiches and wraps, burgers, chicken, salads, bottled beer and wine, desserts, and daily meals made fresh from the Wilds' organic garden and local farmers' market.

Guests can enjoy an exclusive, adults-only overnight stay in a private yurt at Nomad Ridge or at The Lodge, a private luxury cabin.

The Wilds is at 14000 International Rd., Cumberland; (740) 638-5030; thewilds.org. Open Oct only on Sat and Sun, 10 a.m. to 4 p.m. Also open daily May through Sept, 10 a.m. to 4 p.m. Admission: adults $20; senior citizens $19; children (ages 4 to 12) $15.

Eastern Ohio, western Pennsylvania, and northern West Virginia were once the center of the US glassware industry, and Cambridge, Ohio, was an important city for the glass business. The large Cambridge Glass Company dominated glass production in Guernsey County, opening in the spring of 1902 and shutting down half a century later. Although the boom in glassmaking has since passed, *Mosser Glass* preserves the heritage of the industry and offers free tours of its factory to the public. Mosser manufactures glass pitchers, goblets, candleholders, lamps, and animal figures such as frogs, owls, cats, and rabbits.

During the tour, guides explain glassmaking, from heating glass powder to 2,000 degrees in the furnace to forming molten glass in a cast-iron mold. After being pressed in a mold, the shaped glass goes under a flame "glazer," which smooths the surface by reheating the exterior. From there, the molded hot glass cools in a special oven called a Lehr, which uniformly reduces the temperature to prevent shattering. Mosser Glass cranks out 150 pieces of glass per hour.

Mosser Glass is 1/2 mile west of I-77 on US 22 at 9279 Cadiz Rd., Cambridge; (740) 439-1827; mosserglass.com. Tours are given from 8 to 10 a.m. and 11 a.m. to 2:30 p.m. Mon through Fri. No tours the first 2 weeks of July or the last 2 weeks of Dec. No admission charge.

You will find *Georgetown Vineyards* surrounded by 5 acres of planted grapes, sitting on top of a ridge overlooking the city of Cambridge. The family-owned business produces a variety of wines. The list includes familiar whites, reds, and blushes. However, in addition to that more familiar Chardonnay or Merlot, those looking for something a little different will find sweet fruit wines such as apple, cherry, or blackberry as well. The wines, along with selected Ohio-made and -grown products, are available in the retail shop. Wine tastings are available for 25 cents a tasting. Georgetown Vineyards is located at 62920 Georgetown Rd., Cambridge; (740) 435-3222; georgetownvineyards.com. Open Mon through Sat from 11 a.m. to 5 p.m.

The *Pine Lakes Lodge* gives you both the chance to work up an appetite and to sleep like a baby. Guests at the lodge can hike the trails and bird-watch while walking the grounds of this 550-acre working cattle ranch. Other activities include clay shooting, seasonal bow hunting, horseback riding, and fishing. ATVs and John Deere Gators can be rented for four-wheeling fun. If the view across the stocked ponds or fields isn't quite expansive enough, you can climb up the wildlife observation tower. For the less adventurous, a visit to the petting zoo will give you a close-up encounter with white-tailed deer, goats, emus, llamas, donkeys, and miniature horses.

After all this communing with nature, you can settle in to one of the 5 suites. A plush robe is provided so you can wrap up after your relaxing bath in a two-person whirlpool tub. Each suite is well appointed and decorated using a ranch-rustic motif, and each suite also has a balcony or deck.

A full breakfast is also included with your accommodations. For an additional charge you can also have a luncheon picnic basket prepared for your tours around the area or for a quiet lunch on the meadows near the lodge. Indoor areas in the lodge also are very welcoming with 3 fireplaces and warm, inviting areas to sit and relax.

Pine Lakes Lodge is located at 61680 Buskirk Ln., Salesville; (740) 679-3617; pinelakeslodge.com. Rates: $165 to $295 per night.

Roscoe Village served as an important canal port during the Ohio and Erie Canal's boom years in the 1840s and 1850s, with wheat and wool exports traded for coffee and calico. The 308-mile canal extended from Cleveland to Portsmouth, contained 146 locks, and cost more than $7 million to build. Construction of the canal took seven years, ending in 1832 when the canal completed the link between Lake Erie and the Ohio River.

Located near the confluence of the Muskingum, Walhonding, and Tuscarawas Rivers, the 23 brick and frame buildings in the village have been restored to their appearance during the canal's heyday, making Roscoe Village (originally called Caldersburgh) Ohio's only complete canal town restoration. Seven new buildings also have been added to this historic village.

Seven exhibit buildings, shops, restaurants, and horse-drawn canal boat rides on the replica *Monticello III* all contribute to the appeal of this unique village. You can purchase tickets to the exhibit buildings and craft demonstrations at the Edward E. and Frances B. Montgomery Visitor Center, which is open year-round. This three-story structure offers a wide-screen film presentation of the history of the canal and the village, and displays a large, detailed map of the locks and elevation changes along the canal's more than 300-mile span.

Costumed interpreters and craftspeople welcome visitors to the 19th-century buildings, including the blacksmith's shop, the print shop, the one-room schoolhouse, and the 1840s period home of Dr. Maro Johnson. You'll see rugs and wall hangings being woven on 2 antique looms, and the village potter throwing pots, bowls, and vases on an old-fashioned kick wheel.

In one of the exhibit buildings, the Toll House, Roscoe's first toll collector, Jacob Welsh, registered incoming canal boats and collected passage fees. Also on display is the compass used in the construction of the canal in the 1820s and 1830s, a canal boat model that travels through a set of double locks, and a working model of a gristmill.

Roscoe Village is on OH 16 and OH 83 near OH 36, Coshocton; (740) 622-9310, (800) 877-1830; roscoevillage.com. Guided tours are available daily Apr through Dec at 11 a.m. and 2 p.m. Self-guided tours are available on Fri, Sat, and Sun from June 14 to Labor Day. Canal boat rides daily except Mon in the summer, weekends in Sept and Oct. Festivals and special events are held throughout the year. Admission to exhibit buildings: adults $9.95; children (ages 5 to 12) $4.95.

Those fond of guitars, dulcimers, and the like will want to stop in at **Wildwood Music.** Here you will find one of the largest selections of acoustic guitars in the US. More than 600 instruments fill 5 showrooms.

Owner and musician Marty Rodabaugh carries a large stock of hand-crafted fretted and hammered dulcimers. Fine mandolins, banjos, autoharps, specialty tapes and CDs, and music books round out the inventory.

Wildwood Music is at 672 Whitewoman St., by the Roscoe Village Visitor Center, Coshocton; (740) 622-4224; wildwoodmusic.com. Open Wed through Fri, noon to 6 p.m.; Sat, noon to 5 p.m.

The **Johnson-Humrickhouse Museum,** located in Roscoe Village, contains 5 major galleries, each with its own theme. American Indian artifacts including baskets, pottery, beadwork, blankets, and weapons are represented and range from prehistoric to more recent times. Of particular note are the Inuit totem poles, scrimshaw, and carved argilite, ivory, and bone artifacts.

The Historic Ohio Gallery celebrates yesterday in Ohio with a re-created pioneer home and furnishings, plus antique tools, farm implements, rare firearms, dolls, clocks, pottery, and glassware. An extensive treasury of Asian artifacts features Chinese and Japanese porcelains, lacquerware, embroidery, metals, wood sculptures, and splendid carvings in jade, bone, ivory, soapstone, and horn. A Japanese samurai warrior, fully armored, stands guard beside a case filled with Japanese swords.

One gallery is devoted to fine European and American decorative arts and includes cut and pressed glassware, delicate china, precious metals, wood carvings, and an unusual collection of knife rests.

For a mystery that has never been solved, see the Newark Holy Stones, a set of controversial stone artifacts discovered in the 1860s in the Newark earthworks. The four objects are said to suggest a link between the "Lost Tribes of Israel" and the mound builders.

The Johnson-Humrickhouse Museum is located at 300 N. Whitewoman St., Roscoe Village, Coshocton; (740) 622-8710; jhmuseum.org. Open daily, May through Oct, noon to 5 p.m.; Nov through Apr, Tues through Sun, 1 to 4:30 p.m. Admission: adults $4; children (ages 7 to 18) $3.

Farmer and engineer George Crise took three years, from 1915 to 1918, to build the fine old structure that is today the **White Oak Inn.** He used white oak from his land for the soul of his home and red oak to produce intricate flooring.

Some of the antiques that complete the 10 guest rooms at the White Oak Inn are Crise family originals, and each room in the main building is named for the type of wood that predominates in it. All rooms have private baths; the queen-size first-floor suite features a wood-burning fireplace and whirlpool tub. The former chicken house has become a spacious guesthouse with 3 rooms, all with fireplaces. The latest additions to the inn are 2 luxury cottages of log cabin construction, each with fireplace, two-person whirlpool tub, and private deck.

Guests congregate in the light and spacious living room, mingling, reading, or just rocking in front of the fire. Innkeepers Ian and Yvonne Martin offer full breakfasts for their guests, and dinners can be arranged by advance reservation. The inn's remote location invites walks or bicycle rides down country roads, far away from city noise and hassle. On clear nights, the sky dazzles with brilliant star displays.

The White Oak Inn is 4 miles east of the junction of OH 36 and OH 62 at 29683 Walhonding Rd. (OH 715), near Millwood; (740) 599-6107, (877) 908-5923; whiteoakinn.com. Rates: $140 to $215 per night, double occupancy, with full breakfast. Reservations and a deposit are required; there is a two-night minimum stay most weekends.

Tim and Maureen Tyler undertook a country inn/bed-and-breakfast odyssey; they spent 2 1/2 years and traveled more than 20,000 miles searching for the perfect home to restore as a bed-and-breakfast. Determined to abandon the rat race of New York City, they stumbled on

yankeepens "dixie"

I wonder how Confederate soldiers and sympathizers would have reacted if they had known that a Yankee from Mount Vernon, Ohio, had written their beloved anthem, "Dixie"? Probably would have spit out their grits.

Daniel Decatur Emmett was a minstrel performer who had moved to New York City when he penned "Dixie" in 1859. It later was played in the South and was quickly adopted as the battle cry for secession. Dan Emmett returned to Mount Vernon and died there in 1904.

Mount Vernon en route to Kentucky and discovered what is today the **Russell-Cooper House.**

This ornate structure grew in stages over a period of 60 years, originally constructed in 1829 as a modest federal-style residence. By 1895 the dwelling had been transformed into a one-of-a-kind mansion masterpiece, a Tudor-Italianate Victorian Gothic villa! The Russell-Cooper House is the former home of two prominent Ohio families. Dr. John Russell, physician and surgeon, was the first American to employ a female physician, Dr. Jane Payne, in 1852. His son-in-law, Colonel William Cooper, had a distinguished career as an attorney, US congressman, and Ohio's adjutant general.

When the Tylers acquired the property in 1987, it was no longer the proud residence of the past, but 3 "modern" apartments. Their restoration of the home's Victorian grandeur was massive, necessitating the removal of 13 major walls, 3 baths, 5 closets, 5 furnaces, and 3 water heaters. After nine months of seven-days-a-week restoration, this award-winning mansion inn now boasts 6 guest rooms with private baths, a cherry-bookcased library, a dining hall with an embossed tin ceiling, a grand ballroom with a restored 1856 hand-painted ceiling, a four-season sunroom, and a professional art gallery and studio.

The inn is furnished almost entirely with 19th-century antiques, many recovered from Russell-Cooper descendants. The 2 third-floor guest rooms, accessed via a new grand staircase of cherry and sassafras, offer a primitive, pre-Victorian style, with hand-hewn beams. Tom Dvorak acquired the property post-renovation and is now the innkeeper at the Russell-Cooper House.

The Russell-Cooper House is at 115 E. Gambier St., Mount Vernon; (740) 397-8638; russell-cooper.com. Rates: $85 to $95 per night, double occupancy, including breakfast. Reservations and a deposit required.

Approximately 200 million years ago, a layer of hard flint pushed toward the earth's surface in an area now known as Flint Ridge. Erosion exposed some of the flint, attracting Native Americans to the area 8,000 to 10,000 years ago.

Although the weathered flint on the surface was too brittle to be of much value, the Native Americans discovered a vein of high-quality flint 1 to 10 feet below and established crude quarries to extract the material. Using tremendous physical effort and large hammer stones, they pounded bone and wooden wedges into the flint, breaking it into removable chunks.

State Gemstone and Fossil

The Columbus Rock and Mineral Society led the charge to honor flint as Ohio's official state gemstone. They pointed to its importance to Native Americans in Ohio for making knives, arrowheads, and spear points, its use for flintlock guns and millstones by early white settlers, and its value as a semiprecious stone when cut and polished. In 1965, the Ohio General Assembly concurred, designating flint as Ohio's state stone.

Twenty years later, lawmakers were at it again, this time to recognize a state fossil. Despite numerous jokes suggesting that some of the older members of the General Assembly were in the running for this honor, the actual winner was the trilobite, an extinct marine crustacean found in the limestone and shale beds of southwestern Ohio, among other places.

They used the flint to form arrowheads and spear points, scrapers, and other tools, and to start fires. Because of the demand for flint in prehistoric times, Flint Ridge was considered neutral ground, with members of any tribe allowed to quarry there. White settlers later rediscovered Flint Ridge, using the mineral for buhrstones in gristmills and as roadbed on a nearby section of the National Road.

Today the ***Flint Ridge State Memorial*** museum is built around one of the prehistoric Native American quarries, and native mannequins stand ready to break up the rock with a stone maul. The museum features an impressive collection of scrapers, drills, hoes, knives, and projectile points. One flint sample contains an excellent impression of a coral animal, created during one of the times when this part of Ohio was under the sea.

A large topographical map illustrates the extent of the ridge in eastern Licking and western Muskingum Counties. Other displays include an explanation of the calendar of geological time and descriptions of the various layers of rock in the region, from the surface to 468 feet underground.

A thick forest of beech, maple, and oak surrounds the museum, and hiking trails pass by old quarries and exposed outcroppings of red, yellow, brown, and creamy flint. One trail takes hikers by 2 small streams, and abundant wildlife, including deer, squirrels, chipmunks, and birds, can be observed in the park. The park is open year-round.

Flint Ridge State Memorial is at 7091 Brownsville Rd. SE (CR 668), 3 miles north of Brownsville; (740) 787-2476, (800) 283-8707; ohiohistory.org. The museum is open June through mid-Oct, Sat, 9 a.m. to 5 p.m.; Sun, 10 a.m. to 5 p.m. Admission: adults $3; children (ages 6 to 18) $1.

August Heisey was born in Hanover, Germany, in 1842 and came to America with his family a year later. His career in the glass industry began in Pittsburgh in 1861 but was interrupted by his service with the Union army during the Civil War.

After the war and several sales positions in the glass business, in 1893 Heisey began formulating plans for his own glass company. He chose Newark as the site for this new enterprise because of its abundance of natural gas and low-cost labor. The factory opened in 1896 and grew to employ several hundred workers.

In 1900 the famous "H within a diamond" trademark was designed by Heisey's son, George Duncan Heisey. Two other sons ran the company, which produced the colored glass and glass animals so popular with collectors today. The company closed for Christmas vacation in 1957 and never reopened; it was no longer competitive in world markets.

Today the best of Heisey Glass is on display at the **National Heisey Glass Museum.** The museum is housed in what was once the home of Samuel Dennis King, a prominent Newark attorney. It was built in 1831 and was moved to Veterans Park in 1973. The museum is run by the Heisey Collectors of America. In 1993 the collectors constructed a new wing at the museum, adding 2 large galleries and a media center where a 26-minute video is shown. Inside, you browse through room after room of Heisey glass; hundreds of patterns are displayed, including pieces in all production colors. Examples of experimental pieces, photographs, molds, and tools complete the collection.

The National Heisey Glass Museum is at 169 W. Church St., Newark; (740) 345-2932; heiseymuseum.org. Open Tues through Sat, 10 a.m. to 4 p.m.; Sun, 1 to 4 p.m. Winter hours (Dec through March 15) are Thurs through Sun, noon to 4 p.m. The museum is closed on Sun in Jan and Feb. Admission: adults $4; children free if accompanied by an adult.

Housed in a block-long complex of historic buildings, **The Works: The Ohio Center of History, Art, and Technology** is a unique center dedicated to lifelong learning. Through its four primary subject areas—Digital

Works, Glass Works, Art Works, and Museum Works—students of all ages experience technology and the arts in provocative settings. The state-of-the-art digital lab enables students to create multimedia presentations using Photoshop, Freehand, Illustrator, Flash, InDesign, and other software. Design students from area colleges work on real projects for real clients in the community. Art Works classes include everything from watercolors to papier-mâché sculpture, from bead-work to painting with dyes on silk.

In the Glass Works, the furnace melts the batch at 2,300 degrees Fahrenheit and keeps it at a 2,100-degree working temperature. The studio has one glory hole, which heats the glass as it is being formed, and a bench equipped with basic glass tools—blowpipes, jacks, shears, etc. Students learn time-honored glass-blowing techniques, and some of the work is available for purchase in the gift shop. The Museum Works occupies the Scheidler Machine Works building, which was constructed in 1861. Built by Reinhard Scheidler, the factory was used to manufacture steam engines and line shaft sawmills. On display are a renovated interurban car, an operating factory, historical landmarks of Licking County and Ohio, Shops of Yesterday, plus many other exhibits.

The Works is at 55 S. First St., Newark; (740) 349-9277; attheworks.org. Open Tues through Sat, 9 a.m. to 5 p.m.

The 1,650-acre **Dawes Arboretum,** established by Bertie Burr and

ohio'sstate tree/juice

There was a time when being called a "buckeye" was an insult, the equivalent of being labeled a "hick." Its origin as a put-down comes from the fact that rural Ohio pioneers used wood from buckeye trees to build their cabins and carve their furniture.

Attitudes about the term gradually changed, and the tree's fruit—a brown nut—was described as resembling the eye of the noble buck deer. In 1953, the buckeye was officially designated Ohio's state tree, and Ohio has been the Buckeye State ever since.

The recognition of Ohio's state beverage has been less successful. In 1963 Governor James Rhodes took office and launched a campaign to promote the consumption of Ohio products.

Since tomatoes are a significant crop, he encouraged the drinking of tomato juice. What started as a joke—the naming of tomato juice as Ohio's state beverage—became law in 1965. Cheers.

Beman Gates Dawes in 1929, blends rolling meadows, deep woods, and cultivated gardens. Perhaps the most beautiful area is the Japanese garden designed by noted landscape architect Makoto Nakamura. In Nakamura's design, a small lake with islands connected by arched bridges and plantings of pine, flowering cherries, Japanese yew, and Japanese maple creates a tranquil environment. Another popular area is the cypress swamp, where southern native bald cypress trees grow and produce "knees."

The holly collection contains more than 100 distinct types of holly, and the sugar maples at Dawes provide the sap for the annual production of maple syrup. One section of the arboretum consists of the deciduous climax forest that once blanketed central Ohio. In a climax forest, tree seedlings are able to grow in the shade of parent trees, thus reproducing the forest indefinitely in a cycle of growth and regeneration.

One feature of the arboretum can be fully appreciated only from the air—a 2,100-foot-long series of hedges that spells out "Dawes Arboretum." Other collections at Dawes include oaks, crab apples, flowering shrubs, and conifers. In addition to the forests, meadows, and gardens, there are three ponds and a lake. The visitor center offers nature exhibits, a bird-watching area, an indoor beehive, which the bees enter from the outside through a clear plastic tube, and a fine bonsai display.

Beman and Bertie Dawes moved into the Daweswood House in 1916. Built in 1867, this two-story brick home contains antique furnishings and other of the Daweses' possessions, including portraits of famous family members William Dawes, who rode with Paul Revere, and Charles Gates Dawes, who served as vice president in the Coolidge administration. Guides conduct tours of the home on Sat and Sun at 3:15 p.m.

The Dawes Arboretum is on OH 13, 5 miles south of Newark at 7770 Jacksontown Rd., SE; (740) 323-2355, (800) 443-2937; dawesarb.org. The visitor center is open Mon through Sat, 8 a.m. to 5 p.m.; Sun and holidays, 10 a.m. to 5 p.m. Grounds are open during daylight hours. No admission charge except at Daweswood House.

Perhaps Ohio's prettiest small town, Granville dates its founding to 1805, by settlers from Granville, Massachusetts, and Granby, Connecticut. The 19th-century shops and homes in the picture-postcard community are painstakingly maintained. Up on a hill is Denison University, and a more perfect setting for spending college years is difficult to imagine.

In addition to the crafts and antiques shops, Granville boasts historic inns providing overnight accommodations. Orrin Granger built the ***Buxton Inn*** (known as The Tavern in Granger's day) in 1812, and the inn has operated continuously since then. The inn housed Granville's first post office and served as a stagecoach stop on the Columbus-Newark line. An addition in 1851 formed the U-shaped structure with center courtyard that exists today. The Buxton is named for one of its more colorful proprietors, Major Buxton, who owned the inn from the close of the Civil War until his death in 1905. The present owners, Mr. and Mrs. Orville Orr, purchased it in 1972 and spent two years researching and completely restoring this outstanding structure, which is now listed on the National Register of Historic Places.

The Buxton serves fine cuisine in tasteful period dining rooms, each unique in mood and ambience. Antiques are proudly displayed throughout the inn, and the brick-floored center courtyard provides a delightful outdoor dining area. Blooming plants in hanging baskets and small potted trees combine with the splash of a nearby fountain and candlelit tables to make the courtyard a most pleasing place.

For dinner, choose from seafood such as fresh Atlantic salmon and, one of my favorites, seafood Chesapeake (shrimp, scallops, and whitefish in a rich pecan cheese sauce over Buxton rice en casserole). Other dinner menu options include roast duckling with orange-cranberry sauce; Louisiana chicken (chunks of chicken breast rolled in seasoned cornmeal and sautéed, then topped with rich mushroom pimento sauce, artichoke hearts, and toasted almonds); and grilled porterhouse pork chop with roasted red-skinned potatoes. Be sure to order the Southern-fried brie with raspberry drizzle and toasted baguettes for an appetizer. The tempting desserts include gingerbread with hot lemon sauce and the five-layer white chocolate raspberry torte.

Luncheon selections such as salads, soups, and sandwiches like the corned beef Reuben join entrees that include quiche, crepes, eggs Florentine, and seafood Chesapeake.

Stagecoach drivers once cooked their meals on an open fire in the stone-walled basement of the inn and slept on straw beds around that fire. With its rough beams and imposing stone fireplace, the basement tavern retains the flavor of those early years. The tavern serves a casual menu of sandwiches and appetizers.

Buxton Inn's Bonnie Ghost

If an inn has a ghost or two in residence, it is best if they are happy lodgers! Such is the case at the Buxton Inn. According to legend, and those who have had the pleasure of a meeting, the resident spirits of the Buxton Inn are just continuing to play the role of host and hostess.

If the feminine fragrance of gardenia perfume wafts heavily across the air on the stairway, the Lady in Blue is nearby. This spirit is supposed to be that of Ethel Bounell, better known as "Bonnie." The former actress turned innkeeper was the owner and operator of the inn from 1934 until 1960. She died in room 9. She is reported to have had a theatrical streak and was known for both her gardenia perfume and her love of blue dresses.

In life and death she apparently loves the inn. According to staff and guests, she often is heard walking up and down the stairs or opening and closing doors. Guests have reported being awakened by a woman, who generally expresses concern over their comfort.

While Bonnie may be tending guests, the tales of the inn say that she doesn't have to handle that duty alone. The first innkeeper, Major Buxton, also has appeared to both staff and guests. The nattily attired gentleman, sporting a mustache, is apt to show up in the bar or come up behind staff, perhaps just to check that all is running smoothly.

While the occasional ghostly footsteps, door banging, or mysteriously rearranged objects sometimes have given visitors a start, the ghosts also give the Buxton a unique character. Since the inn traditionally receives high ratings for service, who can blame the former innkeepers for hanging around just to make sure that your stay is something special.

The Buxton Inn also offers overnight accommodations in guest rooms furnished with antiques. Lodging ranges in price from $90 to $100 per night for single occupancy and $100 to $110 for double occupancy. A continental breakfast is included with lodging.

The Buxton Inn is at 313 E. Broadway St., Granville; (740) 587-0001; buxtoninn.com. The inn serves a continental breakfast daily, full breakfast Sat and Sun mornings. Lunch is served Tues through Sat, 11:30 a.m. to 2 p.m.; Sunday brunch, 11 a.m. to 3 p.m. Dinner hours are Tues through Sat, 5 to 8 p.m.

Across the street from the Buxton sits the Tudor-style *Granville Inn,* built in 1924 by the president of the Sunday Creek Coal Company, John Sutphin Jones. Offering the elegance of an English manor house, the lobby is furnished with splendid antiques and lush Oriental rugs. The dining room features high ceilings, ornate brass chandeliers, and sandstone fireplaces. In warm weather, meals are also served outside the tall French doors on the flagstone terrace, which is surrounded by a manicured lawn, gardens, and towering trees.

The evening menu at the Granville Inn features a variety of steaks, chops, seafood, chicken, and house specialties such as steak Diane and crab and cauliflower risotto. Another favorite is the scallops Lavallee, pan-seared day-boat sea scallops served over mushroom, bacon, and asparagus hash. For a tasty appetizer, try the Heartland cheese plate, a changing presentation featuring fine Ohio handcrafted cheese, seasonal fruits, and crisps. (Yes, crackers, but they call them crisps.)

Luncheon selections include soups, salads, and sandwiches. With any meal at the Granville Inn, the house specialty desserts are chocolate hazelnut praline terrine with salty caramel sauce, Ohio apple tarte tatin with Velvet vanilla ice cream, and creamy cheesecake.

The Acorn Pub offers sandwiches, bangers and mash, fish and chips, and appetizers. The pub specializes in creative cocktails such as the Byrn du Julep with Maker's Mark bourbon and simple syrup muddled with fresh mint and lemon. The 587 martini is a tasty mixture of sparkling wine, Mathilde pear liqueur, and St. Germain.

The Granville Inn's 27 guest rooms and 3 suites are individually decorated and have an understated charm and dignity. Prices range from $130 to $255 per night, including a continental breakfast.

The Granville Inn is at 314 E. Broadway St., Granville; (740) 587-3333, (888) 472-6855; granvilleinn.com. Lunch is served Mon through Fri, 11 a.m. to 2 p.m. Dinner is served Mon through Thurs, 5 to 9 p.m.; Fri and Sat, 5 to 10 p.m.; and Sun, 4 to 7 p.m. Brunch is offered on Sun from 11 a.m. to 4 p.m.

A focal point of Granville life, the *Robbins Hunter Museum* at 221 E. Broadway St. is one of the most prominent residential examples of American Greek revival architecture. Built in 1842 by successful businessman Alfred Avery, the home was a private residence until 1903, when it served as the home of Denison University's Phi Gamma Delta fraternity, and from 1930 until 1956 it was home to the Kappa Sigma fraternity.

Robbins Hunter Jr. was a collector with a vision for the future. The Avery Downer House that visitors see today is a result of Hunter's foresight and hard work. Hunter lived in the house from 1956 to 1979; even then his goal was to see it become a museum. To make that possible, Hunter gathered antiques he believed would be lovely additions to the Grecian building. Hunter also left provisions in his will that would ensure the Avery Downer House would survive long after his death. Opened as a museum in August 1981, the house has been restored to its former grandeur and seems a fitting legacy for the man who loved this beautiful landmark.

The Robbins Hunter Museum, (740) 587-0430, robbinshunter.org, is open Wed through Sat from 1 to 4 p.m. No admission charge.

The growing season in Ohio welcomes a variety of fruits and flowers to **Lynd Fruit Farm,** and Lynd Fruit Farm welcomes visitors to pick the best from the fields. Home of Ohio's largest apple orchard, Lynd has 80,000 trees, and during September and October, you can pick your own apples. Fall also brings pumpkins and squash to pick or cornstalks to use for autumn decorating. A "show" apple orchard tells the history of the fruit. Apples from colonial times hang on trees next to the latest test varieties. You may also want to hop on a hayride, and let one of the farm's 10 antique John Deere tractors give you a ride around the farm. In addition to these seasonal activities, the farm hosts other events, such as cooking and plant propagation demonstrations. Call ahead for dates and times.

The Lynd Fruit Farm Market is open daily from 9 a.m. to 6 p.m. from mid-July until the end of the growing season. The family is known mostly for their apples but they also grow peaches, plums, pears, nectarines, berries, sweet corn, pumpkins, and more. Also sold at the market are produce and products from local farmers, many of whom are Amish. Local items featured at the market include baked goods, salsa, granola, honey, candy, maple syrup, spices, popcorn, and frozen custard.

Lynd Fruit Farm is located at 9090 Morse Rd. SW, Pataskala; (740) 927-1333; lyndfruitfarm.com. A devastating fire at **Ye Olde Mill** near Utica in April 1986 completely destroyed the hundred-year-old structure. Only the 18-foot, 2,000-pound waterwheel and the quarry stone survived the blaze.

But the Velvet Ice Cream Company, which operates the mill and has its headquarters next door, set about building a new Ye Olde Mill of rough-sawed oak and poplar. This new building now sells country crafts and other gift items, and, not surprisingly, Velvet Ice Cream, a Dager family tradition since 1914.

The 1870-vintage building destroyed by fire was not the first mill on this site—a sawmill was erected here in 1817, and a larger one went up in 1827. You can find out about this and more at the museum of milling history and ice cream that is part of Ye Olde Mill. In fact, the ice-cream museum, Ohio's first and only, traces the history of ice cream from Roman times to the present.

Once you've picked up a cone full of your favorite ice-cream flavor, step outside to the 20-acre parklike picnic area. Relax at the picnic tables while watching the ducks frolic in a picturesque pond. The mill also houses a down-home restaurant, complete with deli sandwiches, soups and salads, and finger food. A petting zoo, nature trail, historic 1817 gristmill with water wheel, and tours of the ice-cream factory round out your visit.

Ye Olde Mill is located 10 miles north of Newark on OH 13 at 11324 Mt. Vernon Rd., Utica, (800) 589-5000, (740) 892-3921; velveticecream.com. Open daily, May through Oct, 11 a.m. to 7 p.m. (to 8 p.m. during the summer, 5 p.m. in Oct).

Imports dominate the basket industry in the US today, but one Ohio family continues four generations of handcrafted basket making. Before the turn of the 20th century, John Longaberger began weaving baskets for his neighbors and local potteries, which used them for storing and shipping fragile products. John's son, J.W. Longaberger, expanded the business after World War I and taught his 12 children the art of basket making in the evening, after he worked a full day at a nearby paper mill. But over the years, inexpensive cardboard, plastic, and metal containers drastically reduced the industrial demand for Longaberger's baskets, and production slowed to a trickle.

In the 1970s, however, J.W.'s son, Dave, revived the business after becoming convinced a new market existed for good quality, handmade baskets. Today nearly 75 weavers produce an average of 500,000 baskets each year at the Longaberger Company. Basket weavers make from 12 to 100 baskets each per day, depending on the size and style, with each weaver making an average of 35 baskets daily. It must be a good job—most weavers have been with Longaberger more than 20 years.

The baskets are constructed of hard maple from Ohio, Michigan, Pennsylvania, Wisconsin, New York, and Maine. As a testament to the emphasis on quality at Longaberger, each weaver initials and dates each basket. Nearly 50,000 independent Longaberger home consultants sell the baskets, along with pottery, wrought-iron products, and fabric accessories in home shows throughout the US.

Upon a visit to the headquarters, shaped like a giant basket including the handles, visitors can see baskets being made and see product displays at the Longaberger Manufacturing Campus before heading next door to the *Longaberger Homestead.* You can dine at the Terrace Cafe, the Longaberger Heartland Deli, or the Longaberger Homestead Restaurant. For a sip of tea and something sweet, you may want to drop in to the Sentimental Rose Tea Garden. The Longaberger at Home Building features unique gifts and home decorations.

For a fun experience, visitors can make their own Longaberger basket for $59.95. Choose from 3 basket styles along with choice of trim and chain weave colors, plus themed ornaments that adorn the top band of the basket. Don't worry if you are not a skilled weaver. Experienced Longaberger professionals are there to make sure your basket turns out nicely. The lovely one I made now sits on my kitchen counter (and I had never woven a basket before).

The Longaberger Homestead is on OH 16 at 5563 Raiders Rd. in Frazeyburg; (740) 322-5588; longaberger.com/visitus.aspx. Open Mon, Tues, and Thurs, 10 a.m. to 5 p.m., Fri and Sat, 9 a.m. to 6 p.m.; Sun, noon to 5 p.m.

As the name indicates, the *National Road–Zane Grey Museum* actually houses 2 museums—one presenting the story of the building of the National Road connecting the western territories with the original eastern states, and the other commemorating author Zane Grey, the Zanesville, Ohio, native known through his travels and writing as the High Priest of the Outdoors.

Built in stages from 1811 to 1838, the National Road stretched from Cumberland, Maryland, to Vandalia, Illinois. George Washington originally conceived the idea of constructing a road into the new nation's western lands, and the ninth US Congress approved funds for this first federally supported road in 1806.

Workers earned $1 per day to clear a 66-foot-wide path and to build a 30-foot-wide roadbed of broken stone using hand tools, mules, oxen, and horses. The National Road was vital to the development of the frontier—as each section of the road opened, settlers loaded their Conestoga wagons and headed west.

The museum displays horse-drawn carts, buggies, and wagons (including a Conestoga wagon), plus antique bicycles and automobiles—all methods of transportation utilized on the National Road (which eventually became US 40 and reached all the way to California). A 136-foot diorama depicts the chronology of the road, from its construction and use by early settlers moving west to farmers herding their livestock on the road and the road's revival after the invention of the bicycle and automobile. Other exhibits include photographs of sections of the road under construction and fully equipped interiors of blacksmith and wheelwright shops.

Author Zane Grey, born in 1875, acquired his passion for hunting and fishing around Dillon Falls, near his home in Zanesville. Grey attended dental school at the University of Pennsylvania, where he also played on the college baseball team. But he abandoned his dental career to write, achieving national prominence with his 60 western novels, many of which were later filmed as motion pictures. He used the money from his books and movies to finance his worldwide fishing trips and big-game hunting expeditions.

The museum displays many of Zane Grey's books, magazine articles, and posters from his motion pictures, plus the lures and hunting rifles used on his travels. There is also a complete replica of the study he added to his Altadena, California, home, where he penned many of his works.

The National Road–Zane Grey Museum is at the Norwich exit of I-70, 10 miles east of Zanesville at 8850 East Pike; (740) 872-3143, (800) 752-2602; ohiohistory.org/museums-and-historic-sites/museum--historic-sites-by-name/national-road/National-Road---Old. Open from May 1 through October 31, Wed through Sat, 10 a.m. to 4 p.m.; Sun, noon to 4 p.m. Admission: adults $7; senior citizens $6; children (ages 6 to 12) $3.

A fairly unremarkable brick building in downtown Zanesville houses a very unique enterprise. The *Alan Cotrill Sculpture Studio and Gallery* is where the Zanesville artist both creates and displays his art. Cotrill and a cadre of artists and artisans bring his work from idea to bronze.

The second-floor gallery shows off numerous bronze sculptures created by Cotrill, as well as photographs of larger Cotrill pices and installations.

But visitors can also get a unique look behind the scenes by visiting areas of the studio to see how the process of creating a bronze sculpture begins, from drawing to preparing molds for casting. While the actual pouring of the bronze is done at a foundry, most other steps are undertaken at the studio.

The Alan Cotrill Studio and Gallery is located at 110 S. Sixth St., Zanesville; (740) 453-9822; alancottrill.com. Open Mon through Sun, 9 a.m. to 5 p.m. Call for an appointment at other times.

Spend a peaceful respite in a fragrant apple orchard at **Cabin in the Orchard Bed and Breakfast,** located 10 miles south of Zanesville off OH 555 at 2230 Irish Ridge Rd. The two-bedroom, two-bath, fully furnished luxury log cabin is in the Thomas Family Orchard. Amenities include a hot tub, fireplace, gas grill on the patio, large porch overlooking a pond, orchard, and vineyard. The refrigerator is stocked with breakfast food for guests to prepare at their leisure. Rates are $175 to $205 for one to four guests. Call (740) 674-6814 or (800) 915-9903 or check the website at cabonintheorchard .com.

Learn about famed astronaut John Glenn in New Concord. Across the street from the entrance to Muskingum College (alma mater of the senator, astronaut, and former resident) is Glenn's boyhood home. The home was donated to Muskingum College in 1999. The college leased the building to the John and Annie Glenn Foundation, which moved the house to its current site and restored it to its late 1930s condition. The building is now home to the *John and Annie Glenn Historic Site.*

Senator Glenn's father built the home in 1923. The modest-looking frame house was opened as the John and Annie Glenn Historic Site in 2002. Visitors to the site will see a 20-minute video presentation on the lives of John and Annie Glenn and can tour the first-floor rooms. Glenn's bedroom looks much like it did in his boyhood, complete with model airplanes and a crystal radio set. Exhibits showcasing the Glenns' hometown of Concord are also part of the site's displays of Ohio living history.

The John and Annie Glenn Historic Site is located at 72 W. Main St., New Concord; (740) 826-3305, (800) 752-2602; johnglennhome.org. Open May through Oct, Wed through Sat, 10 a.m. to 4 p.m.; Sun, 1 to 4 p.m. Admission: adults $7; senior citizens $6; students $3; children younger than age 6 free.

Places to Stay in East Central Ohio

ASHLAND

The Winfield Bed & Breakfast
1568 OH 60
(419) 281-5587,
(800) 269-7166
winfieldbb.com

BERLIN

Donna's Premier Lodging
½ block off Main Street on East Street
at 5523 East St.
(330) 893-3068,
(800) 320-3338
donnasofberlin.com

Garden Gate Get-A-Way
just outside of Berlin
at 6041 Township Rd.
(330) 893-3999,
(330) 674-7608
garden-gate.com

Zinck's Carriage House
5453 East St.
(330) 893-6600
(800) 435-6600
zincksinn.com

BOLIVAR

Enchanted Pines Bed and Breakfast
1862 Old Trail NE
(330) 874-3197,
(877) 536-7508
enchantedpines.com

CANAL FULTON

Fulton House on Pleasant Hill Bed & Breakfast
451 E. Cherry St.
(330) 854-4645
fultonhousebb.com

CHARM

The Guggisberg Swiss Inn
5025 OH 557
(330) 893-3600
guggisbergswissinn.com

DELLROY

Atwood Lake Resort
2650 Lodge Rd. SW
(800) 735- 2211
atwoodlakeresort.com

GRANVILLE

Welsh Hills Inn
2133 Cambria Mill Rd.
(740) 321-1493
welshhillsinn.com

LOUDONVILLE

Blackfork Inn
303 N. Water St.
(419) 994-3252

Mohican State Park Lodge and Cabins
OH 3, just north of Loudonville
(419) 938-5411,
(800) 282-7275
mohicanresort.com

MILLERSBURG

Inn and Spa at Honey Run
3 miles northeast of Millersburg,
off OH 214 at 6920 CR 203
(330) 674-0011
innathoneyrun.com

MILLWOOD

White Oak Inn
29683 Walhonding Rd.
(OH 715) 4 miles east of junction of US 36 and US 62
(740) 599-6107
whiteoakinn.com

MOUNT VERNON

Russell-Cooper House
115 E. Gambier St.
(740) 397-8638
russell-cooper.com

SALESVILLE

Pine Lakes Lodge
61680 Burskirk Ln.
(740) 679-3617
pinelakeslodge.com

HELPFUL WEBSITES

Ohio Division of Travel and Tourism:
discoverohio.com

Canton/Stark County Visitors Bureau:
visitcantonstark.com

Holmes County Chamber of Commerce:
holmescountychamber.com

Tuscarawas County Visitors Bureau:
traveltusc.com

Wayne County Visitors Bureau:
wccvb.com

ZANESVILLE

Cabin in the Orchard
2230 Irish Ridge Rd.
(740) 674-6814
(800) 915-9903
cabinintheorchard.com

Places to Eat in East Central Ohio

CHARM

Grandma's Homestead Restaurant
4450 OH 557
(330) 893-2717
grandmashomestead.com

GRANVILLE

Buxton Inn
313 E. Broadway
(740) 587-0001
Lodging is also available.
buxtoninn.com

Granville Inn
314 E. Broadway
(740) 587-3333
Lodging is also available.
granvilleinn.com

WAYNESBURG

Cibo's Restaurant
134 W. Lisbon St.
(330) 866-3838
cibosrestaurant.com

WILMOT

The Amish Door Restaurant & Village
1210 Winesburg St.
(330) 359-5464,
(888) 246-7436
Lodging is also available.
amishdoor.com

River Region

At the conclusion of the Revolutionary War, Congress passed the Ordinance of 1787, which opened up new land west and north of the Ohio River for settlement. A group of soldiers and officers from the Revolutionary conflict, along with other New Englanders, formed the Ohio Company of Associates to settle in this frontier territory. On April 7, 1788, a party of 48 men on a crude barge followed the Ohio River to the Muskingum River, arriving at today's location of Marietta, Ohio. By July of that year, Governor Arthur St. Clair had established the first civil government west of the Allegheny Mountains in Marietta, with the settlement destined to be Ohio's first city and gateway to the Northwest Territory (Ohio, Michigan, Indiana, Illinois, Wisconsin, and part of Minnesota). The city was named for Queen Marie Antoinette, in gratitude for the support France had provided the colonies during the war with the British.

Rufus Putnam, a general under George Washington during the Revolution, led that 48-man party in April 1788 and supervised the construction of a walled fortification

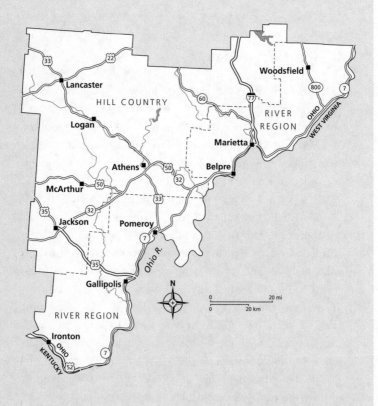

with 4 blockhouses to discourage Indian attacks. Putnam's home was part of that fortification and still exists today, completely enclosed in the *Campus Martius Museum.* Putnam coined the name Campus Martius, which means "field of wars," but the Treaty of Greenville in 1795 virtually ended hostilities in the region.

Putnam's 200-year-old home rests on its original foundation and contains furnishings from the Putnam family. Guides describe the hardships of early pioneer life and explain the use of the various kitchen and household implements on display.

The museum also exhibits hundreds of items from Marietta's early days, such as the compasses and surveyors' chains used to plat the city. Other collections include Dr. John Cotton's surgical equipment (he practiced medicine in Marietta from 1815 to 1847), antique musical instruments, and a very unusual studio portrait camera from the early 1900s.

One entire gallery contains 19th-century ladies' apparel—the lavish gowns and dresses worn during that era. An outdoor patio features an outstanding assortment of Franklin stoves, a water pumper (ca. 1853) used to fight fires, and the enormous pilot wheel from the stern-wheel towboat *J.C. Risher,* which worked the Ohio River from 1873 until it sank in 1919. A military display includes the sword used by General Putnam during the Revolutionary War (he later gave this sword to George Washington), old rifles and muskets used by early settlers in the area, uniforms and dress swords from the War of 1812, and a Confederate flag captured at the Civil War battle of Chancellorsville, plus uniforms, saddlebags, and a fife and drum used by Civil War soldiers.

The Campus Martius Museum is at the corner of Washington (OH 7) and Second Streets at 601 Second St., Marietta; (740) 373-3750, (800) 860-0145; campusmartiusmuseum.org The museum is open year-round Mon and Wed through Sat, 9:30 a.m. to 5 p.m.; Sun noon to 5 p.m. Admission: adults $7; students (kindergarten through college) $4; children (ages 5 and under) free. A one-day pass to both the Campus Martius Museum and the Ohio River Museum is $9 adults, $5 students (kindergarten through college), free for ages 5 and under.

With their tall smokestacks puffing black ash and their paddleboards splashing the waters of the Ohio and Muskingum Rivers, the great stern-wheelers plied these waterways carrying freight and passengers during the

BEST ATTRACTIONS

Campus Martius Museum	Our House
Ohio River Museum	Bob Evans Farm
Valley Gem	Buckeye Furnace
Levee House Cafe	Lake Katharine State Nature Preserve
Rossi Pasta Factory Outlet	
Lafayette Hotel	

19th century. Marietta was once a thriving port; its history is interwoven with that of the rivers and the steamboat era.

The ***Ohio River Museum*** stands on the bank of the Muskingum River, just down the street from Campus Martius. The museum actually consists of 4 separate buildings connected with covered outdoor walkways. One building's maps, models, and illustrations trace the origins of the Ohio River—the role of glaciers in its development and the natural history of the region. A half-hour multimedia presentation describes the river's more recent past, from its early exploration to modern-day commercial and recreational usage.

The most popular building features dozens of detailed models of stern-wheeled paddleboats, with the statistics and a narrative of each vessel provided, plus other riverboat memorabilia such as newspaper clippings, passenger tickets, bills of lading, and stern-wheeler travel brochures. The museum also houses a fine collection of steam whistles and a complete set of woodworking tools used for shipbuilding.

The major outdoor attraction at the Ohio River Museum—the 175-foot, 342-ton *W.P. Snyder, Jr.*—was the last steam-powered stern-wheeled towboat to operate in America. It is now permanently docked on the Muskingum River right behind the museum; visitors walk the gangplank to explore this proud vessel from engine room to pilothouse. Built in 1918, the *W. P. Snyder, Jr.* plied America's rivers until 1955.

Other outdoor exhibits include a skiff built in 1885, believed to be the oldest such boat in the inland lakes region, which was used during one of the many floods that rampaged in Marietta prior to the installation of flood-control dams. The museum also has a replica of an early flat-boat, the flat-bottomed, square-cornered boat used to float heavy cargo downstream. Propelled only by the river's current, flatboats were dismantled (their wood sold for construction projects) upon arriving at their destination.

The Ohio River Museum is at the corner of Front and Saint Clair Streets at 601 Front St., Marietta; (740) 373-3750, (800) 860-0145; campusmartius-museum.org/river. Open March 30 through Oct, Memorial Day through Labor Day, Mon, and Wed through Sat, 9:30 a.m. to 5 p.m.; Sun, noon to 5 p.m. Admission: adults $7; students (kindergarten to college) $4, children (ages 5 and under) free. A one-day pass to both the Campus Martius Museum and the Ohio River Museum is $9 adults, $5 students (kindergarten through college), free for ages 5 and under.

Given the importance of stern-wheelers to Marietta's past, it seems only proper to survey the city and surrounding area from aboard one— the **Valley Gem,** which docks adjacent to the Ohio River Museum. The ship's captain pilots this 300-passenger excursion vessel down the Muskingum and Ohio Rivers on 50-minute cruises.

During the trips, he points out the historic places of interest along the shoreline, including the location of Fort Harmar (built in 1785). Large stone blocks spelling "Marietta" mark the landing once used by arriving steamboats, and this landing is now the site of the annual stern-wheeler festival. Graceful stern-wheelers come from all parts of the inland waterway system to compete in races, and generally show off during this annual weekend of activities.

The *Valley Gem* departs from the landing under the Washington Street Bridge at Front Street, Marietta; (740) 373-7862; valleygemsternwheeler.com.

ohio'sstatesong

Ohio's state song, "Beautiful Ohio," was written in 1918 by Ballard McDonald and Mary Earl. But the song is not about the state of Ohio; rather, its focus is the Ohio River. That did not stop the General Assembly from designating it as Ohio's official state song on October 24, 1969.

Even more curious was the selection of "Hang On Sloopy" as Ohio's state rock song in 1985. Made popular by the McCoys, a Dayton rock band, "Sloopy" is a favorite of the Ohio State University Marching Band.

During the summer, she sails daily at noon for a 90-minute cruise and every other Saturday for a dinner cruise. Check the schedule for dinner cruise dates and times. Cruise rates: adults $12; children (ages 3 through 12) $6. Dinner cruise rates: adults $37, senior citizens $35, children (ages 3 through 12) $27.

A delightful dining option is the ***Levee House Cafe,*** the only remaining original Marietta riverfront structure. Built in 1826 or earlier for Dudley Woodbridge Jr., the first merchant in the Northwest Territory, this historic building later served as a hotel, restaurant, and saloon.

Today the menu changes seasonally and features entrees as varied as root beer pork tenderloin, peppercorn tuna, crab cakes, and bowtie chicken pasta. The adventurous might want to sample the shrimp Diablo—a spicy blend of shrimp with spinach, onions, and tomatoes served over pasta in a zesty tomato cream sauce.

Johnny Appleseed Apparition

As you travel throughout Ohio, you may want to conjure up a mental image of the famous Johnny Appleseed. Many of the state's apple orchards, as well as countless lone apple trees, stand as a monument to the man who brought seeds to the farmers of Ohio. A more formal monument at the Washington and Noble County line was dedicated to his memory on September 25, 1942, the 168th anniversary of his birth.

Some say that this is not the only reminder of the famous wanderer that a visitor can experience in this area of Ohio. Just after the monument was dedicated, people began reporting that the man himself was coming back to visit. Some folks were pretty amazed to look up into one of Johnny's apple trees and see a smiling man with a long gray beard swinging his legs and calling out a greeting.

Because Johnny adhered to a religious sect that believed in communication with the departed, local tale tellers say it seems natural that he would try to make an appearance in some of his former haunts.

If you travel through Appleseed country, you may catch a glimpse of a shadow of a man in baggy pants held up with one suspender. You may wonder at the appearance of a man who reaches up to adjust the cooking pot he wears for a hat. But whether or not you see Johnny's spirit as an apparition, you certainly will see his spirit in the strong limbs and the glistening fruits of Johnny's apple trees.

Your dinner starts with appetizers such as fried ravioli, Tuscan shrimp, or spinach artichoke dip and concludes with your choice of freshly baked pies and cakes.

The Levee House Cafe is at 127 Ohio St., Marietta; (740) 374-2233; leveehousemarietta.com. Open Mon through Thurs, 11 a.m. to 2 p.m. and 5 to 9 p.m.; Fri and Sat, 11 a.m. to 2 p.m. and 5 to 10 p.m. Reservations recommended for dinner.

One of the finest examples of Gothic revival architecture in Ohio can be found in a mansion in Marietta known as *The Castle.* The Castle was built in 1855 and was home to Ohio senator Theodore Davis. The house, listed on the National Historic Register, had fallen into disrepair, but was rescued by the Bosley family, who began renovations in the 1970s. Some restoration projects continued past the year 2000. The home's distinctive features make it easy to see why it's called the "castle." It has a wonderful octagonal tower and stone-capped spires. The attic has a trefoil window and the master bedroom and other rooms have stained-glass windows, which have been salvaged and returned to their former glory. Mosaics and intricate woodwork have also been restored or replaced. The fireplace has a scagliola fireplace surround, which is plaster carefully colored and polished to resemble marble. The papier-mâché moldings are another unusual feature. They follow a fashion begun in the mid-18th century when papier-mâché was used to craft delicate and detailed molding and painted to resemble wood or precious metals.

capitalofthe territory

During the days of the Northwest Territory, the capital of the territory was wherever the territorial governor and judges convened. In July 1788, Arthur St. Clair, the first territorial governor, arrived in Marietta and instituted the first government under the Ordinance of 1787. By 1790, Governor St. Clair had moved his headquarters to Cincinnati, making it the capital of the territory.

By 1798, the territory had 5,000 white male inhabitants, and Congress gave it permission to elect a legislature. In 1799, 22 representatives and Governor St. Clair met in Yeatmen's Tavern in Cincinnati. By the September session, when William Henry Harrison was elected the first territorial delegate to Congress, a new two-story frame building on Main Street was the home of the new legislature.

On the grounds, a lovely gazebo, once the covering for the well, has been returned to the mansion grounds to grace the gardens. The cast-iron fence and herb garden have been restored as well. Decorations and furnishings reflect the period in which Senator Davis would have occupied the home.

Start your tour in the restored carriage house, where a videotape presentation and introductory exhibits will set the scene. Check the website for seasonal and special programs at the Castle. Holidays such as Christmas and Easter mean special decorations, and exhibits and musical programs are often held during the winter months. Tours are offered every half hour and take about 50 minutes.

The Castle is at 418 Fourth St., Marietta; (740) 373-4180; mariettacastle .org. Open April 1 through May 31, Mon, Thurs, and Fri, 10 a.m. to 4 p.m.; Sat and Sun, 1 to 4 p.m.; June 1 through August 31, Mon, Tues, and Thurs through Sat 10 a.m. to 4 p.m.; Sun, 1 to 4 p.m.; September 1 through December 31, Mon and Thurs through Sun 1 to 4 p.m. Admission: adults $7; senior citizens $6.50; children (ages 5 to 17) $4; children (ages 5 and under) free.

Marietta is also home to a world-famous gourmet pasta maker, **Rossi Pasta.** Though most of its pasta is sold by catalog and through upscale restaurants and retailers like Williams-Sonoma, in Marietta you can stop by the Rossi Pasta factory shop.

The success of Rossi Pasta can be attributed to a high-quality product and an intriguing selection of pasta cuts and flavors. These include everything from spinach basil garlic fettuccini to Italian spice linguini, from vino Rosso linguini made with Cabernet sauvignon to calamari fettuccini. Not only does Rossi have three sauces to top off the pasta, they also will recommend the perfect wine to complete your meal.

Rossi Pasta Factory is at 106 Front St., Marietta; (740) 376-2065, (800) 227-6774; rossipasta.com. Open Mon through Sat, 9 a.m. to 8 p.m., Sun 11 a.m. to 5 p.m. (Pasta-making times are variable, typically before noon.)

During your visit be sure to take a walking or driving tour of Marietta's stately residential neighborhoods. The city contains hundreds of 19th -century homes, many on charming brick streets.

For overnight accommodations, the **Lafayette Hotel** is at the landing where steamboats once unloaded their passengers and cargoes on cruises between Pittsburgh and Cincinnati. Nautical memorabilia decorate the lobby, restaurants, and lounge in this building, including brass pilot instruments, a pilot wheel, and paintings and photographs of the stern-wheelers that once traveled the nation's rivers.

The hotel's 77 guest rooms have been renovated and feature classy Victorian-style furnishings. Four even offer private balconies facing the river. Special Marietta lodging and entertainment packages are also available at the historic Lafayette.

The first liquor license in Marietta was issued to the Lafayette Hotel on January 19, 1934. Toast that special day with a drink in the Riverview Lounge, where the large hardwood bar was handcrafted by Amish workers. Overlooking the Ohio River, the lounge celebrates its river ambience with original riverboat paintings and model stern-wheelers.

Opened in 1931, the Rufus Putnam Dining Room reflects the graciousness of yesteryear. Even if you are not dining there, peek into the Gun Room Dining Room. Adorning the Gun Room are reminders of the hotel's river heritage, including a boat's telegraph, steering arms, steamboat instruments, a bell, a compass, and bell pulls.

The Gun Room is known most for its famous collection of long rifles, handcrafted and dating from 1795 to 1880. Each rifle is numbered and a description with a brief history hangs just inside the entrance to the room. One of the most unusual weapons is a percussion rifle made by J.J. Henry and sons, who accompanied Benedict Arnold to Quebec in 1775. The company later went on to make muskets for the US Army.

The Lafayette Hotel is at the corner of Front and Greene Streets at 101 Front St., Marietta; (740) 373-5522, (800) 331-9336; lafayettehotel.com. Rates: $85 to $290 per night.

How many people can say they had a massage in a grain bin? You can as a guest at the **Stockport Mill Inn.** The inn is housed in an impressive mill built in 1906, the last surviving mill building on the Muskingum River. After its long career as, primarily, a flour mill, the building now houses an inn with 14 guest rooms and the Restaurant on the Dam. In the basement of the mill, safely located behind glass, guests can view the 100-year-old double turbines that generate hydroelectric power. Too corroded to restore and use, the mill's original turbines have been replaced by these twins from the same era, which now produce about 800,000 kilowatt hours of electricity each year—enough to supply the electrical needs of the mill, with some extra to sell to the local utility company.

A restaurant, gift shop, and a wheelchair-accessible guest room are housed on the first floor. The original train bin that is now home to the massage therapy room is on the second floor. Unique guest rooms are on the second floor too, as well as the third and fourth, and even the cupola. The riverboat rooms are named for Ohio riverboats and have private baths with claw-foot tubs, all with private terraces with views of the river. One suite, the Captain Hook, which sleeps 8, has a large sitting area, and a stairway up to the Mill's cupola. No, it was not named for the famous fictional pirate. It was named for Isaac Newton Hook, a riverboat captain in the 1800s. A couple of notes for the traveler: Stockport is a dry town, so do not plan to order wine or a drink with dinner. However, diners are welcome to bring their own wine or drink to the restaurant. Also, this inn is in a historic building, so don't expect the uniformity in heating and ventilation systems that you would find in a more modern building.

The Stockport Mill Inn is at 1995 Broadway, Stockport; (740) 559-2822; stockportmill.com. Rates: $89 to $299 per night.

The settlement of Gallipolis resulted directly from what had to be one of the first land speculation schemes in US history. A congressman and his business associates received a congressional grant for 3.5 million acres in southern Ohio. These investors planned to secure the funds to pay for this land by reselling large tracts to Europeans. They formed the Scioto Company and dispatched a sales representative to France, who easily sold tracts to 500 upper-class French citizens ready to leave the turmoil in their country. These 500 men, women, and children set sail for America in 1790, but by the time they arrived in the New World, the Scioto Company had failed, leaving the immigrants without their property.

After negotiations with Congress, the French were given frontier land on the Ohio River. Since these immigrants were largely noblemen, professionals, and artisans, pioneer life quickly took its toll. Half of the party deserted the frontier during the first two years for "more civilized" areas.

But those remaining in what is today Gallipolis endured, and the town's strategic location on the river spurred its growth. In 1819, Henry Cushing constructed a tavern and inn, and that two-story building still exists, now a museum known as ***Our House.***

The doors, floors, and even the lock on the front door at Our House are all original. A grandfather clock built in 1780 still keeps time, and the museum contains Chippendale and Hepplewhite furnishings that belonged to early Gallipolis settlers. In the dining room, for example, is a magnificent cherry dining room table set with delicate French plates and serving trays. The second-floor ballroom still has the original carved wooden chandeliers.

The name Our House comes from the sales pitch its owner, Henry Cushing, would give when he met boats arriving at the docks. To keep the newcomers from going to the other inn in town, he would tell them, "Come to our house." The inn's most famous guest was the French general and statesman Marquis de Lafayette. After his first trip to the colonies in 1777 to fight with the Americans against the British, Lafayette returned to France and convinced his countrymen to enter the war against England. America never forgot Lafayette's aid during the Revolution, and in 1825 he made a triumphant return to the US, which included a 2.5-hour visit to Gallipolis and Our House on May 22. The coat he wore and one of the violins used to entertain him are displayed at the museum.

Another important Frenchman planned to come to Gallipolis with the original 500 settlers but at the last minute he let his fiancée go without him. Had he made the trip to America, history would have been dramatically altered. His name was Napoleon Bonaparte; his fiancée's portrait hangs above a fireplace at Our House.

Our House is at 434 First Ave., Gallipolis; (740) 446-0586, (800) 752-2618; ohiohistory.org. The museum is open Memorial Day through Labor Day, Wed through Sat, 10 a.m. to 4 p.m.; Sun, 1 to 4 p.m.; Labor Day through October 31: Sat, 10 a.m. to 4 p.m., Sun 1 to 4 p.m. Admission: adults $4; children $1.

Bob Evans has made his mark in two related businesses—as a manufacturer and distributor of his country sausage and as the proprietor of the Bob Evans Restaurants. After World War II, Evans opened a 12-stool restaurant near Gallipolis. Not satisfied with the sausage available commercially, he started making his own. This blossomed into a sausage business, and he devoted more and more of his time and energy to it. Once Bob Evans Farms Sausage was firmly established in the marketplace, he once again concentrated on the restaurant business, opening a second location in 1962 and coordinating a major expansion in the late 1960s. Today, Bob Evans operates nearly 600 restaurants in 18 states and is a leading producer of pork sausage under the Bob Evans and Owens brand names.

The **Bob Evans Farm** is home to the Homestead Museum, the Craft Barn, the original Bob Evans restaurant, and many unique events. The museum reflects the history of the company, and guests sit at the reconstructed counter for the first restaurant owned by Bob Evans. Visitors also browse the thousands of homemade arts and crafts in the Craft Barn. Special events throughout the year include a bluegrass festival, an antique car and power equipment show, and a gospel sing. The most popular event is the Farm Festival, which celebrates the harvest season as it was in rural America of yesteryear.

Bob Evans Farm is on OH 588, 1 mile east of Rio Grande at 791 Farmview Rd. in Bidwell; (740) 245-5305, (800) 944-3276; bobevans.com. The farm is open daily April through Dec 23, 10:30 a.m. to 5:30 p.m.

Hill Country

The 100-mile-long, 30-mile-wide belt of southern Ohio and northern Kentucky known as the Hanging Rock Iron Region once produced the iron demanded by the booming Industrial Revolution. Eighty charcoal furnaces operated in this region from 1818 to 1916, furnishing iron ingots used to manufacture railroad and farm equipment, heavy machinery, and even the cannons and gunboats used in the Civil War. Abundant quantities of the iron ore, limestone, and timber needed for iron production caused the proliferation of furnaces in the region, and furnace communities sprang up near these facilities.

While many of the region's sandstone stacks today stand in silent memory of this once vital industry, at **Buckeye Furnace,** Ohio's only restored charcoal furnace, all buildings have been reconstructed. Visitors learn the history of the Hanging Rock region and the basics of iron making by reading the many signs along Buckeye's self-guided tour.

The furnace was built into a hillside, and the raw materials (iron ore, limestone, and charcoal) were brought by wagon to the top of the hill, where the charcoal was stored under a stock shed to keep it dry, and the limestone and ore were graded and sorted. (The charcoal was produced at a separate location by slowly burning timber under mounds of earth.)

Laborers mixed and poured enormous quantities of these materials into the top of the furnace: In a 12-hour shift, they would measure and load 57,000 pounds of ore, 1,900 pounds of limestone, and 800 bushels of charcoal. As the charcoal burned, temperatures in the furnace reached 600 degrees, causing the impurities in the iron ore to mix with the limestone, forming a waste product called slag. Since molten iron is heavier than slag, the iron could be removed from the bottom of the furnace by opening a stone dam at its base. The liquid iron flowed into sand molds known as pigs. The process of loading raw materials (the "burden") and drawing off the slag and molten iron was continuous—the furnaces operated 24 hours a day.

Down the hill from the stock shed and loading area, the Buckeye Furnace general store contains merchandise typical of the 19th century. The companies often paid the laborers in scrip, rather than currency, which could only be used at the company store or to pay for company lodging. As a result, some workers were continually in debt to their employers.

The discovery of richer and more easily transported Lake Superior iron ore caused the decline of the Hanging Rock Iron Region. Buckeye Furnace shut down for the last time in 1894, closing a chapter in the state's industrial history.

Buckeye Furnace is off OH 124, 10 miles east of Jackson, at 123 Buckeye Park Rd., Wellston; (740) 384-3537, (800) 860-1144; buckeye-furnace.com. Open daylight hours year-round. Museum and gift shop open Sat and Sun, noon to 4 p.m. No admission fee.

Northwest of Jackson, the *Lake Katharine State Nature Preserve* contains 2,019 breathtaking acres of rolling wooded hills, dense vegetation, and a cool, clear lake. Stop by the manager's office for maps of the main

moresaltplease

Long before white settlers explored what is today Jackson County, Native Americans came to Salt Creek for its salt. The first whites to take advantage of the creek did so in 1798. They drew water from 30-foot wells and boiled it away in huge kettles. Due to the low salinity of the water, up to 15 gallons of water were required to produce each pound of salt. Because of the importance of salt in preserving meats, both Congress and the Ohio Legislature passed laws regulating the Jackson saltworks. The discovery of other saltworks both more accessible and with higher salinity led to the decline of Salt Creek's commercial value.

hiking trails (which are located across the lake from the office) and walk down the path near the office for your first view of tranquil Lake Katharine.

It's a scenic drive to the parking area adjacent to the start of the 3 main trails on the east side of the lake. The Calico Bush Trail, a favorite in late April and May with wildflower lovers, leads hikers past abundant calico bush (mountain laurel) in full bloom on and between the exposed sandstone formations.

The Pine Ridge Trail crosses Rock Run, a gurgling stream that supplies Lake Katharine's sparkling water, and follows the lakeshore. This 2-mile trail then rises through a ridge of pines to a spectacular overlook.

Ohio's Youth Conservation Corps completed the preserve's most demanding trail in 1979—Salt Creek Trail. Traveling 2 miles through steep hills, wooded ravines, cliffs, and creeks, hikers pass abandoned drift mines, early Native American work sites, and burial pits.

Visitors to this pristine preserve frequently spot varied wildlife, including wild turkey and deer, and occasionally a bobcat or king snake. Because this is a nature preserve, no bank fishing, swimming, or picnicking is allowed, and nonmotorized watercraft are permitted on the winding lake by written permit only, with a maximum of 5 boats allowed per day.

Lake Katharine State Nature Preserve is 3 miles northwest of Jackson off US 35 on CR 59 at 1703 Lake Katharine Rd.; (614) 286-2487; dnr.state.oh .us/location/lake_katharine/tabid/904/Default.aspx. Open daylight hours; no admission charge.

Just north of Lake Katharine, under a protective roof, rests a large slab of black hand sandstone with some remarkable Native American carvings— the *Leo Petroglyph.* Probably carved by the Fort Ancient Indians more than 700 years ago, the petroglyph has 40 carved figures, with a fish, a bird, and three human feet plainly visible. The most intriguing carving shows an Indian wearing an elaborate headdress. Nature trails penetrate the deep woods and skirt the upper cliffs of the gorges and forests surrounding the petroglyph.

The Leo Petroglyph is on CR 28, off US 35, 4 miles northwest of Jackson; leopetroglyph.com. Open daylight hours; no admission charge.

Sue and Jim Maxwell created a most unusual lodging experience in southeast Ohio: a replica of a 12th-century Norman castle known as *Ravenwood Castle.* Longtime Anglophiles, the Maxwells traveled extensively throughout England and Scotland and were attracted to castles and the medieval period. Surrounded by the Wayne National Forest and just 7 miles from the Hocking Hills, Ravenwood Castle sits atop a wooded hill. More than 100 acres of forest and large rock formations surround the castle.

Ravenwood's crenelated towers contain the guest rooms and suites. Although the building is new, the Maxwells collected architectural antiques for several years. Each guest room or suite has a stained-glass window, usually in the bathroom, a fireplace with Victorian mantel and gas logs, antique light fixtures, and many feature wonderful old doors. The wood moldings around the doors and windows and the castle's 5 stairways are inspired by centuries-old motifs from Great Britain's stately homes and castles. Each room also has a balcony or private deck overlooking the forest.

Common areas include the Great Hall, with 3 large stained-glass windows from an old church at one end and a huge arched stone fireplace at the other. Ornate and heavily carved museum-quality Gothic tables and chairs furnish the Great Hall, where guests dine in a convivial "old English" atmosphere. On the lower level is a library stocked with books on a wide variety of topics, a game room, and the charming Rose and Thistle Pub.

Jim and Pam Reed loved staying at Ravenwood Castle. It was one of their favorite getaway spots. When the Reeds heard that the Ravenwood was for sale in early 2012, they decided to write the next chapter in the magical tale of the lovely castle.

The fairy-tale castle has 7 guest rooms—Rapunzel's Tower, the Duke's Dungeon, the Queen Elizabeth Suite, the Queen Victoria Suite, the Empress Matilda Suite, the Shakespeare Suite, and the King Arthur Suite. Rates are $119 to $299 per night, double occupancy, including full breakfast.

A small village of medieval-style cottages, each with a whirlpool bath, fireplace, and kitchenette, provides another unique lodging option. Surrounding the Castle, the village cottages offer themes in keeping with their names—the Candlemaker's Cottage, the Merchant's Cottage, the Spinster's Cottage, the Woodcutter's Cottage, the Clock Tower, the Silversmith's House, and Cinderella's Coach House. Rates are $159 to $250 per night, double occupancy.

A short drive or walk from the castle are the Fairy Tale Village Cabins—Little Red Riding Hood, Frog Prince, Snow White, Hansel and Gretel, and Sleeping Beauty. The cabins are $99 to $109 per night, double occupancy.

Vinton County Wild Turkey Festival,
McArthur, May;
(740) 596-9889, (740) 591-1118;
vintoncountytravel.com/turkeyfestival
.htm

Moonshine Festival,
New Straitsville, May;
(740) 334-2239;
athensohio.com

Oak Hill Festival of Flags,
Oak Hill, May;
oakhillfestivalofflags.org

Commercial Point Homecoming,
Commercial Point, June;
(740) 983-4836

Poston Lake Bluegrass Festival,
Guysville, June;
(740) 667-0437;
athensohio.com

Appalachian Uprising,
Scottown, June;
(740) 533-7271;
appalachianuprising.net

Gallipolis River Recreation Festival,
Gallipolis, July 4th weekend;
(800) 765-6482;
galliacounty.org

Lawrence County Fair,
Proctorville, July;
(304) 544-5255;
lawrencecountyohiofair.com

Fireman's Old Time Festival,
Laurelville, July;
(740) 332-4691;
laurelvillevfd.com/fest.htm

Civil War Encampment Days,
Malta and McConnelsville, July;
(740) 962-4909;
visitmorgancountyohio.com

Lancaster Festival,
Lancaster, July;
(740) 687-4808;
lanfest.org

Jackson County Fair,
Wellston, July;
jacksonohio.org

All-American Soap Box Derby,
Akron, July;
(330) 733-8723;
aasbd.com

Pig Iron Day,
Jackson, Aug;
(740) 286-2707;
jacksonohio.org

Parade of the Hills,
Nelsonville, Aug;
paradeofthehills.org

Sweet Corn Festival,
Millersport, Sept;
sweetcornfest.com

Baltimore Festival–Canal Lock Days,
Baltimore, Aug;
baltimorefestival.org

Ohio River Sternwheel Festival,
Marietta, Sept;
(800) 288-2577;
ohioriversternwheelfestival.org

For a fun camping experience, try the Gypsy Wagons. The heated wagons include ceiling fans and kitchenettes. Guests bring their own sleeping bags or air mattresses. The Gypsy King's Wagon and Ezmerelda's Wagon are $59 per night, double occupancy.

Ravenwood Castle serves dinner in the Great Hall on most Fridays and Saturdays at 7 p.m. Reservations are required. The Raven's Roost Pub is open most Fridays and Saturdays from 5 to 10 p.m., offering beer, wine, and mixed drinks as well as pub food.

Ravenwood Castle is near the intersection of OH 56 and OH 93 at 65666 Bethel Rd., New Plymouth; (740) 596-2606, (800) 477-1541; ravenwoodcastle .com.

Ohio's state parks offer hundreds of cabins throughout the state, most of them modern, two-bedroom deluxe models. For those seeking more rustic and less expensive lodging, **Lake Hope State Park** provides the widest selection of types of cabins in the state park system. In addition to deluxe cabins, Lake Hope has 21 standard cabins with wood-burning fireplaces. These cabins, available April through October, accommodate up to 6 people in 4 rooms and contain complete kitchens. A third type, the sleeping cabins, have 1 to 4 bedrooms, fireplaces, and refrigerators, but no cooking facilities. As with the modern deluxe cabins, the sleeping cabins are available year-round.

The 3,000-acre park includes 120-acre Lake Hope, with its large beach and swimming area, in a heavily wooded section of Vinton County. The park has miles of hiking trails, as does the adjacent state forest. Lake Hope State Park also contains the remains of an old charcoal furnace—Hope Furnace.

Opened in December 2012, the $5 million **Lake Hope Lodge** has arisen like a phoenix from the ashes of the original 1950 structure, which burned to the ground in 2006. The new 14,645-square-foot lodge, built of local timber cut from the Zaleski State Forest, overlooks Lake Hope. The lodge includes a restaurant, cafe, park office and cottage check-in, and gift shop. A banquet hall and caterer's kitchen are located on the lower level.

The lodge restaurant offers home cooking with an emphasis on using Ohio products. A traditional barbecue pit is fired by pure hickory wood. The restaurant is open year-round Mon through Thurs, 11 a.m. to 8 p.m.; Fri and Sat, 11 a.m. to 9 p.m.; Sun, brunch 10 a.m. to 2 p.m., dinner 4 to 8 p.m. Call the Lodge at (740) 596-0601.

Lake Hope State Park is at 27331 OH 278, 5 miles north of Zaleski in McArthur; (740) 596-5253, (866) 644-4938; lakehopestatepark.com. Cabin rates range from $60 to $95 per night.

Southeast Ohio contains thousands of acres of rugged, hilly countryside covered with thick forests, but the most geologically intriguing area may be the 10,000-acre *Hocking Hills State Park and Forest.* Steep hills, deciduous and evergreen forests, caves, rivers, waterfalls, and abundant plant and animal life provide outstanding recreational opportunities.

A warm, shallow ocean covered Ohio some 300 million years ago and deposited the bedrock of shale and black hand sandstone found in the area. Black hand sandstone is so named because of a large black hand drawn on a slab of the stone near Newark. Probably drawn by Native Americans, the hand may have served as a marker pointing the way to the outcroppings of flint found at Flint Ridge.

Though primitive man may have used the caves, recesses, and cliffs in the Hocking Hills for shelter as long as 7,000 years ago, pottery fragments confirm the Adena Indians lived here from the time of Christ to AD 800. White settlers did not discover the lush forests and flowing streams in these hills until the 1790s.

Old Man's Cave, one of the 6 major formations in the park, so awed Richard Rowe with its natural beauty in the early 1800s that he decided to live at the cave as a hermit for the rest of his days. Rowe was the "old man" for whom this cave is named. A deep gorge runs along the cave, which is actually a major recess in the sandstone cliff, and water flowing through the bottom of the gorge is hurled over 2 waterfalls and into the Devil's Bathtub, a large pothole formed in the sandstone by swirling rock and gravel in the stream water. Hiking trails follow the ridges on both sides of the gorge, and a third trail snakes through the hemlocks, beeches, and yews at the bottom of the gorge.

Decades of erosion have created another spectacular sandstone formation called Ash Cave, a 700-foot horseshoe-shaped rock ledge that forms a recess 100 feet deep. Mounds of ash found here by early settlers indicated that this large rock roof was a popular camping site for Native Americans. Hiking trails run along both ridges and the floor of the gorge, past a 90-foot waterfall.

The Rock House, a massive recess completely enclosed by rock except for the open "windows," is the most cavelike formation in the

ALSO WORTH SEEING

Wayne National Forest,
Athens

Burr Oak State Park,
Glouster

Slate Run Living Historical Farm,
Lithopolis

park—certainly more so than Ash Cave or Old Man's Cave—yet of the three it is the only one not named a cave. Another misnomer is nearby Cedar Falls, a waterfall named by pioneers who mistakenly identified the dense forest as cedar, when in fact it is hemlock.

In addition to the 6 major formations in the park, hiking trails explore thousands of acres in the thickly wooded state forest. The park has 40 deluxe cabins in a secluded, peaceful setting. The cabins are available year-round but are rented for full weeks only during summer months, with rates of $140 per night. Other park features include campsites, a 17-acre fishing lake, and a summer naturalist program, plus picnic tables, barbecue grills, and shelters scattered throughout the area.

Hocking Hills State Park is 14 miles west of Logan, at 19852 OH 664 South; (740) 385-6841 (cottage office), (740) 385-6842 (park office), (866) 644-6727 (reservations); parks.ohiodnr.gov/hockinghills.

The original innkeeper's ambitious goal when he conceived of *Glenlaurel*, his Scottish country inn and cottages, was to build the premier romantic getaway of the Midwest. Situated on 140 wooded acres and backing up to the rocks of Camusfearna Gorge, Glenlaurel welcomed its first guests in 1994.

This full-service resort is a great country escape any time of the year. The 8 stone fireplaces of the Manor House and its guest rooms take the chill out of a fall day. A double whirlpool tub in each private bath overlooks the hemlock and trillium. The Carriage House and the Manor House both offer rooms and suites—3 rooms and 3 suites total. Tucked away in a dense woods, each of the 6 features an open-air hot tub on a private deck and a kitchenette.

Then there are the crofts, a smaller version of a cottage. A croft is about 450 square feet, compared with a cottage, which is about 700 square feet.

Glenlaurel offers 4 East Crofts on Thistle Ridge and 3 West Crofts overlooking Brannock Burn Ravine. Each croft has a kitchenette, living room, queen bedroom, gas log fireplace, screened porch, and hot tub on a private deck.

Glenlaurel is famed for its gourmet cuisine served with a Scottish flair. Dinner consists of three-, six-, and seven-course meals served by candlelight with bagpipe music and Scottish poetry. Gourmet dining includes legendary light-as-air Belgian buttermilk waffles topped with maple cream and strawberry-rhubarb sauce. A "typical" dinner: orange-tomato-basil soup, mixed greens with balsamic vinaigrette, soy-sesame-ginger-marinated salmon over basmati rice with roasted vegetables, finished with a slice of mixed-berry sour cream pie.

Glenlaurel is 5 miles west of US 33, just off OH 180, at 14940 Mt. Olive Rd., Rockbridge; (800) 809-7378; glenlaurel.com. Rates are $189 to $229 for rooms, $219 to $299 for suites, $249 to $299 for crofts, and $299 to $349 for cottages, per night, double occupancy, including full breakfast. The resort also has a spa, wellness center, and Scottish Links golf course.

It took more time and money than its creators ever imagined, but the *Inn and Spa at Cedar Falls* was worth the wait. Situated on a hillside meadow, surrounded on three sides by the Hocking Hills State Park, the inn represents 2 1/2 years of work and an investment of a half million dollars.

First, shingle and plaster were removed from the 1850s-vintage farmhouse, purchased from an 86-year-old woman who was born here, to reveal its original log-and-mud construction. A second log building was moved on site, and the union of these structures now houses a gourmet kitchen and 2 indoor dining areas. The plank flooring and period pieces give this room a pioneer ambience—it's a place where guests watch culinary artistry in progress. The aromas of American country cooking fill the inn—apple-smoked pork loin, bean soup, bread pudding with whiskey sauce, or chicken with morel sauce.

The inn's garden supplies herbs and edible flowers. Meals are prepared with the local growing season in mind. Guest chefs from Columbus and elsewhere are invited to spend an evening in the kitchen, explaining their technique to guests as they perform their magic. Exceptional breakfasts, lunches, and dinners are then served either in the log house or out on the patio.

The Inn and Spa at Cedar Falls offers most unusual accommodations for its overnight guests. Housed in a modern, barn-shaped building are

9 guest rooms. Though similar in design to contemporary motel rooms, with individual heating and air-conditioning units, they are furnished with antiques and wood floors. Each has an up-to-date private bath, but no telephone or television. Rocking chairs and tables make the second-floor balcony a delightful spot for reading or just soaking up the hilly landscape. Twelve cozy cottages have been built, each with a gas log stove, a large whirlpool tub, and a private deck. Five log cabins are scattered throughout the inn's 75 acres, each with privacy, cooking facilities, and its own personality.

The Spa at Cedar Falls is a secluded retreat of luxurious simplicity tucked gently in these Hocking Hills. From traditional massages to body mud wraps, guests will feel the stress of everyday life ease beneath the hands of their therapist. The Spa at Cedar Falls is surrounded by the fresh air and natural environment of the Hocking Hills—a wilderness retreat inspired by the land it borders. A section of the prairie meadow that predominates here has been mowed, so guests can stroll down the hill to an outstanding lookout. Here you might encounter deer, fox, or raccoon, while birders view yellow finches, bluebirds, woodpeckers, ruffed grouse, and wild turkey.

Although the inn occupies a clearing right on OH 374, wooded hiking trails meander nearby. The Buckeye Trail, which connects Old Man's Cave with Ash Cave, is easily joined from here. Or hike to Rose Lake for some trout fishing. Cross-country skiing is a winter favorite.

Innkeepers Ellen Grinsfelder and Terry Lingo want their guests to enjoy the natural wonder of this area as much as they do. And although the kitchen serves overnight guests, others are welcome for dinner if they call ahead and make reservations. Seasonal delights are prepared at mealtime, when visitors come together to share their day's adventures. Lunch is served daily from 11:30 a.m. to 1:30 p.m. Holidays are special times here—the inn provides those without family nearby (or those escaping relatives!) a homey retreat full of holiday spirit.

The Inn and Spa at Cedar Falls is located at 21190 OH 374, 10 miles southwest of Logan; (800) 653-2557; innatcedarfalls.com. Rates: $135 to $379 per night, double occupancy, including full breakfast. Open year-round.

Wyandot Woods is a welcome retreat for those seeking to get off the beaten path, with 6 cabins nestled in the trees around a spring-fed lake.

The cabins are well separated from one another, and each has a private dock on the lake—a perfect spot to fish for largemouth bass, yellow perch, and bluegill, or to launch one of the rowboats provided for guests. Lake swimming is a favorite summer pastime here, or you can loll and sunbathe out on the diving platform floating in the center of the lake. Whatever you choose to do here, the limited number of cabins ensures that you will never encounter a crowd.

Cabins here range from one-bedroom single stories to the bi-level Cedar House with two large decks, an indoor hot tub, and two-plus bedrooms. Each cabin at Wyandot Woods has a deck, porch swing, wood-burning stove with glass front for fire watchers (as well as electric heat), and an outdoor barbecue grill. All are comfortably furnished in pleasing earth tones, and they have plenty of windows looking out on the dense forest. Complete kitchens round out the facilities here.

Wyandot Woods is east of Laurelville, off OH 180; (877) 365-8009, (740) 335-1020; wyandotwoods.com. Rates: $150 to $244 per night, depending on the size of the cabin, day of the week, and season. Open year-round. Reservations are required.

Another Hocking Hills lodging option, set on 100 wooded acres, is **Old Man's Cave Chalets.** These 16 A-frames, sprinkled on a hillside, are three-room structures, complete with lofts. Each chalet sleeps four and has a deck with a private hot tub, a wood-burning fireplace (plus central heating and air-conditioning), and an efficiency kitchen.

In addition to the A-frames, 15 larger luxury log homes, sleeping four to eight people, are situated in more secluded locations throughout the hills. These deluxe log homes feature large stone fireplaces, private hot tubs, TVs and DVDs, central air, handmade furniture, and fully equipped kitchens. Four large lodges accommodate groups of up to 16 guests. Three cottages and 12 cabins are also available.

The quiet, isolated location makes this an ideal year-round retreat. Facilities also include a large outdoor swimming pool and recreation area. More than 800 acres of state forest adjoin the property and are available for hiking and exploration.

Old Man's Cave Chalets is at 18905 OH 664 South, south of Logan; (800) 762-9396, (740) 385-6517, (740) 385-8941; oldmanscavechalets.com. Rates: $169 to $989 (for a 7-bedroom lodge) per night, double occupancy. Reservations required.

In addition to hiking and camping, canoeing and horseback riding are popular in the Hocking Hills. *Hocking Valley Canoe Livery and Fun Center* provides rental equipment along the picturesque Hocking River, with trips ranging from two hours to three days at rates from $20 to $60 per canoe. The livery is at 31251 Chieftain Dr., Logan; (800) 686-0386, (740) 385-8685, (740) 385-2503; hockinghillscanoeing.com. Canoe rentals are available Apr through Oct; daily between June and Aug, on weekends or by appointment in Apr, May, Sept, and Oct. Kayaks, rafts, go-karts, miniature golf, and a driving range also are available.

A unique way to experience the natural beauty of the Hocking Hills is riding the rails. The *Hocking Valley Scenic Railway* departs from its Nelsonville Depot for leisurely jaunts through the woods. The route between Nelsonville and Logan was once a part of the original Hocking Valley Railway's Athens Branch. The Hocking Valley was eventually merged into the Chesapeake & Ohio Railway in 1930.

The Hocking Valley Scenic Railway offers diesel-powered rides through the beautiful rolling hills of southeastern Ohio aboard vintage equipment. The primary locomotive was built for the Chesapeake & Ohio Railway in October 1952 by the Electro-motive Division of GM. In the 1970s, along with a few other C&O "Geeps," it was transferred to the Chicago, South Shore & South Bend Railroad for use in the C&O subsidiary's freight service. It has been restored and returned to its 1952 as-delivered paint scheme.

The coaches used were built in 1927 by the Standard Steel Car Company for the Chicago, Rock Island & Pacific Railroad. Each coach can seat 100 passengers and weighs in at 95,200 lbs. They were used for commuter runs between Chicago and Joliet, Illinois. The coaches are heated in the winter, so a comfortable and enjoyable ride is to be had with Santa Claus during the annual Santa trains. Other vintage rolling stock is under restoration and on display.

The Hocking Valley Scenic Railway departs from 33 E. Canal St. (US 33), Nelsonville; (740) 753-9531, (800) 967-7834; hvsry.com. Trains depart every Sat and Sun between Memorial Day and the last weekend in Oct. Train times are noon and 2:30 p.m. Special event trains operate throughout the year. Check the schedule for special holiday train trips. Santa specials run the last weekend in Nov and the first three weekends in Dec, Sat and Sun, at 11 a.m. and 2 p.m., plus 7 p.m. the first three Fri nights in Dec. Rates: adults $16 to $18; children (ages 3 to 12) $11.

ohio's bulgaria liberator

The man hailed as one of the greatest figures in the history of Bulgaria was born on a farm near New Lexington in 1844. Januarius MacGahan, the "Liberator of Bulgaria," hoped to be a teacher but was unable to land a job with the local school district. Instead, in the early 1870s, he traveled throughout Europe and eventually became a war correspondent in the Balkans, where he filed eyewitness accounts of Turkish atrocities. His reporting shifted British public opinion regarding their support for Turkey and encouraged Russian intervention. MacGahan crossed the Danube with 100,000 Russian soldiers and received a hero's welcome. MacGahan lived out his life in Constantinople and died there in 1878. His body was returned to the US; he's buried at New Lexington's Maplewood Cemetery.

Nature herself has given this site its name, Wahkeena, which is a Native American word meaning "most beautiful." The 150-acre **Wahkeena Nature Preserve,** at the edge of the Hocking Hills, is blessed with so many natural assets that it serves as a center for both outdoor education and nature study.

But the casual visitor won't have to study too hard to see how the preserve got its name. Much of the area is forested with lovely tulip trees as well as oaks. Mountain laurel, brilliant rhododendron, a host of wildflowers, and more than two dozen kinds of fern grace the landscape. While you may not think of Ohio as home to the exotic orchid, Wahkeena boasts 8 native varieties of the flower, including the pink lady's slipper.

Visitors can hike 3 trails into the preserve and may be able to catch glimpses of the permanent residents: white-tailed deer, woodpeckers, maybe even a hawk or an owl. The land itself is noteworthy, with sandstone cliffs part of the preserve's vista, the famous black hand sandstone.

Although you can do your own exploring, naturalists also offer guided hikes and walks focusing on wildlife, plant life, or even the ways of the early pioneers in the area. Check in advance for topics, dates, and times.

The Wahkeena Nature Preserve is located at 2200 Pump Station Rd., Sugar Grove; (740) 746-8695, (800) 297-1883; dnr.state.oh.us/location/dnap/wahkeena/tabid/969/default.aspx. Open Apr through Oct, Sat and Sun, 8 a.m. to 4:30 p.m. No admission fee.

Square 13, a National Register Historic District, is one of the original blocks of Lancaster, a block noted by architectural historians as one of the finest collections of 19th-century architecture in a concentrated area in the nation. Within Square 13 on Lancaster's "Main Hill" is the **Sherman House,** the birthplace and early home of noted Civil War general William Tecumseh Sherman, and his brother, Senator John Sherman, author of the Sherman Anti-Trust Act. This museum is furnished as it would have been when the Sherman family lived there (the home was built between 1811 and 1816) and contains an extensive collection of General Sherman's Civil War memorabilia, mementos, and artifacts. One room is the study of William and John's father, Charles Sherman, who was a justice on the Ohio Supreme Court.

The Sherman House is at 137 E. Main St., Lancaster; (740) 687-5891, (740) 654-9923; shermanhouse.org. Open Apr through mid-Dec, Tues through Sun, noon to 4 p.m. Admission: adults $6; students (ages 6 to 18) $2.

The **Decorative Arts Center of Ohio** is a statewide organization that promotes the appreciation of decorative arts and finds its impressive home in the Reese-Peters House. Within this venue there are permanent and special exhibitions, plenty of art classes and workshops for children and adults, and a gift shop where you can find a souvenir or a book to help you learn more and celebrate decorative arts.

The house itself is a piece of art. The grand, Greek revival–style home was built around 1835 by William James Reese, the son of a wealthy merchant. After getting a degree in law, Reese came to settle in Lancaster and married into a famous family. His wife, Elisabeth Sherman, was the sister of Secretary of State John Sherman and General William Tecumseh Sherman.

Reese ultimately lost the magnificent house in the financial panic of 1837. Luckily, after the house went through a series of owners, the final private owners donated it to Fairfield County. The house was renovated and became the home to the Decorative Arts Center, thanks to the authorization of more than $1 million in capital funds from the Ohio State Legislature.

The Decorative Arts Center is located at 145 E. Main St., Lancaster; (740) 681-1423; decartsohio.org. Open Tues through Sat, 10 a.m. to 4 p.m.; Sun, 1 to 4 p.m. No admission charge.

After a day of exploring the Sherman House or attending a class at the Decorative Arts Center of Ohio, you may be ready to relax in a charming and relaxing setting. The **Henry Manor Bed and Breakfast** is a lovingly restored 1869 Tuscan-Victorian home situated on 10 acres of woodlands. Guests can enjoy the outdoors just by sitting in the gazebo or get a little exercise on the woodland trails.

Two guest rooms on the second floor of the home have private baths. The Angel Room's bath is down the hall from the bedroom, and the Yellow Rose Room's bath features the original, old-fashioned claw-foot tub. Both rooms have a romantic feel and are graced with some lovely antiques. A full breakfast is included with the room. Guests select the breakfast menu and dining time.

Henry Manor Bed and Breakfast is located at 1755 Cedar Hill Rd., Lancaster; (740) 689-8589, (740) 215-5303; henrymanor.com. Rate: $125 per night.

The Georgian, an elegant two-story brick mansion, sits on a hill looking down on Lancaster's central business district, just as it has for the past 180 years. Constructed in 1831 for prominent businessman Samuel Maccracken, the Georgian mixes federal architecture with Regency features and Empire furnishings. The federal influence can be seen in the symmetrical placement of doors, windows, and fireplaces, while the Regency features are exemplified by the curved bay windows along the west wall. Classic Ionic columns, each containing a complete tree trunk for structural support, form the west portico.

Maccracken came to Lancaster from Big Springs, Pennsylvania, in 1810. Later elected to the state legislature, he introduced the bill funding construction of Ohio's canal system. While serving as Ohio canal funds commissioner, Maccracken raised $6 million in Europe for the project.

This 13-room mansion is furnished with handsome pieces dating from the mid-1800s, including some of Maccracken's possessions. The original pine floors and woodwork remain intact, as do the original doors, door frames, and ornate arches. The spiral staircase features a cherry spindle handrail, and a large skylight allows light to spill down the stairs.

Splendid blue marble fireplaces from the quarry in King of Prussia, Pennsylvania, grace the 2 large parlors, as do matching French chandeliers (ca. 1820). One of the upstairs bedrooms contains a fine Regency bed (ca. 1800)—the type of bed preferred by generals in the Civil War, since it could be assembled and disassembled easily by the troops. One unique item in the museum is a 1792 senility cradle. Similar in design and function to a baby's cradle, cradles such as this were used by old people who were no longer ambulatory.

Hanging on the wall in one of the stairways are original Fairfield County land grants signed by Presidents Jefferson and Madison. Also on display is an American flag with 18 stars—the US flag from 1816 to 1820. The basement houses the kitchen, equipped as it was in the 1830s, and a unique dry well, where groundwater from the surface drained by way of pipes and was dispersed into the ground beneath the basement.

The Georgian is at 105 E. Wheeling St., on the corner of East Wheeling and North Broad Streets, Lancaster; (740) 654-9923; georgianmuseum .org. Open Apr through mid-Dec, Tues through Sun, 1 to 4 p.m. Admission: adults $6; students (under age 18) $2.

After your tour of the Georgian, be sure to walk up East Wheeling Street for a view of the magnificent restored homes in a hilly, shaded section of Lancaster. If lunch or dinner is the next item on your itinerary, try a 1940s hotel that is making a comeback. Just across the street from the Georgian, **Shaw's Restaurant and Inn** features food, libations, and lodging in a delightful setting. Nine of the inn's 25 rooms and suites feature whirlpools and themed decor.

With rich wooden doors and trim, potted greenery, and distinctive floral wall coverings, the main dining room of the hotel has candlelit tables and indirect lighting, creating a cozy atmosphere. The dinner menu changes daily and is known for its sophistication.

Shaw's serves fresh homemade pies and cakes, and the house-made hot fudge sauce is a standout. Due to the popularity of lunch and dinner selections, the dining rooms accept reservations for both meals.

Shaw's has received the prestigious Wine Spectator Award of Excellence, noting the depth of the selections of vintage California red wines. In addition to the extensive wine list, a dozen varieties are served by the glass.

Shaw's Restaurant and Inn is at 123 N. Broad St., Lancaster; (740) 654-1842, (800) 654-2477; shawsinn.com. Rates: $74 to $218 per night, double occupancy, including full breakfast.

Abundant clay deposits in eastern Ohio, particularly in Perry and Muskingum Counties, encouraged the manufacture of pottery and ceramic wares in this section of the state. Pottery production in these counties dates to the early 19th century, and 22 major pottery companies once generated clay products in the area. Only eight of those firms remain in business, but the **National Ceramic Museum and Heritage Center** preserves the history of the industry and displays samples of the diverse output of those factories.

Set on a hilltop in a cluster of trees, the center consists of 5 open-air exhibit buildings. Guides provide the background and explain the processes used to produce the assortment of vases, jugs, pots, and pitchers, plus plates, saucers, and other dinnerware—each unique in shape, color, and clay mixture. Some of the older pieces include stoneware jugs and jars from the 1850s, and even older earthenware, which was made from very soft red clay.

The yellow ware, so named because of its yellow hue, came from the East Liverpool, Ohio, area, as did the most unusual brown Rockingham pottery. Rockingham (also manufactured in Vermont and Great Britain) can be easily identified by the pitcher handles, which are shaped like a dog—a dog that appears to be looking into the pitcher. The guides also explain the obvious similarity in style of pieces from different companies—the firms frequently hired employees away from one another, and these employees often brought to their new employer the techniques and processes used by competitors.

Modern pottery displays include samples of dinnerware and decorative pottery currently in production at the remaining local companies. The museum also exhibits pottery-making equipment such as molds and old potter's wheels, plus examples of industrial uses of ceramics—drain tubes, shingles, chimney liners, and even filters for air-pollution devices. A resident potter demonstrates the craft of hand-throwing vases, bowls, and jugs, and describes glazing and finishing procedures. Two large shelter houses have been added at the

all'spotteryin crooksville

Given its name, you might suspect Crooksville is notable for the poor character of its citizenry. That is not the case. Instead, Crooksville made its reputation as a center of the pottery business.

The rich clays beneath its soil spawned pottery giants such as Crooksville Pottery Company, the Star Stoneware Company, and the Diamond Stoneware Company in the late 19th century. The arrival of rail service in 1890 established Crooksville as "Clay City," and launched a competition with another Ohio pottery town, East Liverpool.

center, where antique pottery is sold on special occasions, the proceeds used to help support this facility.

The National Ceramic Museum and Heritage Center is on OH 93 between Roseville and Crooksville at 7327 Ceramic Rd. NE (CR 96); (740) 697-7021; ceramiccenter.info. The center is open Wed through Sat, 9:30 a.m. to 5 p.m.; Sun, noon to 5 p.m. Admission: adults $4; children $2.

Cattle ranch? Ohio? Yep. The **Smoke Rise Ranch Resort** is a working cattle ranch on 2,000 acres in the rolling hills of southeastern Ohio. Visitors can play cowboy or cowgirl, rounding up strays on horseback, doctoring sick calves, checking fences and water tanks, and driving the herd from pasture to pasture. Or you can just enjoy the scenery, exploring it on foot or in the saddle on the more than 100 miles of trails. Other activities include ranch rodeos, team penning, riding lessons, dinner dances, and music festivals.

A wildlife management area and the Wayne National Forest, totaling more than 30,000 acres, border the ranch. The terrain ranges from rock bluffs to lush green bottomland. The abundant ponds provide water for your trail horse and a great place to stop and fish away an afternoon.

Accommodations range from bunk-style cabins and a fully furnished ranch house to picturesque campsites. And you can cook your own grub (ranch talk for "food"), or dine with the staff at this family-owned resort. Other amenities include a heated swimming pool, a hot tub, and a clubhouse with a full kitchen.

moonshine festival

Legal moonshine? Yes, in New Straitsville in late May you can see demonstrations of moonshine brewing as part of the Moonshine Festival. The character of hill country culture of days past comes back to life in the streets as the music of fiddles and banjos fills the air. There always are plenty of games for the kids, as well as displays and sales of local crafts and plenty of local food specialties.

Smoke Rise Ranch Resort is at 6751 Hunterdon Rd., Glouster; (740) 767-2624, (800) 292-1732; smokeriseranch.com. Open for trail riding daily, 8 a.m. to 6:30 p.m. Lodging is $70 to $175 per night. Office hours are Mon through Sat, 8 a.m. to 8 p.m.; Sun, 8 a.m. to 5 p.m. Hours vary during the off-season of Nov through March.

It was Harriet and Ora Anderson, she a well-known local artist and he a banker and philanthropist, who decided southeastern Ohio was in need of a cultural arts center. Their quest for a home for their vision led them to an unlikely structure: a historic dairy barn, built in 1914, once part of a large farm minutes from the heart of Athens.

By the time the Andersons discovered the **Dairy Barn** in 1977, it was scheduled for demolition in nine days. They rallied area residents and artists and saved it from the wrecking ball. In 1978 the facility was placed on the National Register of Historic Places, protecting it from future demolition.

After a loft renovation, this unique 11,000-square-foot exhibit space today hosts international exhibitions, festivals, performances, and activities for all ages, and all consistent with its mission: to offer exhibitions, events, and educational programs that nurture and promote area artists and artisans, and to draw attention and visitors to southeast Ohio. In the international arts community, the Dairy Barn is best known for its contemporary art quilt exhibition.

The Dairy Barn is at 8000 Dairy Lane, Athens; (740) 592-4981; dairybarn .org. Open year-round, Tues through Sat, noon to 5 p.m. General admission is $8 adults, $5 students.

Places to Stay in Southeast Ohio

GLOUSTER

Smoke Rise Ranch Resort
6751 Hunterdon Rd.
(740) 767-2624,
(800) 292-1732
smokeriseranch.com

LANCASTER

Henry Manor Bed and Breakfast
1755 Cedar Hill Rd.
(740) 689-8589
henrymanor.com

LOGAN

Inn and Spa at Cedar Falls
21190 OH 374
(740) 385-7489,
(800) 653-2557
innatcedarfalls.com

Old Man's Cave Chalets
18905 OH 664
(800) 762-9396
oldmanscavechalets.com

MARIETTA

Lafayette Hotel
Corner of Front and Greene Streets
(740) 373-5522
lafayettehotel.com

HELPFUL WEBSITES

Ohio Division of Travel and Tourism:
discoverohio.com

Hocking Hills Tourism:
hockinghills.com

Athens County Visitors Bureau:
athensohio.com

Marietta Visitors Bureau:
mariettaohio.org

NEW PLYMOUTH

Ravenwood Castle
Intersection of OH 56 and
OH 93
(740) 596-2606,
(800) 477-1541
ravenwoodcastle.com

ROCKBRIDGE

Glenlaurel
14940 Mt. Olive Rd.
(800) 809-7398
glenlaurel.com

ZALESKI

**Lake Hope State Park
Cabins**
OH 278, 5 miles north of
Zaleski
(740) 596-4938,
(866) 644-6727
lakehopestatepark.com

Places to Eat in Southeast Ohio

LANCASTER

**Shaw's Restaurant and
Inn**
123 N. Broad St.
(614) 654-1842,
(800) 654-2477
Lodging is also available.
shawsinn.com

MARIETTA

**Buckley House
Restaurant**
332 Front St.
(740) 374-4400
bhrestaurant.com

Levee House Cafe
127 Ohio St.
(740) 374-2233
leveehousemarietta.com

MCCONNELSVILLE

Boondocks BBQ & Grill
4651 N. OH 60
(740) 962-4100

Scioto Ribber
1026 Gallia St.
(740) 353-9329

Native Beauty

Two thousand years ago, along the rivers of what is now southern Ohio, a great civilization arose. The Hopewell culture flourished for more than 500 years, leaving behind extensive burial mounds, earthworks, and artifacts. They are preserved at the Mound City site of the ***Hopewell Culture National Historical Park.*** Excavation and restoration work was conducted by the Ohio State Historical Society in 1920 and 1921, and the site was declared a National Monument in 1923. Additional excavations were conducted in the mid-1960s.

Some of the artifacts discovered and displayed here may have been used to establish trade and diplomatic ties between distant peoples. The territory we now call southern Ohio was the center of a network of peoples extending from Michigan to southern Florida, and from Kansas to the East Coast. The Hopewell included skilled artisans; they fished and hunted, gathered wild foods, and gardened. They lived along river valleys, in permanent or semipermanent villages near the mounds and earthworks they built. By

BEST ATTRACTIONS

Hopewell Culture National Historical Park	Serpent Mound
	Rankin House
Adena	Signal House
Highlands Nature Sanctuary	Cohearts Riverhouse
Pike Lake State Park	Grant's Boyhood Home
Lake White Club	Grant's Birthplace
Fort Hill State Memorial	Valley Vineyards
Shawnee State Park	

about AD 500 the great Hopewell culture ended, perhaps because of social changes. In addition to the Mound City Group, Hopewell Culture National Historical Park preserves four additional Hopewell sites in Ross County: Hopewell Mound Group, Seip Earthworks, High Bank Works, and Hopeton Earthworks.

Hopewell Culture National Historical Park is 3 miles north of Chillicothe on OH 104; (740) 774-1126; nps.gov/hocu. Open daily, 8:30 a.m. to 5 p.m. Memorial Day to Labor Day the Visitor Center is open 8:30 a.m. to 6 p.m. Admission is free.

Thomas Worthington first came to Ohio from Virginia at the age of 23 in 1796, when he and a small band of men arrived to claim the land promised their fathers and friends after the Revolutionary War. Worthington permanently moved his family to Ohio in 1798 and quickly became active in the efforts to achieve statehood for the territory. He succeeded in that endeavor and served as a member of Ohio's Constitutional Convention in 1802. After being elected as one of the state's first US senators, Worthington built his magnificent hilltop estate, *Adena.* Worthington and his wife, Eleanor, raised their 10 children at Adena and entertained distinguished guests such as President James Monroe, Henry Clay, Aaron Burr, and the Shawnee Indian chief Tecumseh. After building Adena, Worthington was reelected to the US Senate in 1811, and later he served two terms as the governor of Ohio.

More than 300 of the estate's original 5,000 acres are now open to the public, and visitors may explore the spacious two-story sandstone home, the barn, the springhouse, and the smokehouse—all located in a rolling meadow above the Scioto River Valley. Self-guided tours of the 18-room home allow you to browse at your own pace, appreciating the fine antiques described on the fact sheet, which gives the styles and origins of the furnishings in the home. Although many of the pieces on display did not belong to the Worthingtons, they date from the 1780s to 1820s and are typical of the pieces used at Adena.

The large downstairs master bedroom, with its dark ash and oak floors, has a splendid view of the formal gardens. In an adjacent sitting room hangs a most unusual portrait of Thomas Jefferson, created not with paint, but with different colors of wool thread. The enormous state dining room features the actual dining table and chairs used at Adena in 1825. Two large portraits decorate the drawing room; one of Thomas Worthington at age 25 and the other of his sister, who married Edward Tiffin, Ohio's first governor.

State Motto/Animal

In 1866 the Ohio legislature passed a bill adding a motto to Ohio's Great Seal. The motto, *Imerium in Imperio,* translates from Latin to "an empire within an empire." However, the motto's life span was brief. Critics blasted it as pretentious and feudal, and in 1867 the law authorizing it was repealed. For the next 91 years, Ohio had no state motto.

In 1958 Cincinnati sixth grader Jimmie Mastronardo was disturbed to learn that Ohio was the only state without a motto, and he set about to correct this omission. He decided on a biblical verse from Matthew 19:26: "With God all things are possible." He and his classmates launched a petition drive aimed at the legislature, a drive that succeeded in 1959 when the new motto officially was adopted.

Students also were the driving force behind the designation of the white-tailed deer as Ohio's state animal in 1988. In this case, it was a fourth-grade class at Worthington Estates Elementary School that lobbied lawmakers. The students argued that the white-tailed deer's abundance (there are more deer today in Ohio than there were at the time of settlement) and gracefulness warranted the recognition. The legislators agreed and deemed it so.

Two of Adena's most interesting rooms are tucked away down the back stairs: the weaving room, with a large Virginia loom (ca. 1790) and wool and flax wheels, and Worthington's private study. On display in the study is a tomahawk given to Worthington by Chief Tecumseh in 1807. Worthington's musket and his father's sword still hang above the fireplace.

Across the meadow from the home is a scenic overlook of the Scioto River Valley—you can see for miles from this spot. In fact, the splendor of the sunrise over Mount Logan as viewed from Adena is said to have inspired the sunrise design incorporated in the seal of the state of Ohio.

Adena is off OH 104 and Pleasant Valley Road at 846 Adena Rd., 3 miles north of Chillicothe; (740) 772-1500, (800) 319-7248; ohiohistory.org/places/adena. Open from Apr through Oct, Wed through Sat, 9 a.m. to 5 p.m.; Sun, noon to 5 p.m. Admission: adults $8; children (ages 6 to 12) $4.

Built by Governor Tiffin in 1826, the *Guest House Bed and Breakfast* was a wedding gift from Ohio's first governor to his daughter. Situated one block from downtown Chillicothe and listed on the National Register of Historic Places in 1987, the home was "Victorianized" in the 1880s with the addition of a second floor over the east wing of the house with ornate staircases and parquet floors in the hall and dining room. This house was once the home of Edward Tiffin Cook, a gold medalist in pole vault at the 1908 Olympics.

Owners Tom and Kay Binns have traveled extensively—Tom's a retired airline captain—and have brought the best of the amenities they have enjoyed around the world to the Guest House. The Guest House is a two-story brick building with a guest unit on each floor and a separate entrance for each. Look out the window of either unit and enjoy a view of the Old English garden separating the Guest House from the main building. The Guest House offers 5 rooms—3 in the main house and 2 across the yard in the original two-story guest house.

For those who like ghosts, a Confederate soldier is said to sometimes stroll the Guest House. As the innkeepers note, "A ghost lives here with dark hair and beard. On our brick walks, sometimes his footsteps we hear. He wears a draped topcoat and may awaken you at night. But he's friendly, quiet and no cause for fright. He's elusive, evasive and his countenance will fade when there's laundry, yard work or bills to be paid."

The Guest House is at 57 W. Fifth St., Chillicothe; (740) 772-2204; guesthousechillicothe.com. Rates: $125 per night, including full breakfast.

Shawnee leader Tecumseh dreamed of banding together 50,000 warriors from all the western Indian tribes in a force that he hoped would end the white man's westward expansion. The plan obviously failed, and the whites eventually conquered the land north and west of the Ohio River and beyond. Tecumseh's story is portrayed nightly, except Sunday, during the summer at **Sugarloaf Mountain Amphitheatre** in the outdoor drama *Tecumseh!* The Tecumseh Restaurant Terrace serves a buffet dinner each evening prior to the 8 p.m. curtain. Backstage tours also are offered. Immediately following the performance, cast members of *Tecumseh!* gather in the pavilion area to sign autographs and pose for photographs. The Prehistoric Indian Mini-Museum displays prehistoric Indian artifacts from the Scioto Valley. The museum has free admission Mon through Sat from 5 to 7:45 p.m. during the production season.

New in 2013, a "Living History" tour is offered Saturday at 3 p.m. during theater season. The hourlong tour features costumed cast members portraying characters from the world of Tecumseh and the early settlers. Admission is $4.50 for adults and $3.50 for children.

Sugarloaf Mountain Amphitheatre is at 5968 Marietta Rd., east of OH 159, 6 miles northeast of Chillicothe; (740) 775-0700, (866) 775-0700; tecumsehdrama.com. Performances take place from early June to early Sept. Admission: adults $24.95; children (ages 10 and under) $17.95. Advance reservations required.

feastofthe floweringmoon

What child hasn't played at being a Native American or a rugged mountain man? The Feast of the Flowering Moon brings reenactment teams together to bring the days of early Ohio back to Yoctangee Park in Chillicothe. During the weekend festival you'll marvel at the skills of artisans and feel the beat of drums that fire the performance of Native American dancers.

The feast got its name from the American Indian tradition of using 13 lunar months instead of 12 months. At the end of May, tribes would celebrate the end of winter and the annual rebirth of the world. The Shawnee in Ohio called it the Flowering Moon. It was a time to sing and dance and give thanks for surviving the cold and barren Starving Moon.

The Feast of the Flowering Moon is held in late May in Yoctangee Park; no admission charge; feastofthefloweringmoon.org.

"Lemonade Lucy" was the nickname Lucy Hayes, the wife of President Rutherford B. Hayes, given while she lived at the White House because she would not serve alcohol at parties and receptions. Her birthplace, now the *Lucy Hayes Heritage Center,* is modest compared to the president's official residence, but has much to teach us about the life of Lemonade Lucy and of families of the early 1800s. The two-story federal-style home houses period furniture as well as memorabilia from the president and the first lady.

Where's the Capital?

Congress divided the Northwest Territory in 1800 and designated Chillicothe as the capital of the eastern half. The territorial legislature met here in November 1800 in Abrams's Big House, a two-story log cabin and one of the few buildings in the four-year-old village large enough to accommodate the group. The main floor, where the legislature met, also was used for singing schools, dances, and religious services. Upstairs was a bar. Construction began on a statehouse built of stone taken from neighboring hills.

In 1802, when the population of the eastern division of the territory reached 45,000, Congress authorized the election of delegates to create a state constitution. Thirty-five delegates met in the new Chillicothe statehouse on November 4, 1802, and drafted the document in 25 days. Ohio's admission to the Union was in 1803, and the first Ohio General Assembly convened March 1, 1803.

The new constitution called for Chillicothe to remain the capital until 1808, starting an intense competition between towns wanting to be named the permanent capital. Zanesville went as far as building a statehouse and was named the temporary capital in 1809 for its efforts. The brick Zanesville statehouse served as the capital until 1812, when the seat of government was shifted back to Chillicothe.

Meanwhile, Worthington, Lancaster, Newark, Mt. Vernon, Delaware, Dublin, and Pickaway Plains all competed for the permanent site. Dublin was believed to be the front-runner, but legend has it that Dublin lost the favored spot as a result of a card game the night before the legislature was to act on the siting of the permanent capital. The winner was a plot of land across the Scioto River from the town of Franklinton.

The new capital site was heavily wooded and did not even have a name. Though Ohio City was the favorite name with many, the legislature designated the future capital as Columbus. State offices moved from Chillicothe to Columbus on October 1, 1816, and the legislature met for the first time in Columbus that December.

The Lucy Hayes Heritage Center is at 90 W. Sixth St., Chillicothe; (740) 775-5829; lucyhayes.org. Open Apr through Sept, Mon, 10 a.m. to 2 p.m.; Sat, 1 to 4 p.m.

In an area once inhabited by Shawnee and Delaware Indians, **7 *Caves Nature Preserve*** has intrigued visitors since the turn of the 20th century. The park was established as 7 Caves in 1928 and was owned by the Miller family for decades, but went out of business in 2005. It is now part of the nonprofit ***Highlands Nature Sanctuary.***

Highlands Nature Sanctuary's Cave Canyon offers a scenic retreat with miles of hiking trails. In 1995 the Highlands Nature Sanctuary became the headquarters for the Arc of Appalachia Preserve System, whose mission is to reunite and preserve forestland in Ohio. The Arc purchased land that was once part of the 7 Caves tourist attraction. Highlands Nature Sanctuary, including Cave Canyon, now encompasses 2,000 acres, including the deep dolomite canyon known as the Rocky Fork Gorge. Cave Canyon is open to the public and provides nature lovers with access to 3 self-guided trails, a guided hike, and the Appalachian Forest Museum. The 3 self-guided trail walks provide views from the high bluffs and take hikers through an old-growth forest and past amazing rock formations.

To preserve these caves and the habitat they provide for bats, all of the caves are now closed to the public. Additional trails into another 14-acre area are accessible.

Those interested in botany and horticulture will marvel at the more than 200 species of plants, thriving in environments from rock ledges to prairies. More than 60 types of trees can also be found in the preserve. The website provides information on special hikes for those particularly interested in flora.

Birders will also be attracted to this preserve. Multiple types of habitat support a wide variety of feathered residents and visitors. A sampling of the vast array includes wood ducks, great blue herons, osprey, cerulean warblers, hooded warblers, ovenbirds, kingfishers, orchard orioles, and barn owls.

Highlands Nature Sanctuary is 4 miles west of Bainbridge, off US 50 at 7660 Cave Rd.; (937) 365-1935, arcofappalachia.org. Open April through Oct on Sat and Sun from 9:30 a.m. to 5 pm. Entrance is by donation during regular hours only.

When you're traveling through southern Ohio, you can't help but notice the dozens of lakes in the region—lakes providing boating, fishing, swimming, and other recreational activities. For this reason I heartily recommend that when you travel off the beaten path in southern Ohio, you always pack a swimsuit—particularly on hot summer days.

One of these alluring lakes is 13-acre Pike Lake in *Pike Lake State Park,* which offers a delightful spot for swimming, rowing, fishing, or scuba diving. Lifeguards watch over the sandy beach and swimming area during the summer, and rowboats can be rented. Anglers enjoy catching the catfish, largemouth bass, crappie, and bluegill, and divers take advantage of the remarkably clear water.

Although the state park is a modest 600 acres, a densely wooded 10,600-acre state forest surrounds the park. There are numerous hiking trails in the state forest and 7 miles of trails in the park.

Up a shady hill from the lake sit the park's 24 rental cabins—12 deluxe two-bedroom cabins and 12 standard cabins. Some are pet friendly. All are set in secluded locations, and the deluxe cabins offer completely equipped kitchens, baths, living areas, and screened porches. The standard cabins contain a single large sleeping and living area with 4 bunks and a fold-out couch, a kitchen, and a bath. Pike Lake also has 112 campsites, and a park naturalist conducts nature programs during summer months.

Pike Lake State Park is at 1847 Pike Lake Rd., 7 miles south of Bainbridge; (740) 493-2212, (866) 644-6727; dnr.state.oh.us/parks/pikelake/tabid/777/default.aspx. Rates for the cabins range from $75 to $95 per night. Early reservations recommended.

The *Lake White Club* dates back to 1936, but the building housing the club was a log cabin on Pee Pee Creek long before construction of the dam and spillway that created Lake White. The lobby of the restaurant contains the original rough-hewn wooden beams of the cabin, which was built on this spot in the 1820s. The Ohio and Erie Canal could be seen from the windows of that cabin; the canal followed the creek on its way south to Portsmouth. Pee Pee Creek received its name for the initials of Peter Patrick, which he carved in the trunk of a large beech tree beside the stream as a claim on this land in 1785, when this area was still Shawnee country.

The club specializes in down-home country cooking, and the chicken dinners are a house specialty. Other entrees include half a dozen cuts of steak, roast turkey, hickory-smoked ham in raisin sauce, and ham and turkey smothered with a cheese sauce. If the 180-degree view of the lake whets your appetite for seafood, try the broiled or fried pickerel, the lobster tail, the scallops, or the fried shrimp. The club offers prime rib as a special dinner every Saturday night.

The Lake White Club serves generous portions of all its entrees, and the light-wood paneling and bentwood chairs give the dining room a pleasant, not-too-formal atmosphere.

The Lake White Club is at 1166 OH 552, 2 miles south of Waverly; (740) 947-5000, (800) 774-5253; lakewhiteclub.com. Open Thurs through Sat 4 to 9 p.m., Sun noon to 5 p.m. The Lake White Club lounge is open Tues through Sat from 4 p.m. until late and serves appetizers and bar food.

Shawnee State Park, with more than 60,000 acres of parkland and adjoining state forest, consists of ridge upon ridge of thick woods in the splendid southern Ohio countryside. To get perspective on the size of this stunningly beautiful acreage, note that the park contains over 130 miles of roads, not to mention miles of hiking and bridle paths. Shawnee is particularly popular in October, when the changing leaves produce hillsides bursting with reds, oranges, and golds. A 5,000-acre section of the park has been set aside as the Shawnee Wilderness Area, preserving the unspoiled natural beauty of the land. The park's 2 small lakes, Turkey Creek Lake and Roosevelt Lake, both have sandy swimming beaches.

A modern stone-and-timber 50-room lodge provides overnight accommodations in this peaceful park, as do 25 deluxe two-bedroom cabins. Facilities at the lodge include an indoor and outdoor pool, tennis courts, a restaurant, a game room, and an 18-hole golf course with putting green, restaurant, and game room. Lodge rates are $104 to $145, double occupancy. Campsite rates are $19 for nonelectrical and $24 for

thecradleof american dentistry

Bainbridge was a trendsetter in the early 1800s, when Dr. John Harris opened the first school in the US for teaching dentistry. Thanks to Harris, the town has been recognized as the "Cradle of American Dentistry." Harris founded the first US dental school in 1825 in a modest one-story brick building on Main Street. The building today houses a dental museum.

sites with electricity. The cabins are tucked away in an isolated section of the park and come equipped with all kitchen utensils, linens, and blankets. Cabin rates range from $129 to $219 per night, $975 to $1,100 per week. Numerous campsites are also available. Some cabins are pet friendly.

Shawnee State Park is at 4404 OH 125, 12 miles west of Portsmouth; (740) 858-6621, (800) 282-7275; dnr.state.oh.us/parks/shawnee/tabid/788/Default.aspx. Open year-round; reservations recommended.

Fort Hill State Memorial offers the traveler a chance to see one of the best preserved Native American earthworks in all of North America. Archaeologists believe that the 1.5-mile-long earthen enclosure on the hilltop was constructed by the Hopewell people between 100 BC and AD 500. Experts believe that this area also contained at least two ceremonial buildings, and probably a village located in the Brush Creek Valley.

This 1,200-acre preserve lies just at the edge of the glacial boundary and has 11 miles of hiking trails. The hilly region is home to a wide variety of flowers and plants. Along with the hiking trails, visitors can take a break at the picnic grounds. A museum also offers information and exhibits on the area's geology and on the archaeological findings around the region.

Fort Hill State Memorial is located at 13614 Fort Hill Rd., Hillsboro; (937) 588-3221, (800) 283-8905; archofappalachia.org/visit/fort-hill.html. Open daylight hours (closed during deer hunting season, generally the last week in Nov). The museum is open May through Oct, Sat and Sun, 10 a.m. to 5 p.m. No admission charge.

Impressive but still shrouded in mystery is the *Serpent Mound* in southwest Ohio. This huge snake built of mounded earth stretches for nearly a quarter of a mile. The Serpent Mound is the largest serpent effigy mound in the US and one of the few effigy mounds in Ohio. Experts believe that the Adena people built this and other mounds, and lived in this area in Ohio from 800 BC to AD 100. Just what purpose the giant prehistoric mound played in the life and the culture of the Adena remains a mystery. However, archaeologists believe that the uncoiling snake symbolized some mythical or religious principle. Also on this site are smaller conical mounds that contain artifacts from the Adena people and also appear to serve as burial sites.

The Serpent Mound is located at 3850 OH 73, Peebles; (937) 587-2796, (800) 752-2757; arcofappalachia.org/visit/serpent-mound.html. Park and earthworks are open daily, dawn to dusk. Museum and gift shop are open in Mar, Sat and Sun, 10:30 a.m. to 4 p.m.; Apr through mid-May, Thurs through Mon, 10:30 a.m. to 4 p.m.;mid-May through end of August, Mon through Thurs 10:30 a.m. to 4 p.m., Fri 10 a.m. to 5 p.m., Sat 9:30 a.m. to 6 p.m., Sun 9:30 a.m. to 5 p.m. Sept and Oct, Sat and Sun, 9:30 a.m. to 5 p.m.; Nov through Dec 21, Sat and Sun only, 10:30 a.m. to 4 p.m. Admission: per car, $7; bicycles, pedestrians, motorcycles, $2; RVs with 8 or more people, $9.

Rare plants and impressive geological features are waiting to awe the casual hiker or the serious botanist or geologist at the **Davis Memorial Nature Preserve.** This 88-acre site was donated by Davon Inc. and bears the name of its chairman of the board, Edwin H. Davis.

Visitors enjoy two hiking trails in the preserve. Dolomite cliffs, an impressive geological fault, and a cave are among the geological points of interest. The heavily wooded trails give hikers a chance to see bamboo grass, purple cliff brake ferns, great cane, and a rare plant called Sullivantia, which grew here in preglacial times.

The Davis Memorial Nature Preserve is located at Township Roads 126 and 129, 3 miles east of Peebles; (614) 265-6453; enr.state.oh.us/location/dnap/davis/tabid/934/default.aspx. Open daylight hours. No admission charge.

The redbrick two-story house, with its shake roof and white trim, does not at first appear in any way extraordinary. It does offer a marvelous view down the steep hill to the Ohio River, and across the river into northern

birthofthe women'schristian temperance union

On Christmas morning 1873, Eliza Jane Thompson and 75 other women temperance activists visited every Hillsboro saloon and drugstore that sold alcohol. Thompson, daughter of a former governor and wife of a judge, led the charge into those businesses, where the protestors would kneel, pray aloud, and sing hymns. They informed the shocked owners they'd be back the next day and every day until they stopped selling the devil's brew.

The result: They stopped liquor sales in every Hillsboro store but one. Eliza Jane Thompson's protest movement became the Women's Temperance Crusade, which in turn evolved into the Women's Christian Temperance Union.

Kentucky, but there is no outward evidence of this house's role in history. But 150 years ago, rickety wooden steps led from the river up the hillside to this modest home. Those steps became known as the "stairway to liberation," and on moonless nights slaves escaping from plantations in the South crossed the Ohio River and climbed those weathered steps to the *Rankin House,* home of the Reverend John Rankin.

Rankin and his wife, Jean, were conductors on the Underground Railroad, which transported thousands of slaves to freedom in Canada. Rankin's battle against slavery began with his abolitionist preaching as early as 1815, and a series of his letters on the subject were published in a book in 1826. The home he built on "Liberty Hill" protected runaway slaves from the day it was completed in 1828 until 1863. Rankin used an elaborate set of signals, using lanterns in his windows, to communicate the "all clear" message to Dr. Alexander Campbell and other abolitionists in town.

Designated a National Historic Landmark in September 1997, and now open to the public as a museum, the Rankin House contains some of Rankin's possessions, including his personal Bible, published in 1793. The house has dark hardwood floors and high ceilings typical of the period, as well as completely furnished bedrooms and a kitchen stocked with cooking utensils and equipment used in the mid-1800s.

One upstairs room houses a small abolitionist museum, which tells of the more than 2,000 slaves who stayed at Rankin House (often as many as 12 at a time) on their way to freedom. It was Rankin who told Harriet Beecher Stowe the account of a slave named Eliza who carried her children across the frozen, but thawing, Ohio River. Her bravery was rewarded—the bounty hunters pursuing her found the ice broken up by the time they reached the river the next morning, forcing them to abandon their chase. Stowe immortalized the story of Eliza in her book *Uncle Tom's Cabin.* Because of his influence in the abolitionist movement and his work as a conductor on the Underground Railroad, southern plantation owners offered a bounty for Rankin's life.

The Rankin House is just off US 52, west of the central business district in Ripley at 6152 Rankin Rd.; (937) 392-1627; ripleyohio.net/htm/rankin.htm. Open May through Oct, Wed through Sat, 10 a.m. to 5 p.m.; Sun, noon to 5 p.m.; closed Mon and Tues. Admission: adults $4; children $2.

One of the homes that signaled the Rankin House when the waterfront was clear of bounty hunters, dogs, and slave owners during those

Underground Railroad days was on the corner of Locust and Front Streets in Ripley and is today known as ***The Signal House.*** Built in the 1830s in Greek Italianate style, this home is now a delightful bed-and-breakfast owned by Vic and Betsy Billingsley.

The Billingsleys first caught sight of the stately white structure while cruising the Ohio River on their houseboat. When they decided they were ready to leave suburban Cincinnati for a more rural environment, they came to Ripley. Initially they bought The Signal House to be their home and nothing more. But encouraged by friends enchanted with the place, they decided to share it with others and began operation as a bed-and-breakfast in 1989.

Furnished with family antiques, The Signal House features 3 porches, twin parlors, and river views from every room. The 2 guest rooms share a bath at $95 per night, double occupancy, including full breakfast. Breakfast here can range from homemade breads, muffins, jams, and spreads to sausage and cheese strata.

Guests also can choose to rent the 2 rooms and have a private bath for $150 per night with full breakfast.

The Signal House is at 234 N. Front St., Ripley; (937) 392-1640; thesignalhouse.com. The Signal House closes for the winter in mid-Dec and reopens in May.

For lunch or dinner in Ripley, stop by ***Cohearts Riverhouse.*** Sisters Joanne May and Roberta Gaudio, veterans of the Cincinnati restaurant scene, restored this 1840s structure and opened for business in 1989. The second-floor screened porch offers a great view of the river. Roberta does the cooking, using produce from local farms, handmade pasta, and Amish cheeses. Dinner selections range from pasta and barbecue ribs to chicken, fish, and steaks. Lunch options include soups, salads, and sandwiches.

Cohearts Riverhouse is at 18 N. Front St., Ripley; (937) 392-4819. Open Thurs through Sat, 11:30 a.m. to 9 p.m.; Sun, 11:30 a.m. to 7 p.m. Personal checks accepted.

The modest but solid roots of Ulysses S. Grant (known as Hiram Ulysses Grant as a boy), commander of the Union forces during the Civil War and 18th president of the US, are obvious when you visit ***Grant's Boyhood Home*** in rural Georgetown. Built by his father, Jesse Grant, in 1823, the

TOP ANNUAL EVENTS

Feast of the Flowering Moon,
Chillicothe, May;
(740) 887-2979;
feastofthefloweringmoon.org

Yellow Springs Street Fair,
Yellow Springs, June;
(937) 767-2686;
yellowspringsohio.org/street_fair.shtml

**Ohio River Music and Outdoor
Festival and Ohio River Paddlefest,**
Cincinnati, June;
(513) 232-8230;
coneyislandpark.com

Roy Rogers Festival,
Portsmouth, June;
(740) 259-1195;
royrogersfestival.org

**Tecumseh! Outdoor
Historical Drama,**
Chillicothe, June to Sept;
(740) 775-0700, (866) 775-0700;
tecumsehdrama.com

Wheels of Progress Festival,
Greenfield, July;
greenfieldrotary.org

Fayette County Fair,
Washington Court House, July;
(740) 335-5856;
lafayettecofairoh.com

Cityfolk Festival,
Dayton, July;
(937) 223-3655;
cityfolk.org

Sweet Corn Festival,
Fairborn, Aug;
(937) 305-0800;
fairbornsweetcornfestival.org

Ohio Renaissance Festival,
Renaissance Park, 317 Brimstone Rd.,
Wilmington, early Sept to mid-Oct;
(888) 695-0888;
renfestival.com

home is designated a National Historic Landmark. The Grants expanded the home in 1825 and again in 1828. Grant lived here from the age of 1 until he left to attend West Point at 17, the longest period spent at any residence during his lifetime.

Early 19th-century furnishings and Grant memorabilia are on display. The white gloves President Grant wore to his inaugural ball and a velvet dress belonging to his wife, Julia Dent Grant, are among the more noteworthy items.

A multiyear $1.4 million restoration of Grant's Boyhood Home was completed in 2013. The restoration returned the home to its appearance in 1839, the year Grant left for West Point.

Highland County Fair,
Hillsboro, Sept;
(937) 393-9975;
highlandcountyfair.org

Montgomery County Fair,
Dayton, Sept;
(937) 224-1619;
montcofair.com

Circleville Pumpkin Show,
Circleville, Oct;
(740) 474-7000;
pumpkinshow.com

Sauerkraut Festival,
Waynesville, Oct;
(513) 897-8855;
sauerkrautfestival.com

Hallzooween,
Cincinnati, Oct;
(513) 281-4700, (800) 944-4776;
cincinnatizoo.org/events

Fall Festival of Leaves,
Bainbridge, Oct;
fallfestivalofleaves.com

Springboro Christmas Festival,
Springboro, Nov;
springborofestivals.org

Historic Clifton Mill Light Display,
Clifton, late Nov to Dec;
(937) 767-5501;
cliftonmill.com/christmas.htm

**Historic Lebanon Horse-Drawn
Carriage Parade & Christmas
Festival,**
Lebanon, Dec;
(513) 932-1100;
lebanonchamber.org

Grant's Boyhood Home is at 219 E. Grant Ave., Georgetown; (937) 378-9470; ohiohistory.org/museums-and-historic-sites/museum--historic-sites-by-name/grant-boyhood-home. Open Memorial Day to Labor Day, Wed through Sun, noon to 5 p.m., plus weekends in Sept and Oct, noon to 5 p.m. Rates: adults $3; children (ages 6 to 12) $1.

Queen City

A three-room cottage was the birthplace of a man who would become the highest elected official in the land. The *Grant Birthplace* is a simple one-story home built in 1817. Hiram Ulysses Grant was born in the humble home five years later, on April 27, 1822. (Grant did not become "Ulysses S." until his application to West Point incorrectly identified him as such, a mistake with which he concurred.) Grant's father worked at a tannery, which was next to the Grant home.

Before the home was restored and preserved for all of us to visit, it was loaded on a railroad flatcar and transported on a tour around the US. Now returned to its original site, it is open to the public and furnished in the style of the early 1800s.

The Grant Birthplace is at 1551 OH 232, Point Pleasant; (513) 553-4911; ohiohistory.org/museums-and-historic-sites/museum--historic-sites-by-name/grant-birthplace. Open Apr through Oct, Wed through Sat, 9 a.m. to noon and 1 to 5 p.m.; Sun, noon to 5 p.m. Admission: adults $3; senior citizens $2; children (ages 6 to 12) $1.50.

Take time to walk through the historic Milford central business district. Housed in restored commercial buildings, stores on Main Street include early antiques and gift shops.

Valley Vineyards offers special holiday meals and cookouts on Friday and Saturday nights. In the warmer weather, July through October, they add Sunday dinners as well. In the cold weather, the cookouts are actually cook-ins, using a huge indoor grill. The rest of the year, Ken Schuchter's Valley Vineyards produces almost 50 fine wines from its 50 acres of American and French hybrid and vinifera grapes.

Grape growing and winemaking have been popular in southern Ohio for more than 150 years, and the Schuchters planted their first vines at Valley Vineyards in 1969. The winery, in a recent chalet-style building, offers a tasting tray with 1-ounce servings of 9 wines—the perfect way to investigate and appreciate the vineyard's quality blends. I particularly enjoyed the Vidal blanc, the winner of many awards.

The winery has indoor and outdoor seating, with cookout dinners every Friday and Saturday (Sunday also during the summer) on the large patios. Cheese plates and pizzas are always available. The Schuchter family also creates craft beers under its label Cellar Dweller.

Valley Vineyards is on combined OH 22 and OH 3 at 2276 E. OH 22 and OH3, Morrow; (513) 899-2485; valley-vineyards.com. Open Mon through Wed, 11 a.m. to 6 p.m.; Thurs, 11 a.m. to 10 p.m.; Fri and Sat, 11 a.m. to 4 p.m.; and Sun, 1 to 6 p.m. Cookouts, July through Oct, Fri through Sun, 5:30

to 8:30 p.m.; Nov through June, Fri and Sat, 5:30 to 8 p.m. Adults $29.50; children $16.50.

If you are looking for a unique shopping experience or for handcrafted 18th- or 19th-century reproduction furniture, then a trip to the **Workshops of David T. Smith** should be on your itinerary. The site actually features many buildings housing woodworking and pottery areas. Visitors are welcome at the showroom and design center.

Each piece of furniture is unique and reflects a period of American furniture building. You can buy a simple table that looks like something the Pilgrims would have used during the first Thanksgiving or a Windsor chair with delicately turned legs. You could come home with a decorative spoon holder or contract to have your entire kitchen renovated with handmade cabinetry.

Pottery is also produced in the workshops. The potters specialize in Redware Pottery, formed from slabs of red clay that is either pressed into molds or thrown on a potter's wheel. Collectors will find a variety of pots, plates, lamps, and sculpture pieces from which to choose.

The Workshops of David T. Smith are at 3600 Shawhan Rd., Morrow; (513) 932-2472; davidtsmith .com. Open Tues through Sat, 10 a.m. to 5 p.m.

On December 23, 1803, Jonas Seaman received a license to operate a "house of public entertainment" at the site today occupied by one of Ohio's premier historic hotels, the **Golden Lamb.** The present building replaced Seaman's cabin in 1815, and the Lamb now provides travelers with fine dining and period accommodations in picturesque Lebanon.

notsogoldrush

You missed the Ohio gold rush of 1868? Well, you didn't miss much. The discovery of what was thought to be gold at Batavia right after the Civil War set off a panic and prompted the establishment of the Batavia Gold Mining Company. Speculators sold shares in this venture for $100 each—big money in those days. Oh, there was gold here, but just minute traces too small to ever be profitably mined. The Batavia gold rush was over as quickly as it started.

During its nearly two centuries, distinguished guests at the Golden Lamb have included 10 American presidents, Henry Clay, Mark Twain (who performed at the Lebanon Opera House in the late 19th century), and

Charles Dickens, who, it is told, complained vociferously during his visit in 1842 when informed the inn did not serve "spirits." Dickens would maintain his composure if he visited the Golden Lamb today, for the Black Horse Tavern provides complete bar service at the inn. And after some "refreshment," he might well enjoy browsing in the extensive gift shop on the lower level.

With a reputation for serving challenging dishes, the Lamb offers a dinner menu that includes delights such as timbale of fillet of sole and salmon mousse with lobster sauce; roast duckling; broiled veal medallion topped with asparagus, crabmeat, and béarnaise sauce; and roast leg of spring lamb with mint jelly. More traditional entrees include steaks, ham, roast pork loin with dressing, and baked salmon. Lunch is also served at the Golden Lamb, with tasty soups, salads, and sandwiches, plus luncheon entrees including broiled petite filet mignon with béarnaise sauce and roasted chicken with dressing.

After eating in one of the 4 cozy downstairs dining areas, venture past the classy blue-gray lobby and up the stairs to the second floor. There you will discover 5 opulent private dining rooms. One is the Henry Clay Room (he visited the inn frequently on his trips between Kentucky and Washington, DC). Decorated in greens and pinks, this room is furnished with a gorgeous dark hardwood table and matching chairs for 10. With their splendid period pieces, these private dining rooms truly conjure up images of a bygone era.

The second floor also has the most expensive guest room at the inn—the Charles Dickens Room. The massive carved headboard towers 12 feet in the air, as do the mirror and frame on the marble-topped washstand. The third and fourth floors contain the other 17 guest rooms, each unique in its appointments and named for one of the noteworthy guests who have stayed at the Golden Lamb. The De Witt Clinton Room, for example, is named for the New York governor who traveled to Lebanon in 1825 to attend the opening of the Ohio canal system, and it is furnished with a canopied four-poster bed and antique maple chests.

The fourth floor of the Lamb also houses the inn's Shaker museum, which is full of pieces collected from the former Shaker community called Union Village.

The Shakers migrated to Warren County from New Lebanon, New York, and established a religious communal village. But one of their religious convictions was celibacy, which doomed the sect to a relatively short existence.

Shaker furnishings are simple and functional, devoid of ornamentation. The Shaker Pantry has the characteristic wall pegs for hanging utensils, herbs, and even chairs not in use. The Shaker Retiring Room contains a simple rope-spring bed with trundle, a maple rocker, a pine cupboard, and a very rare Shaker embroidery hoop. Perhaps the most interesting display room—Sarah's Room—belonged to Sarah Stubbs, a young girl who came to live in the hotel with her aunt and uncle after the death of her father in 1883. The room has the furniture that was Sarah's more than 130 years ago.

The Golden Lamb is at 27 S. Broadway, Lebanon; (513) 932-5065; goldenlamb.com. Open daily for lunch and dinner except Christmas Day. Lodging rates: $119 to $149 per night.

On a bluff overlooking Lebanon just a few blocks south of the Golden Lamb sits one of the best examples of Greek revival architecture in the Midwest: *Glendower.* Constructed by John Milton Williams, a young attorney, for approximately $5,000 in 1836, the residence was inhabited by the Williams family during Williams's career as county prosecutor and state legislator. Brigadier General Durbin Ward, another influential area politician, purchased Glendower from Williams, and the home remained in the Ward family until the turn of the 20th century.

Knowledgeable guides lead visitors through the home's 14 rooms and basement, explaining the history and significance of the lavish furnishings, most of which date from the mid-1800s. In the downstairs drawing rooms, the symmetry characteristic of Greek revival architecture is readily apparent: With matching placement of doors, mirrors, and fireplaces, one side of each room is the mirror image of the other. The original brass deadbolt still secures the front door, and the luxurious ash and walnut floors were installed when the home was built. The formal dining room contains a silver sugar bowl with a lock on it (to keep the servants from pilfering this then-expensive commodity), and the old Regina music box plays flat metal discs, as it has for decades.

In addition to the furnished bedrooms upstairs, one room has a sizable collection of antique dolls and the 1865 sewing machine that won first prize at the Warren County fair. The basement display cases contain pioneer tools such as axes, woodworking equipment, and a carpenter's vise. Other items include old-fashioned irons, candle molds, bootjacks, spectacles, and

Ohio Renaissance Festival

Once upon a time in a kingdom about 5 miles east of Waynesville there was held the Ohio Renaissance Festival. In some ways, to call this a festival is a great understatement. From humble beginnings, a village of sorts has grown up in a farm field. Several streets of a 16th-century English village have and continue to evolve into a real town of make-believe.

A king and queen reign over the town and over amazingly realistic jousting matches. Combatants actually mount horses and, in full armor, race toward each other and attempt to knock the opponent from his mount. One generally ends up bouncing on the ground (although we suspect that they probably decided who was going to take the blow before the match began). No blood is spilled, and no bones are broken, although falling from a galloping horse is a little rough on the body, even with choreography.

Throughout the village are more than 150 costumed shopkeepers and entertainers. Modern times do occasionally intrude in interesting ways. There is something a little odd about seeing a gentleman in tights and tunic holding a crossbow in one hand and a soft drink can in the other. A comical and talented array of performers entertains on several stages scattered throughout the village. Jugglers, tightrope artists, and a variety of clowns, magicians, and musicians take turns entertaining the crowds.

If you want to participate in medieval activities, you can buy a ticket and try the ax throw or spear chuck, or toss overripe tomatoes at the guy in the medieval equivalent of a dunk tank. There are plenty of unusual craft and artisan shops. Buy a talisman or a fake sword or a pouch to hang at your waist to hold your ducats. More modern souvenirs such as jewelry, glass art, and candles also are plentiful.

The Renaissance Festival is open weekends from late August through mid-October. Admission is charged. Be prepared to park in a farm field and walk a bit to the "village gates." For specifics, call (513) 897-7000 or for tickets, (888) 695-0888. The website also provides a good deal of information: renfestival.com.

snuffboxes, plus the compass used to map the village of Lebanon, and a wonderful assortment of fancy hand-turned horseshoes made by Matt Burdett, the village smith in the 1890s.

Glendower is on US 42 at 105 Cincinnati Avenue, just south of the business district in Lebanon; (513) 932-1817; wchsmuseum.org. Open from June through Aug, Wed through Sat, 1 to 4 p.m. Admission: adults $5; senior citizens $4.50; children (ages 5 to 18) $3.50.

If you are fascinated with unraveling the riddles of prehistory, you should visit **Fort Ancient.** This prehistoric settlement is a significant archaeological site in North America. Two thousand years ago, Native Americans during the Hopewell culture built a walled enclosure, probably with crude digging tools, such as deer antlers or shoulder bones. The walls, which are earthen, run for 18,000 feet, and consist of 550,000 cubic yards of soil, which was transported in baskets, each capable of holding 35 or 40 pounds of earth. From the site, archaeologists have determined that parts of the walls were actually designed and constructed to align with the sun and the moon to create a calendar for the community. They believe that Fort Ancient served as a ceremonial and social center.

Visitors enjoy hiking the trails not only for the historic value of the site, but also for the beauty of the natural surroundings. The site also features the Museum at Fort Ancient, which has numerous interactive exhibits and highlights 15,000 years of Native American history in the Ohio valley. A prehistoric garden demonstrates crops grown 2,000 years ago.

Fort Ancient is at 6123 OH 350, Oregonia; (513) 932-4421, (800) 283-8904; fortancient.org. Open Apr through Nov, Tues through Sat, 10 a.m. to 5 p.m.; Sun, noon to 5 p.m.; Dec through March, Sat, 10 a.m. to 5 p.m.; Sun, noon to 5 p.m. Admission: adults $8; senior citizens $5; children (ages 6 to 12) $4.

With more antiques shops per square mile than any other city or town in Ohio, Waynesville is a browser's paradise. It has more than 40 individual shops, plus 3 large buildings where dozens of dealers display their goods on consignment, and it has become a major antiques marketplace, attracting out-of-state buyers and Ohioans alike. Waynesville's antiques boom started inauspiciously in the mid-1960s with the opening of a handful of shops, but the number has grown steadily ever since. Now many of the town's commercial buildings, a substantial number of former residences, and even one of the town's churches house antiques stores—in fact, on one block on Main Street, there are nine shops in a row!

Among the many quality shops, one favorite is at 274 S. Main St.: **Spencer's Antiques and Imports.** The two-story house with a large front porch and 4 adjoining buildings hold an impressive inventory. Careful perusal of this 15,000-square-foot shop, with its hundreds of items, takes time, but it will be time enjoyably spent. George and Fay Spencer's inventory includes a large selection of oak furniture—tables, chairs, washstands, chests, wardrobes, and beds—plus many large walnut and poplar pieces. The basement of the main building is filled with old trunks, toys, and stained glass, while the second floor has many antique kitchen gadgets, such as meat and sausage grinders, iron pots, and skillets. Spencer's acquires most of its inventory from southwestern Ohio. Spencer's is open from 11 a.m. to 5 p.m., Tues through Fri and on Sun. Saturday they open at 10 a.m. The shop is closed on Mon. (866) 897-7775; spencersantiques.com.

Caesar Creek Lake and the surrounding recreation area are managed by the Army Corps of Engineers primarily as a flood-control project. However, the 2,830-acre lake provides terrific recreation opportunities. The 1,200-foot-long beach welcomes swimmers, and the lake is a great place for fishing or boating. Remember to bring your fishing license if you want to try your luck at hooking bluegill, saugeye, crappie, largemouth, smallmouth, white, or spotted bass.

The visitor center is a good place to begin your trip to Caesar Creek Lake. It provides an overlook of the park and the dam and has lots of educational information about various features of the lake and the recreation area, including trail maps. The more than 10,000 acres of wildlife area includes forests, meadowlands, and the Caesar Creek Gorge with rushing waters. Visitors enjoy day hikes. Trails range from a 3-mile, easy-to-moderate hike to a 13-mile trek for the serious hiker. Backpacking in the park area is allowed, but you need to stop at the visitor center and get a permit first. The area is also a favorite for bikers and horseback riders.

You can also pick up a free permit and directions to prepare you for a fossil hunt. The fossils here date back to the Ordovician age, when Ohio was covered by a shallow ocean. When a spillway was excavated, the area that was disturbed became a great fossil-hunting zone. Brachiopods (which look like seashells) and the remains of cephalopods (which resemble today's octopi) are chief among the fossils you can discover on your hunt. This is one of the only areas where you can legally remove fossils and keep them as souvenirs of your adventures. If you are planning to bring a group along for picnicking, 2 shelters are available. One costs $75 per day and must be reserved. The second is free of charge and available on a first-come, first-served basis. Be sure to call ahead to check availability and to reserve the shelter.

To reach Caesar Creek Lake recreation area, take exit 38 west off I-71 or exit 45 east from I-75. The visitor center is at 4020 N. Clarkesville Rd., Waynesville; (513) 897-1050; caesarcreekstatepark.com. While recreation may be the current focus of the Caesar Creek Lake area, its history is rich and long. This region was home to the prehistoric Native American tribes, the Hopewell and Adena, and later to the Miami and the Shawnee.

According to local historians, Caesar Creek was named for a black slave, Caesar, who was captured by the Shawnee. The Shawnee must have been favorably impressed by Caesar—they gave him the area around Caesar Creek as his hunting ground. The villages that grew up in the area in the 1700s and 1800s became a Quaker settlement and an important stop on the Underground Railroad, supporting the flight of slaves on their way to freedom in the North.

When the Army Corps of Engineers was clearing land and preparing to dam the river in 1978, log homes dating back to the 1700s were found in the woods. These historic buildings were moved to the *Caesar's Creek Pioneer Village.* Some of the buildings in Pioneer Village were actually erected there and stand on their original sites. Walking through the reconstructed village, visitors can see the log cabins, as well as some of the homes built in the early 1800s, the Quaker meetinghouse, and the tollhouse. The grounds are open daily, but the houses are only open on special occasions or if you prearrange a tour. Pioneer Village is in Waynesville, on the southeast side of Caesar Creek Lake. From Waynesville, go east on Route 73 for about 1 mile. Turn right on Clarksville Road, then left on Oregonia Road, then left again on Pioneer Village Road. The Village is at 3999 Pioneer Village Rd., Waynesville; (513) 897-1120; caesarscreekpioneervillage.org.

It will take a little effort to visit the *Harveysburg Free Black School.* The school is not open to the public on a regular basis, but tours can be arranged by calling (513) 897-6195.

This unassuming one-room schoolhouse has a special place in Ohio history. It was the first free school for black children in the state. Jesse and Elizabeth Harvey, the founders of Harveysburg, founded the school in 1831 after finding out there were no educational opportunities for black children. The Quaker community supported the school that allowed black and Native American children the then-rare opportunity to enter elementary school and continue in that tiny schoolhouse until they received a high school diploma.

The schoolhouse is a simple brick structure with a modest cupola on the roof to house the school bell. The school was acquired by the Harveysburg bicentennial committee in 1976 with a mission to preserve it as a part of the community's history. Primers, historical documents, and slate blackboards remain from this important chapter in the history of education and the search for freedom in Ohio.

The school is at 23 North St. in Harveysburg. Contact the Harveysburg Historical Society at (513) 897-6195. Open by appointment. Admission is $5 for adults and $3 for children.

Many visitors to Warren County are attracted to the area because of southern Ohio's most popular amusement park complex: *Kings Island.* Its 7 themed areas, dozens of rides including 14 coasters, live shows, international shops, and restaurants delight the millions who visit the park during its late-April-through-October season.

Other favorites include Soak City, a 30-acre water park that originally opened in 1989 as a 12-acre water park named WaterWorks. Over the years, the popular attraction grew and during the 2011–2012 off-season, Kings Island undertook a $10 million expansion of the water park and renamed it Soak City. The park features many ways to get wet, including a massive 650,000-gallon wave pool.

Planet Snoopy is a fun collection of rides and attractions with the theme of Peanuts cartoon characters for every age, including 4 kids' roller coasters. Planet Snoopy also features a live stage show and daily times to meet beloved Peanuts characters including Charlie Brown, Linus, Peppermint Patty, and of course, loveable beagle Snoopy.

In 2011 extinct dinosaurs came "alive" again in a new Kings Island attraction called Dinosaurs Alive! The largest animatronics dinosaur park in the world features more than 60 life-size, moving dinosaurs in a 12.5-acre Jurassic forest outdoor setting. Four of the dinosaurs have interactive consoles so that guests can guide dinosaur movement to see how scientists think the gigantic beasts once moved their arms, eyes, mouths, and tails. A kid-size paleontological "dig" lets children uncover "prehistoric fossils." A large gift shop features, of course, dinosaur-related gifts. Dinosaurs Alive! costs an extra $5 in addition to the Kings Island admission.

Kings Island is on I-71 at Kings Mill's; (800) 288-0808; visitkingsisland .com.

An 80-year-old train station that houses 3 superior museums and an OMNIMAX theater? That's the incomparable *Cincinnati Museum Center.* This magnificent, 500,000-square-foot Art Deco railroad station, built in 1933 as a center of regional travel, is now a center of fine exhibits and spectacular film showings. During its heyday as a rail hub, hundreds of trains arrived and departed from here each day. And while it is still an Amtrak station (one eastbound and one westbound daily, both in the middle of the night; call Amtrak at 800-872-7245), the crowds gather now not to greet passengers, but rather to discover the past.

One attraction at the Cincinnati History Museum is the world's largest S-scale city model, called "Cincinnati in Motion." It combines model trains with trolleys, homes, and city buildings. Interpreters help take the visitor back in time and tell the story of Cincinnati and its early days as a bustling river town. Children will find their own kind of fun at the Duke Energy Children's Museum, where they can explore interactive exhibits that use simple machines, balls, and a water play area to stimulate young imaginations. The Museum of Natural History and Science has walk-through re-creations of limestone caves and an Ice Age exhibit, as well as a Fossil Prep Lab that lets visitors observe scientists at work.

The Robert D. Linder Family OMNIMAX Theater wraps you in sight and sound, highlighted by a five-story, 72-foot, domed screen. Dramatic films that depict flight and rapid travel appear to pull you into the action, while spectacular landscapes completely surround you.

Cincinnati Museum Center is at 1301 Western Ave., Cincinnati; (513) 287-7000, (800) 733-2077; cincymuseum.org. Open Mon through Sat, 10 a.m. to 5 p.m.; Sun, 11 a.m. to 6 p.m. Admission: adults $12.50, senior citizens $11.50; children (ages 3 to 12) $8.50; toddlers (ages 1 and 2) $4.50. The OMNIMAX Theater requires a separate ticket, or the purchase of a ticket

ALSO WORTH SEEING

Cincinnati Art Museum

Cincinnati Zoo and
Botanical Gardens

Irwin M. Krohn Conservatory,
Cincinnati

Dayton Art Institute

that combines the entrance fee for the museum and the theater. Call for OMNIMAX show times and ticket prices.

European elegance with a musical backdrop graces the intimate ***Symphony Hotel***. The full-service bed-and-breakfast welcomes guests into a graceful 1871 building, furnished in turn-of-the-20th-century antiques but modernized to provide private baths, telephones, televisions, and air-conditioning. A European-style breakfast also is included in the room rate.

The Symphony Hotel is across the street from the Cincinnati Music Hall, which was constructed in 1878. The musical theme continues into the hotel. Every guest room is dedicated to a composer, including Mozart, Brahms, Bach, and Beethoven. The dining room serves a special fixed-price, 5-course meal ($45) prior to performances at the music hall. Dinner guests must make reservations in advance. Sunday brunch is served from 10 a.m. to 1 p.m. Reservations can also be made for special events such as parties, meetings, or luncheons.

The Symphony Hotel is at 210 W. 14th St., Cincinnati; (513) 721-3353; symphonyhotel.com. Rates: $99 to $149.

One of the finest small art museums in the US, the ***Taft Museum of Art*** is a National Historic Landmark. Built in 1820, this federal-period building is home to nearly 700 works of art, including the work of European and American Masters. However, this stunning building served first as a residence for Martin Baum. During his ownership of the property from 1829 to 1863, Nicholas Longworth began a tradition of artistic patronage that was expanded by the last private owners of the house, Charles Phelps Taft and Anna Sinton Taft. They acquired and decorated their home with treasures ranging from French Renaissance enamels and Italian decorative arts to Chinese porcelains and European and American oils.

The home and collections were donated as a gift to the people of Cincinnati in 1927, and the house opened as a museum in November 1932. With its slender Tuscan columns, the Taft Museum is a federal-period country villa. The central section of the structure features delicate elliptical windows, while the southeast facade has a distinctive upper and lower columned porch.

The collection includes works by such masters as Rembrandt, Hals, Gainsborough, Sargent, Ruisdael, Turner, and Corot. There's an extensive presentation of French Renaissance Limoges enamels and watches of the 17th and 18th centuries.

The Lindner Family Cafe at the Taft Museum offers light lunches as well as wine and beer. The exhibitions provide inspiration for the cafe's culinary staff. For example, the African-American art exhibition inspired the Gumbo Yaya, a tasty combination of chicken and smoked turkey sausage with tomatoes, onions, filé gumbo, and black roux over rice. When the weather is good, dine on the garden patio. The cafe is open Wed through Fri from 11 a.m. to 2 p.m., Sat and Sun from 11 a.m. to 3 p.m. Reservations recommended. Call the cafe at (513) 352-5140.

The Taft Museum of Art is at 316 Pike St., Cincinnati; (513) 241-0343; taftmuseum.org. Open Wed through Fri, 11 a.m. to 4 p.m.; Sun, 11 a.m. to 5 p.m. Admission: adults $8; college students, teachers, and senior citizens $8; children (ages 12 to 17) $4. Admission is free every Sun. The museum has free on-site parking.

Letters from President William Howard Taft's mother to her relatives in the East proved invaluable in the restoration of Taft's childhood home. The **William Howard Taft National Historic Site** was the childhood home of the 27th president of the US. It is Greek revival in design; square and symmetrical with decorative trim. The home has been restored and is much as it must have been in the mid-1800s. The Taft family has provided many personal effects, including portraits and books that would have been in the Taft household when the young William was growing up.

Congress designated the house a National Historic Site and monument to the president in 1969, and placed it under the administration of the National Park Service. The William Howard Taft National Historic Site is at 2038 Auburn Ave., Cincinnati; (513) 684-3262; nps.gov/wiho. Open daily 8 a.m. to 4 p.m. The last guided tour of the day starts at 3:30 p.m. Closed on holidays. Free parking.

In 1833, the daughter of the new president of Lane Seminary moved into a stately residence on the campus. This house, the **Harriet Beecher Stowe House,** has now been renamed to acknowledge the legacy of the former resident.

Harriet Beecher Stowe wrote the landmark story *Uncle Tom's Cabin,* which dramatically portrayed the cruel and dehumanizing effects of slavery. The Stowe House is now a black history, education, and cultural center.

The Harriet Beecher Stowe House is located at 2950 Gilbert Ave., Cincinnati; (513) 751-0651, (800) 847-6057; stowehousecincy.org. Open May through Labor Day, Tues through Thurs and Sat, 10 a.m. to 2 p.m.; after Labor Day through Nov, Tues, Wed, and Sat, 10 a.m. to 2 p.m.; Feb through Apr, Wed and Sat 10 a.m. to 1 p.m. Closed from Thanksgiving through Jan. No admission charge.

If you're in the mood for mouth-watering barbecued ribs and chicken, plus ice-cold beer, try Ted Gregory's **Montgomery Inn.** This popular restaurant claims to serve the "world's greatest ribs," a designation with which few customers would argue. Although the menu at the Montgomery Inn does include selections such as steaks, pork chops, and fillet of sole, the restaurant is known for tender ribs and chicken dripping with a zesty sauce.

While waiting in the bar for your table, you'll see photographs of the likes of Tommy Lasorda and Billy Carter displayed on the wall, each autographed and extolling the virtues of Ted Gregory's barbecue. On the rough wood paneling in the comfortable dining rooms are photos and paintings of Gregory's other passion—horse racing. You'll even find some bridles and jockeys' shirts displayed throughout the inn.

For those unable to decide between barbecued ribs and barbecued chicken, try some of each with the half-and-half dinner, which is served with crisp tossed salad and the inn's famous Saratoga chip potatoes. The management thoughtfully provides bibs for those partaking of the sauce-laden barbecue.

If you're not hungry for barbecue (which seems inconceivable once you experience the aroma in this restaurant), other menu selections include Cantonese-style fried Oriental shrimp with sweet 'n' hot sauce, Wisconsin's Pride duckling, and a number of sandwiches (including a barbecued beef sandwich).

The Montgomery Inn is at 9440 Montgomery Rd. (exit 12 off I-71), Montgomery; (513) 791-3482; montgomeryinnribs.com. Open Mon through Thurs, 11 a.m. to 10:30 p.m.; Fri, 11 a.m. to 11 p.m.; Sat, 3 p.m. to 11 p.m.; Sun, 3 to 9:30 p.m.

Founded in 2003, the **Tri-State Warbird Museum** set lofty goals for itself, including being recognized as one of the most-admired museums dedicated to military and historic aviation. This museum honors both the pilots and planes that defended America during wartime, particularly during World

War II. The planes and exhibits on display pay tribute to our rich military aviation history, recognizing the creativity, commitment, and sacrifice of so many during the crucial conflict in the 1940s.

Among the collection are such treasures as the P-51D Mustang, *Cincinnati Miss*. Smartly painted with a black and yellow checkered nose and yellow tail sections, she represents the definitive version of the P-51 single-seat fighter. Powered by a supercharged Merlin engine to a single prop, the D version delivered 1,695 horsepower, had a maximum speed of 437 miles per hour, a service ceiling of 41,800 feet, and a combat range of 1,000 miles. This long-range fighter aircraft entered service in 1943, featured six .50-caliber machine guns, and is still regarded as one of the best piston-engine fighters ever built. Nearly 8,000 P-51 D/K Mustangs were built.

Another mid-war entrant was the TBM-3 Avenger. Aptly named, the Avenger was designed and built to retaliate against the Japanese Navy after its attack on Pearl Harbor. Grumman and General Motors produced 9,836 Avengers, equipping them with a power-operated gun turret, heavy 22-inch torpedoes, bombs, rockets, and depth charges. The Wright Cyclone 14 engine delivered 1,726 horsepower, giving the Avenger a maximum speed of 276 miles per hour, a ceiling of 30,100 feet, and a range of more than 1,000 miles. It was a torpedo attack by British-flown Avengers that sank two of the world's largest battleships, the Japanese *Musashi* and *Yamato* in October 1944 and April 1945, respectively.

An equally proud member of the museum's collection is its twin-engine B-25 Mitchell bomber. Approximately 10,000 of these bombers were built by North American Aviation. Although designed for bombing runs at medium altitudes, they frequently were used for treetop-level missions against Japanese airfields and shipping in the Pacific. Powered by twin Wright Cyclone engines, each producing 1,850 horsepower, the B-25 had a top speed of 275 miles per hour, a combat range of 1,350 miles, and a ceiling of 25,000 feet. The most famous wartime use of B-25s was the 1942 Doolittle Raid, where pilots flew off the aircraft carrier USS *Hornet,* bombed Tokyo and then crashed in China. It was also a B-25 that collided with the Empire State Building in New York City in 1945.

Many pilots in the US Navy, Air Force, and Marines and the British Royal Air Force learned to fly at the controls of a T-6 Texan. A total of 15,495 Texans, a single-engine, advanced trainer aircraft designed by North American Aviation, trained tens of thousands of wartime pilots. The museum's yellow and red Marine AT-6D version—*Tweety*—features a 600-horsepower radial engine, with a maximum speed of 208 miles per hour and a range of 730 miles.

Another common trainer was the Stearman Model 75 biplane. The museum's bright blue and yellow one is an excellent example of this popular trainer, originally built during the 1930s. Its rugged construction and open-air dual cockpit seating made it a popular crop duster and leisure aircraft once the war concluded.

One of the most intriguing exhibits at the 20,000 square-foot Tri-State Warbird Museum is not even an airplane. It's the ANT-18 Link Trainer. This was the first flight simulator trainer, built of wood in 1932 by Edwin A. Link, who used bellows and other parts from his father's Link Piano and Organ Company.

World War II produced a tremendous demand for new pilots, and cadet pilots could become proficient in instrument flying in 50 hours using the ANT-18. By war's end, 10,000 of the trainers had been built, teaching many of the 190,000 pilots trained in the US during World War II.

The museum also honors Cincinnati-area military aviation veterans, such as Tom Griffin, who flew with Lieutenant Colonel Jimmy Doolittle, and Russell B. Witte Jr., a B-25 bomber pilot with more than 50 missions flying from North Africa over Sicily and Italy. He was awarded the Distinguished Flying Cross and nine Air Medals. Many of the museum's aircraft are still airworthy and can often be found at regional air shows and similar events.

The Tri-State Warbird Museum is at 4021 Borman Dr., Batavia; (513) 735-4500; tri-statewarbirdmuseum.org. Open Wed, 4 to 7 p.m.; Sat, 10 a.m. to 3 p.m. Admission is $12 for adults, $7 for students and veterans. Admission is free for World War II veterans and all veterans in uniform.

The founders of the Mariemont Company designed and constructed the village of Mariemont as a totally planned community modeled after the "garden city" villages in England. In the 1920s, they envisioned Mariemont as a rural alternative to bustling Cincinnati nearby.

Although it's no longer in the country (Mariemont is now in the suburban ring surrounding Cincinnati), this quaint village, with its Tudor commercial buildings and peaceful, tree-lined residential neighborhoods, does provide the tranquil existence sought by its founders. The entire village is listed on the National Register of Historic Places.

The **Mariemont Inn,** a member of Historic Hotels of America, offers visitors a charming place to imbibe, dine, and spend the night. It is set facing the circle in the center of the commercial business district, and the striking Tudor exterior is rivaled by the interior decor in this classic structure. Each of the 45 guest rooms contains the dark, heavy woods and rich colors typical of the Tudor period; the spacious suites come furnished with ornate canopy beds, and there are antiques throughout the inn. Your day starts off with complimentary coffee or juice, delivered to your room at your convenience.

Visitors unwind in Southerby's Pub, a cozy old-English pub. The popularity of the National Examplar dining room for breakfast, lunch, and dinner with area residents and businesspeople speaks for the excellent food. An innovative breakfast-brunch-lunch menu featuring omelets, homemade soups, fine salads, and a wide selection of sandwiches is served from 7 a.m. until 2:30 p.m. The varied dinner selections include fresh seafood, pasta, veal, and many great steaks, with appetizers and desserts to accompany these dishes. The inn is now part of the Best Western hotel group.

The Mariemont Inn is at 6880 Wooster Pike (US 50), Cincinnati; (513) 271-2100, (877) 271-2211; mariemontinn.com. Lodging rates: from $179 to $239 per night.

After your meal, enjoy a stroll, jog, or bike ride in the picturesque village, or stop by the gift shop, bookstore, ice-cream parlor, or other shops adjacent to the inn. Though downtown Cincinnati is only 15 minutes from Mariemont, when you're walking through this peaceful community, the big city seems worlds away.

It is the last of its kind in Clermont County. The **Stonelick Covered Bridge** has become not just an icon of a bygone era, but a magnet for tourists and the inspiration for local artists. This covered bridge, also known as the Perintown Covered Bridge, was built in 1878, restored in 1971, and placed on the National Register of Historic Places in 1974. The 140-foot-long bridge is supported by an impressive 12-panel Howe Truss system, patented by William Howe in 1840. This system uses vertical iron rods instead of vertical timber posts, and crossed timber members forming the familiar X-shaped supports. The bridge spans Stonelick Creek. The bridge was closed in 2010 for major renovation and is scheduled to open at the end of 2013.

The Stonelick Covered Bridge is on Stone-Williams Corner Road (CR 116) in Clermont County, 0.2 mile west of the junction of US 50 and OH 222 (go north on Stone-Williams Road).

The Benninghofens were an affluent family in the late 1800s. Their Italianate home was built in 1861. The *Benninghofen House* has 13-foot ceilings beautifully painted and adorned with heavy moldings. Cherry wood-work, parquet floors, and chandeliers are original to the home, which was placed on the National Register of Historic Homes in 1973.

The home itself is a wonderful reflection of the times, but the visitor also will find various collections in the home noteworthy. Civil War enthusiasts will want to note the field desk, sword, and flag from the Ohio Volunteer Infantry. Dolls, surveying equipment, pottery, and vintage furniture all provide color and life to this slice of Ohio history.

The Benninghofen House is at 327 N. Second St., Hamilton; (513) 896-9930; bchistoricalsociety.com/house/html. Guided tours are available Tues through Sat, 11 a.m. to 4 p.m. Admission: free, but donations are appreciated.

mt.healthy

In 1817 John La Boiteaux and Samuel Hill founded Mt. Pleasant in Hamilton County. Although the town was known as Mt. Pleasant for years, the post office urged the residents to rename it, to avoid confusion with the "other Mt. Pleasant." They did, choosing Mt. Healthy as the new name in gratitude for being spared the cholera epidemic that struck Cincinnati in the late 1840s.

Cincinnati lost 7 percent of its population to cholera in 1849, during the 19th century's second global epidemic of this once-terrifying disease. Ohio had become vulnerable for the first time due to increased contact with travelers from other parts of the US and the world.

When most of us think of a museum of sculpture, we don't even begin to imagine what awaits us on a visit to the *Pyramid Hill Sculpture Park and Museum.* Yes, there are 35 interesting pieces to view and ponder, but they are set in a 355-acre arboretum. This is one of the four largest sculpture gardens in the US. Your leisurely walk down 3 well-marked trails takes you past gardens, 7 lakes, and a wide variety of trees. You'll even see the remains of a 19th-century stone pioneer home.

These outdoor features provide a backdrop for the nearly three dozen sculptures. Some, like *Eve* by Marc Mellon, are traditional. *Age of*

Stone by Jon Isherwood evokes the feeling of a mystic place filled with ancient druids. The park also features a series of one-way roads that allow visitors to view the art from their private cars. The park provides bus tours, but you need to make a reservation for this guided tour. Pyramid Hill offers many special children's programs in the summer months, as well as music programs that provide a blending of arts that will enchant the entire family.

The park also features a 10,000-square-foot Ancient Sculpture Museum with Etruscan, Greek, Egyptian, and Roman sculpture thousands of years old. The Ancient Sculpture Museum is open daily, noon to 5 p.m.

Sorg Opera House Ghost

Since 1891 the Sorg Opera House has been a place where the starstruck come and linger. More than 100 years ago, a wealthy entrepreneur, Paul Sorg, built the theater. Famous actors and grand productions were invited to the Middletown stage to perform with Jeannie Sorg, Paul's wife and a great fan of the performing arts.

Over the life of the theater, the likes of George M. Cohan and Bob Hope have taken their place on center stage. It became a movie house in the 1920s and hosted the first "talkie" shown in town. A fire damaged the building in 1935, but it was renovated and reopened four years later.

The legend of the theater centers on Paul Sorg. As owner, the well-dressed business baron is reported to have always claimed the best seat in the house when he attended performances. In the 1890s those seated in the orchestra or the first balcony arrived at the opera house in full evening dress. Paul Sorg was a fixture at his theater, dressed in fashionable garb and seated in his favorite seat in the first row of the first balcony.

Through the years and even today, staff and patrons sometimes claim they catch a glimpse of the nattily attired Sorg taking his place in the first balcony. When asked to describe the man, many ghost spotters have described him as he appears in his portrait, which hangs in the theater lobby. Sometimes only his footsteps are heard crossing the stage or walking overhead on the catwalks. So, while actors and actresses have come and gone, the first owner maintains his star status as the legend of the Sorg Opera House.

The Sorg Opera House is located at 63 S. Main St., Middletown; sorgopera house.org.

The Pyramid Hill Sculpture Park and Museum is 3 miles southwest of Hamilton on OH 128 at 1763 Hamilton-Cleves Rd.; (513) 861-1234, (513) 868-8336; pyramidhill.org. Open daily year-round, 8 a.m. to 5 p.m. Admission: adults $8; children (ages 5 to 12) $2.

Picture a thoroughfare of pumpkins. In the autumn you can walk past hundreds of pumpkins at the *Barn 'n' Bunk Farm Market.* In warmer weather, the market is filled with bedding plants, hanging baskets, and Amish-made lawn furniture, as well as farm-fresh produce. The market grew out of the family farm of Bev and Tom Theobald.

The century-old barns now house a variety of shops. More than 50 local crafters provide items from candles and baskets to birdhouses and furniture pieces. On the sweeter side, you can also indulge in honeys, jellies, candies, Amish baked goods, and even ice cream. Weekends in September and October feature special fall displays and events, and the market puts on its finest for visitors in the days before Christmas.

The Barn 'n' Bunk Farm Market is on OH 73 and Wayne-Madison Road in Trenton; (513) 988-9211; barnnbunk.com. Open March 25 through December 23, Mon through Sat, 10 a.m. to 5 p.m.; Sun, 10:30 a.m. to 5 p.m.

Invention Trail

The community of Miamisburg has the largest conical burial mound in Ohio—the *Miamisburg Mound.* Artifacts excavated from this 68-foot-high mound, which contains 54,000 cubic yards of earth, indicate the Adena Indians built it sometime between 1000 BC and AD 100. With a circumference of nearly 900 feet at the base, the mound had two burial vaults: one 8 feet from the top of the mound containing a bark-covered skeleton, the other 36 feet down and surrounded by logs but without any skeletal remains.

Visitors to the mound, which today is overgrown with brush and trees, can climb 116 steps to the top of this impressive earthwork for a splendid view of the Miami Valley. A 36-acre park encircles the mound, with picnic tables, barbecue grills, and shelter houses.

The Miamisburg Mound is 1 mile south of OH 725 on East Mound Avenue, Miamisburg; (937) 866-4532; ohiohistory.org/museums-and-historic-sites/museum--historic-sites-by-name/miamisburg-mound. Open daylight hours; no admission charge.

Just south of downtown Dayton, along the Great Miami River, is the landmark **Deeds Carillon,** a 151-foot-high, 57-bell carillon that stands at the entrance to **Carillon Historical Park.** Dedicated in 1942, the carillon was given to the people of Dayton by Colonel Edward Deeds and his wife, Edith. Concerts delight audiences from May through October.

In addition to the bells, this 65-acre park has an outstanding group of exhibit buildings, primarily dedicated to Dayton's invention, transportation, and settlement history. The museum's crown jewel has to be the 1905 Wright Flyer III in Wright Hall, a National Historic Landmark and part of the Dayton Aviation Heritage National Historic Park. Weighing 855 pounds, this plane was the world's first practical aircraft and was described by Orville Wright as the plane in which he and Wilbur learned to fly. Two years after their historic 1903 flights at Kitty Hawk, Wilbur stayed aloft in the Flyer III for 39 minutes at an average speed of 38 miles per hour. Orville Wright later supervised the initial restoration of this aircraft.

Deeds Barn, a replica of the carriage house that stood behind Colonel Deeds's home, houses exhibits that underscore the contributions of Deeds and his friend and contemporary Charles F. Kettering. It was on the second floor of the original barn that Kettering and his "barn gang" revolutionized automobile ignition and lighting systems, and the barn contains a 1912 Cadillac, the first production auto to feature these innovations. Kettering and Deeds went on to found Dayton Engineering Laboratories Company (later called Delco). Kettering's early inventions at National Cash Register Company and Deeds's later accomplishments in developing the Liberty aircraft engine also are displayed.

The two-story log building called **Newcom Tavern,** Dayton's oldest existing building, was the home of George Newcom. It also served as Dayton's first courtroom. The tavern includes many of its original items, such as the china used by Colonel and Mrs. Newcom, and the colonel's favorite rocking chair.

Other displays in Carillon Historical Park include locomotives and railroad cars, a restored canal lock and covered bridge, a working 1930s print shop, and a replica of the Wright brothers' bicycle shop. The Dayton Sales Company automobile showroom has a 1910 Speedwell, a 1923 Maxwell, and a very rare 1908 Stoddard-Dayton.

Carillon Historical Park is at the intersection of Patterson and Carillon Boulevards, east of I-75 at the Edwin Moses/Nicholas Road exit, Dayton;

(937) 293-2841; carillonpark.org. The park is open Mon through Sat, 9:30 a.m. to 5 p.m.; Sun, noon to 5 p.m. (Closed on major holidays.) Admission: adults $8; senior citizens $7; children (ages 3 to 17) $5.

Dayton's historical sites provide interesting glimpses into the lives and work of some of its most famous citizens. The final resting place of some of these notables, **Woodland Cemetery and Arboretum,** is also a quiet spot to reflect on their contributions. This cemetery is one of the five oldest rural garden cemeteries in the country. The 100-acre arboretum and cemetery was planned as the city of Dayton grew, and opened in the 1840s. Such places provided a peaceful alternative to burial in highly populated urban centers. In this cemetery are the graves of poet Paul Laurence Dunbar, both Orville

Victoria Theater

Some of the attractions of the historic Victoria Theater in Dayton are easy for the visitor to see and appreciate. The turn-of-the-20th-century building is graced by lavish period touches, such as gilt trim and green marble pillars. But another attraction is a bit more elusive.

According to legend, the ghost of a young actress occasionally makes an appearance behind the glass and bronze doors of the Victoria. The young lady is winsome, wearing a 1900s black taffeta dress nipped in at the waist and draped softly to the floor. She has a penchant for appearing in the mirror of one of the third-floor dressing rooms.

It is from that dressing room, the legend says, that the ghost, nicknamed Vickie, made her final dramatic exit. In the middle of a production, Vickie is supposed to have forgotten a fan she needed in the next scene and so told the other actors she was returning to the dressing room to get it. She was last seen climbing the stairs. She never returned to the stage. She just vanished.

Did Vickie sneak out of the theater to join a lover? Did she meet with foul play? No one knows for sure, but theatergoers and staff say that she still remains, in spirit.

The door to the fabled dressing room seems to have a mind of its own, and feminine footsteps sometimes can be heard tripping lightly on the stairway. If you hear the rustle of taffeta, detect the scent of rose perfume, or feel the light brush of a young lady passing close to you, then you, too, have experienced the continuing performance of Vickie. Check the website at victoriatheatre.com/venues/victoria-theatre.

and Wilbur Wright, Ohio governor James Cox, and writer and humorist Erma Bombeck.

Visitors enter the cemetery through the impressive Romanesque gateway and chapel. This imposing structure was built in 1889, has an original Tiffany stained-glass window, and is listed on the National Register of Historic Places. This structure also houses the administrative offices where visitors can find walking tour maps or borrow a CD player and headset that provides an audio tour of Woodland's highlights. Special tours can be arranged by calling ahead; special events are listed on the website. More than 3,000 trees and 10,000 monuments are found on the grounds. Some memorials are modern in design, such as the 29,000-pound structure forming the monument for writer Erma Bombeck. Others are more traditional, with statuary of angels, cherubs, and urns or replicas of Greek or Egyptian temples. Some, like the grave of the child Johnny Morehouse, reflect poignant stories. This memorial pictures the faithful dog that pulled the child from a river after he had fallen in, but too late to save him.

Woodlawn Cemetery and Arboretum is located at 118 Woodland Ave., Dayton; (937) 228-3221; woodlandcemetery.org. Open daily, 8 a.m. to 5 p.m. No admission charge.

Art lovers, families, art historians, and those just looking for a glimpse of the unusual can find just what they're looking for at the ***Dayton Art Institute.*** Located in downtown Dayton, overlooking the Great Miami River, the impressive Italian Renaissance–style museum features an impressive collection of more than 12,000 objects spanning 5,000 years of art history. Highlights include an outstanding Asian collection, 17th-century Baroque paintings, and 18th- and 19th-century American art collections. In addition, the institute features innovative exhibits, including a hands-on family "Experiencenter," which let visitors experience art in a new and participatory manner.

The Dayton Art Institute also exhibits some objects never before seen in galleries dedicated to Native American and Oceanic art forms. In addition to the extensive permanent collections, the institute hosts world-class special and traveling exhibits, and art-related educational and cultural events. The historic building also houses an education resource center and an art reference library.

The Dayton Art Institute is located at 456 Belmonte Park North, Dayton; (937) 223-5277; daytonartinstitute.org. Open Tues through Fri, 11 a.m. to 8 p.m.; Sat, 10 a.m. to 5 p.m.; and Sun, noon to 5 p.m. Closed Mon. No admission charge for the museum's permanent collections galleries. Admission to other galleries: adults $8; senior citizens $5; college students (with ID) and children free.

The **Dunbar House State Memorial** was the first state memorial in Ohio dedicated to an African American. This distinction seems fitting, since Paul Laurence Dunbar is often referred to as the poet laureate of African Americans. The turn-of-the-20th-century home of Italianate design was the poet's final residence.

The son of former slaves, Dunbar used his writing to portray the dilemmas faced by a recently freed but still disenfranchised people. Dunbar died at age 34 in 1906, but his mother lived in the Dunbar House until 1934. Thanks to her care in preserving her son's belongings, visitors can view many of his original works and personal items as well as many of the family furnishings.

The Dunbar House State Memorial is located at 219 Paul Laurence Dunbar St., Dayton; (937) 313-2010, (800) 860-0148; ohiohistory.org/dunbar. Open Fri and Sat, 10 a.m. to 4 p.m., or by appointment. Admission: adults $6; children (ages 6 to 12) $3.

Making science fun is the mission of the **Boonshoft Museum of Discovery** in Dayton. Formerly the Dayton Museum of Natural History, today Boonshoft uses a hands-on, interactive environment to foster interest in and understanding of all things scientific.

Travel through time and space at the Caryl D. Phillips Space Theater, where an advanced computer graphics system projects stunning skylines and impressive galaxies. On stage at the Oscar Boonshoft Science Central's Science Theater are live performances showcasing mind-boggling scientific stunts. The Boonshoft also houses an extensive collection of 1.4 million real animal specimens and artifacts, including live animals at the indoor Charles Exley Jr. Wild Ohio Zoo, complete with a variety of native Ohio wildlife such as coyotes, river otters, and bobcats. Other favorite exhibits include the Mastodon Dig and the Sonoran Desert. For a bird's-eye view of the museum's outdoor amphitheater and lush woodland trails, kids climb the Mead Treehouse.

The Boonshoft Museum of Discovery is at 2600 Deweese Parkway, Dayton; (937) 275-7431; boonshoftmuseum.org. Open Mon through Sat, 9 a.m. to 5 p.m.; Sun, noon to 5 p.m. Admission: adults $12; senior citizens $10; children (ages 3 to 16) $9 .

For a look at more modern modes of transportation, be sure to see the more than 300 aircraft and missiles displayed at the impressive **US Air Force Museum.** With 17 acres of exhibit space in the 3 main hangar-type buildings, plus the Presidential and Research/Development Galleries, this may be the world's most complete aviation museum. From a Wright Brothers original to an Apollo space capsule, the museum contains an incredibly comprehensive collection of flying machines. Spads, Camels, Spitfires, Mustangs, the B-29 that dropped the atomic bomb on Nagasaki in 1945, and the enormous Strategic Air Command B-36 bomber—all of these are in one museum.

Located only 3 miles from where the Wright Brothers tested their early designs, the museum, in addition to the aircraft, balloons, and missiles, has hundreds of exhibits that chronicle the history and milestones of military aviation. The newest hangar focuses on the Cold War era to the present day, and features a B-1B bomber, an F-117 Stealth fighter, and a B-2 Spirit stealth bomber. Also new is the Hall of Missiles, including a collection of intercontinental ballistic missiles. And there is an outstanding IMAX theater, which shows spectacular aviation-related films.

The US Air Force Museum is at Wright-Patterson Air Force Base, off OH 4 northeast of Dayton at 1100 Spaatz St.; (937) 255-3286; nationalmuseum .af.mil. Open daily except Christmas, Thanksgiving, and New Year's Day, 9 a.m. to 5 p.m. No admission charge except for the IMAX theater.

The newest addition to the National Park System's Dayton Aviation Heritage History Park is the **Huffman Prairie Flying Field.** While the Wright Brothers may have taken that first flight at Kitty Hawk, this field was where they tested and perfected their flying machines and their flying skills. The experimental planes, the *Flyer II,* built in 1904, and the *Flyer III,* built in 1905, were tested on this prairie land. Along with testing airplanes, this plot of land was also home to the Wright Company flying school from 1910 to 1916, the first flight school in the world. A hangar, similar to the one you would have seen if you visited the Wright brothers, has been erected on the site. In addition to the historic value of the field to flight buffs, this area is also the largest remaining remnant of prairie land in Ohio.

Huffman Prairie Flying Field is located at Gate 16A of Wright Patterson Air Force Base off OH 444; (937) 425-0008; nps.gov/daav. Open daily except

Wed, 8 a.m. to 6 p.m. Closed Thanksgiving, Christmas, and New Year's Day. Admission: free.

Ohio is rich in ancient cultures. One of the best ways to learn more about one of these cultures is to visit *SunWatch Indian Village/ Archaeological Park,* a reconstructed Native American village. This 12th-century village was rebuilt based on the archaeological findings discovered on this site. You'll see pottery and other artifacts typical of the village's era.

The village is named SunWatch because of the advanced system of charting time developed by the village's original inhabitants. During summer months, reconstruction continues at the site, in search of more clues to the past. In season, you'll observe planting, harvesting, house construction, and the manufacture of various artifacts.

SunWatch Indian Village/Archaeological Park is at 2301 W. River Rd., Dayton; (937) 268-8199; sunwatch.org. Open Tues through Sat, 9 a.m. to 5 p.m.; Sun, noon to 5 p.m. Admission: adults $6; senior citizens $4; children (ages 6 to 16) $4.

Daniel Arnold established his 158-acre family farm in 1830 and constructed a farmhouse six years later. The Arnold family worked the farm until 1910, and today this entire farmstead is being restored to its appearance in the 1880s. It's called *Carriage Hill Farm Museum,* and it's part of Carriage Hill MetroPark.

The farmhouse contains furnishings typical of a 19th-century conservative farm family—quilting frame, wood-burning cook stove, and firebox—while bubbles and imperfections in the house's window glass identify it as original. During hot weather, the Arnolds prepared their meals at the outdoor "summer kitchen" to avoid further heating the farmhouse; on many weekends, volunteers now use the cookstove in the summer kitchen to bake fresh bread.

Other demonstrations at Carriage Hill include a blacksmith who operates the old blower, and a woodworker who shapes furniture on a foot-powered lathe.

Like any 1880s farm, Carriage Hill has a variety of farm animals: cattle, chickens, horses, sheep, and pigs. The horses are used to giving hayrides through the reserve's lush meadows and woods. Hiking and bridle trails also wind through the park's acreage. Special events such as square dances, cider pressing, and old-fashioned wheat threshing take place throughout the year at Carriage Hill.

Carriage Hill MetroPark is at 7800 E. Shull Rd., north of I-70 off OH 201, Dayton; (937) 278-2609; metroparks.org/Parks/CarriageHill.

The park is open daily Apr through Oct, 8 a.m. to 10 p.m. and Nov through Mar, 8 a.m. to 8 p.m. Closed Christmas and New Year's Day. The farm museum is open Apr through Oct Tues through Sat, 10 a.m. to 5 p.m.; Sun, noon to 5 p.m.; and Nov through Mar, Tues through Sun, noon to 4 p.m. Closed on Thanksgiving, Christmas, and New Year's Day. No admission charge.

You have to give *Clifton Mill* credit—it has burned down twice, but it has always come back. The first water-powered gristmill at this site on the Little Miami River was built in 1802. Called Davis Mill for its founder, Owen Davis, this first mill prospered until destroyed by fire in the 1840s. But a year or two later, a second mill was erected here, a mill that did its part for the Union army by providing cornmeal and flour to federal troops during the Civil War.

This mill, however, burned down about the time the Confederacy was defeated. In 1869 the Armstrong family built a third mill on this site, which they sold to Isaac Preston 20 years later.

Three generations of Prestons operated the mill until 1948. And although it avoided catching fire again, Clifton Mill did sit idle, deteriorating for 15 years, until Robert Heller bought it and breathed life into it once again. The Satariano family acquired the mill in the mid 1980s, expanding it. A covered bridge now spans the gorge, providing spectacular views.

Today visitors enjoy self-guided tours of this impressive six-story power plant. The huge James Leffel Company turbine on the lowest level, installed in 1908, once provided electricity for farms, homes, and businesses in Clifton, Cedarville, and Yellow Springs at a very modest $1 per month per customer.

Clifton Mill grinds flour, cornmeal, and pancake mix as it has for decades, a process you observe during your tour. And meal and flour, along with homemade breads, pies, and other pastries, are available for purchase, as are fine jams, jellies, syrups, teas, spices, and other specialties. Clifton Mill also serves breakfast, soups, sandwiches, and salads, plus ice cream. On a nice day, take your meal or snack out on the Millrace Deck, and listen to water rushing under your feet on its way to the turbines. At Christmastime the mill is radiant with 2.6 million lights. There's an enormous collection of Santa Clauses and a 100-foot waterfall of lights.

Clifton Mill is at 75 Water St. (OH 72), Clifton; (937) 767-5501; clifton-mill.com. Mill tours: $3. Open Mon through Thurs, 9 a.m. to 4 p.m.; Fri, 9 a.m. to 8 p.m.; Sat, 8 a.m. to 8 p.m.; and Sun, 8 a.m. to 5 p.m. Closed on Thanksgiving, Christmas, and New Year's Day.

Designated a National Natural Landmark by the National Park Service, the *Clifton Gorge Nature Preserve* rates as some of Ohio's most beautiful public land. Over the years, the swift Little Miami River has carved a deep gorge through the thick forest, a process started by the raging meltwaters of the last retreating glacier. The power of the river once turned the wheels of two gristmills in the area—Clifton Mill (described above) and a second mill, the remains of which are still visible in the gorge.

Given the clean vertical drops of the limestone cliffs, Clifton Gorge ranked high with rock climbers until that activity was banned in 1982. Concern for the nearly 350 different wildflowers in the park, which provide an unparalleled spring display, prompted the rock-climbing prohibition.

The preserve has miles of hiking trails along both rims of the gorge and following the river at the floor of the canyon. The adjacent John Bryan State Park contains 11 additional hiking trails, campsites, and picnic areas.

Clifton Gorge Nature Preserve is on OH 343, just west of Clifton at 2331 OH 343. The entrance to John Bryan State Park is on OH 370, near Clifton; (937) 767-1274; dnr.state.oh.us/tabid/882/default.aspx. Open daylight hours; no admission charge.

Another fabulous natural area is Antioch College's *Glen Helen,* a 1,000-acre preserve and outdoor education center adjacent to the college's Yellow Springs campus. Designated a National Natural Landmark by the National Park Service in 1965, Glen Helen has a thick regrown forest canopy, a full array of woodland wildflowers, and undisturbed native wildlife. Scenic features include valleys carved by glacial meltwater, ledges, potholes, cascades, and the Yellow Spring, from which the village gets its name. Flowing at 70 gallons per minute, the spring has built a distinctive hill of travertine deposits that extends from the cliff line down to the valley floor. Numerous hiking trails permeate the landscape.

Nearly two-thirds of Glen Helen is thickly wooded, and the balance is mowed meadow and planted prairie—a diversity that creates varied habitats for many species of animals and birds. A 2.5-mile stretch of the beautiful, free-flowing Little Miami River courses through the glen.

One unique feature of this preserve is its Raptor Center. Here injured birds of prey—hawks, owls, falcons, eagles, osprey, and vultures—are nursed back to health for their return to the wild. The center also serves as a public education facility, permitting visitors to view and better understand these marvelous creatures. The website for the Glen Helen Ecology Institute at Antioch University posts a calendar of events that are open to the general public. These events include wildflower walks, birding walks, and reptile feeding adventures.

Glen Helen is accessible from OH 343 just east of Yellow Springs, or from the Trailside Museum, 405 Corry St., Yellow Springs; (937) 769-1902; glen.antiochcollege.org/glen_helen/visiting_the_glen. Open year-round, daylight hours. No admission charge.

Known as a hotbed of antiwar and counterculture activity in the 1960s and early 1970s, Yellow Springs remains slightly eccentric. The marchers and demonstrators have been replaced by potters and shopkeepers, but Antioch College still provides the youthful emphasis of this uncommon community.

If you've decided you need more time to explore the Yellow Springs area, spend the night at the historic ***Arthur Morgan House.*** No Ohio town seems more suited to the bed-and-breakfast concept than this one, and the Arthur Morgan House fits the bill perfectly. Built in 1921 for the president of Antioch College, Arthur Morgan, this substantial three-story structure has a huge screened porch—a perfect spot to enjoy a morning cup of coffee or the evening breeze.

The innkeeper has created an appropriately peaceful setting with cozy furnishings, including Ohio antiques. Located on a quiet residential street just a half block from the business district, the Arthur Morgan House features 6 guest rooms, each with private bath.

Arthur Morgan House is at 120 W. Limestone St., Yellow Springs; (937) 767-1761; arthurmorganhouse.com. Rates: $105 to $135 per night, double occupancy; includes full breakfast.

Ohio is home to the ***National Afro-American Museum and Cultural Center,*** a repository for preservation, study, and interpretation of the traditions, values, social customs, and experiences of African Americans. The museum's permanent exhibit, *From Victory to Freedom,* chronicles the period from 1945 to 1965—from victory in World War II to freedom through the passage of federal civil rights legislation. Photographs and artifacts re-create a period of social struggle and dramatic change. Particularly impressive is the award-winning film *Music As Metaphor,* which presents the inspiring African-American music of the period and features artists such as Paul Robeson, Fats Domino, Dizzy Gillespie, and many others.

The first phase of this museum opened in 1988, and it is bordered by a scenic wooded area. Additional phases of development are planned. In 2013 a new art exhibit opened that showcases how African Americans have used art to mobilize communities to action in civil rights efforts. The title, *How I Got Over,* is from a song sung by Mahalia Jackson after Dr. Martin Luther King Jr. gave his "I Have a Dream" speech in 1963.

The National Afro-American Museum and Cultural Center is at 1350 Brush Row Rd., Wilberforce; (937) 376-4944, (800) 752-2603; ohiohistory .org/museums-and-historic-sites/museum--historic-sites-by-name/national-afro-american-museum--cultural-center The museum is open Wed through Sat, 9 a.m. to 4 p.m. Admission: adults $6; senior citizens $5; college students with ID $3; children (ages 6 to 18) $3.

Places to Stay in Southwest Ohio

CHILLICOTHE

Guest House Bed and Breakfast
57 W. Fifth St.
(740) 772-2204
guesthousechillicothe.com

CINCINNATI

The Mariemont Inn
6880 Wooster Pike
(513) 271-2100
mariemontinn.com

The Symphony Hotel
210 W. 14th St.
(513) 721-3353,
(888) 281-8032
symphonyhotel.com

PORTSMOUTH

Shawnee State Park
OH 125, 12 miles west of Portsmouth
(740) 858-6652,
(800) 217-2481
ohiodnr.com/?TabId=788

RIPLEY

The Signal House
234 N. Fourth St.
(937) 392-1640
thesignalhouse.com

YELLOW SPRINGS

Arthur Morgan House
120 W. Limestone St.
(937) 761-1761
arthurmorganhouse.com

HELPFUL WEBSITES

Ohio Division of Travel and Tourism:
discoverohio.com

**Cincinnati Convention and
Visitors Bureau:**
cincyusa.com

Cincinnati Enquirer
news.cincinnati.com

**Dayton Convention and
Visitors Bureau:**
daytoncvb.com

Kings Island:
visitkingsisland.com

Places to Eat in Southwest Ohio

LEBANON

The Golden Lamb
27 S. Broadway
(513) 932-5065
Lodging is also available.
goldenlamb.com

MONTGOMERY

Montgomery Inn
9440 Montgomery Rd.
(513) 791-3482
montgomeryinn.com

RIPLEY

Cohearts Riverhouse
18 N. Front St.
(937) 392-4819

WAVERLY

Lake White Club
OH 552, 2 miles south of
Waverly
(740) 947-5000,
(800) 774-5253
lakewhiteclub.com

Rural Roots

Just up the road from Yellow Springs' Antioch College (and across the Greene County–Clark County line) is a most remarkable store—**Young's Jersey Dairy.** Located at a working dairy, Young's caters to the nearby college crowd and the area's year-round residents with fresh breads and pastries, fountain service, and homemade ice cream.

Young's bakes from scratch its vast selection of doughnuts and pastries—turnovers, brownies, pies, cream horns, pecan rolls, coffee cake, fudge, and cookies, plus glazed, whole-wheat, powdered, jelly-filled, and cinnamon doughnuts. The fountain offers shakes, splits, sundaes, and ice-cream sodas created with Young's homemade ice cream. The shakes are particularly good—made in every flavor imaginable. Served regular or extra thick, the calf shake has 2 scoops of ice cream, the cow shake comes loaded with 4 scoops, and the diet-busting bull shake contains 5 scoops.

The Golden Jersey Inn, an authentic frame barn with giant oak timbers fastened with wood pegs, serves country meatloaf, chicken and dumplings, and bacon-wrapped pork chops.

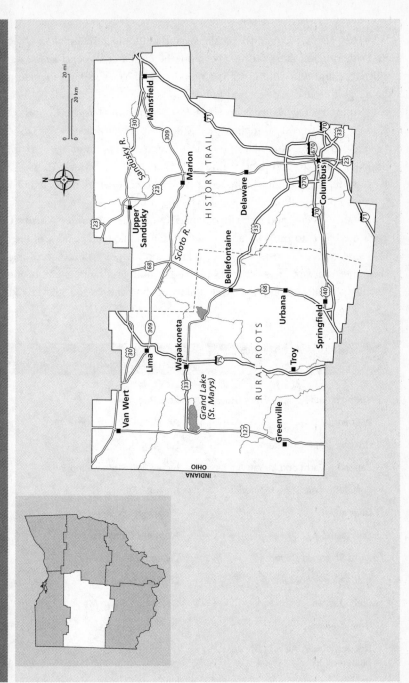

They also serve country breakfasts and a full lunch menu of sandwiches and side orders. After you eat, check out the farm animal petting zoo, wagon rides (Sat and Sun during warmer months), and Young's farm-themed miniature golf course, Udders and Putters.

Young's Jersey Dairy is on US 68 just north of the Greene County–Clark County line at 6880 Springfield-Xenia Rd., Yellow Springs; (937) 325-0629; youngsdairy.com. Summer: open Sun through Thurs, 7 a.m. to 11 p.m.; Fri and Sat, 7 a.m. to midnight. Spring and fall: open Sun through Thurs, 7 a.m. to 10 p.m.; Fri and Sat, 7 a.m. to 11 p.m. Winter: open Sun through Thurs, 7 a.m. to 9 p.m.; Fri and Sat, 7 a.m. to 10 p.m.

With 165 acres and more than 6 miles of trails, the *Brukner Nature Center's* mission is to preserve and present to the public the splendor of the outdoors. Hardwood and pine forests, ridges, and ravines—all are accessible by the center's nature trails. Visitors observe the flora and fauna while hiking by Cattail and Catface Ponds and while following the banks of the Stillwater River.

BEST ATTRACTIONS

Young's Jersey Dairy Farm Store	Fort Recovery
Willowtree Inn	Allen County Museum
Brukner Nature Center	Harding Home
Johnston Farm and Indian Agency	Indian Mill State Memorial
Fort Jefferson State Memorial	Malabar Farm
Bear's Mill	Kingwood Center
Oak Island	Richland Carrousel Park
Zane Shawnee Caverns	Living Bible Museum
Mad River Mountain	Ohio Statehouse
Piatt Castles	Columbus *Santa Maria*
Ohio Caverns	North Market
Neil Armstrong Air and Space Museum	

The spring woodland flora delights visitors with displays of bluebells, trillium, Dutchman's breeches, and delphinium. In summer, Queen Anne's lace, thin-leaved coneflowers, butterfly milkweed, and prairie roses flourish along the trails. Occasional glimpses of hawks, garter snakes, cottontail rabbits, white-tailed deer, and chipmunks give visitors a sample of Brukner's diverse native fauna.

The wildlife rehabilitation unit nurses back to health injured animals brought to Brukner. Those unable to survive in the wild are kept in the animal room on display for visitors to the center. Brukner also hosts a variety of classes and seminars on topics such as quilting, wood carving, gems and minerals, stargazing, beekeeping, and natural history.

Brukner Nature Center is at 5995 Horseshoe Bend Rd., off OH 55 west of Troy; (937) 698-6493; bruknernaturecenter.com. Trails are open during daylight hours. The interpretive building is open Mon through Sat, 9 a.m. to 5 p.m.; Sun, 12:30 to 5 p.m. Admission is $2.50 per person or $10 for a family. Free admission on Sun.

In 1804, for $5 an acre, John Johnston bought the 235 acres he called Upper Pickaway Farms. John and Rachel Johnston, along with their 11 children, lived in the family farmhouse from its completion in 1815 to the 1860s. This historic farm has been restored to its appearance in 1829 and is now the *Johnston Farm and Indian Agency.*

The farmhouse is completely furnished with pieces dating from the early 1800s. The Johnstons used the outdoor fruit kiln to dry apple slices from the farm's 2 orchards. One feature that attracted Johnston to this property was the flowing spring, and he built a springhouse to utilize the cool spring water to refrigerate meats, milk, and produce. Inside the two-story structure, the clear water circles a stone island in the center of the floor. Items requiring cooling were placed either on the stones or in the flowing water. The spring also provided fresh drinking water for the family. When Johnston advertised the farm for sale in 1857, he estimated the spring's output at 10 gallons per minute. The second floor of the springhouse originally contained accommodations for the farm's hired help, but today holds an oak loom (ca. 1750) on which rug making is demonstrated.

The Johnstons' enormous double-pen log barn, constructed in 1808, is the largest log barn in Ohio. Johnston used it for his flock of 100 sheep, and the original pens and beams are still plainly visible. Other attractions at the

Johnston Farm and Indian Agency include canal boat rides on a restored section of the Miami and Erie Canal and an Indian museum dedicated to the tribes prevalent in Ohio from the 17th to mid-19th centuries.

The Johnston Farm and Indian Agency is at 9845 N. Hardin Rd. east of OH 66, north of Piqua; (937) 773-2522, (800) 752-2619; johnstonfarmohio .com . Open from June through Labor Day, Thurs and Fri, 10 a.m. to 5 p.m.; Sat and Sun, noon to 5 p.m. Admission: adults $8; children (ages 6 to 12) $4.

In October 1791, the forces of General Arthur St. Clair built Fort Jefferson as an outpost, one of the chain of defensive forts constructed to protect army supplies from Indians. Named for Thomas Jefferson, then secretary of state, the fort served as a supply base for the campaigns of General St. Clair and General "Mad" Anthony Wayne. It was abandoned in 1796, its location too accessible to the enemy and its water supply too vulnerable.

Today visitors to the *Fort Jefferson State Memorial* find a monument 6 feet square and 20 feet tall made of granite field boulders. The fort exists only in the imagination of those who travel here; none of the structure survived.

Fort Jefferson State Memorial is on CR 24 at OH 121, Fort Jefferson; (937) 547-7370; ohiohistory.org/museums-and-historic-sites/museum--historic-sites-by-name/fort-jefferson. Open daylight hours; no admission charge.

The water of Greenville Creek meanders around a bend in the stream and pushes into a lake surrounded by lily pads. It then cascades over a dam or is forced into the millrace leading to historic *Bear's Mill.*

In 1824 President James Monroe granted the site of the mill, as well as water rights, to Major George Adams. In 1849 Gabriel Bear constructed Bear's Mill. One hundred and thirty years later, Terry and Julie Clark, a local family, discovered the mill for sale while taking a leisurely drive in the country. Terry, having a fascination for anything old, immediately was drawn to the property. They decided this noble, rustic building and its adjoining property were perfect for them. After two years of renovation, the Clarks reopened Bear's Mill in 1981.

Today Bear's Mill is listed on the National Register of Historic Places and is an operating, water-powered, stone-grinding flour mill. It is owned by the Clarks and run by a nonprofit organization, the Friends of Bear's Mill.

Terry oversees the milling of cornmeal, rye, cracked-wheat, and whole-wheat cake flour. All of these are stone ground on the original 1849 French buhrstones, which have a porous and abrasive quality favored by old-world millers. The grinding process is slow and cool, which preserves the nutrients in the flour.

Julie makes wheel-thrown and hand-built pottery, both functional and decorative, which is available for purchase. The rustic specialty shop offers wholesome stone-ground flour, as well as a selection of home, gift, and gourmet items. These include organic grain products and cereals, pancake and soup mixes, gourmet coffees, preserves, and sauces. Handcrafted wood items, garden accessories, tableware, handmade jewelry, soaps, and candles are also available. Visitors are welcome to take a self-guided tour of the four-story mill.

Bear's Mill is off OH 36 at 6450 Arcanum-Bear's Mill Rd., 5 miles east of Greenville; (937) 548-5112; bearsmill.com. Open Jan and Feb, Thurs through Sun, 11 a.m. to 5 p.m. Open Mar through Dec daily, from 11 a.m. to 5 p.m. Closed holidays.

General Anthony Wayne arrived in Greenville in 1793 and built the largest fortification on the western frontier. After the signing of the Treaty of Greenville between Wayne and representatives of the Wyandot, Delaware, Miami, Shawnee, Pottawatomi, Chippewa, Ottawa, Kickapoo, Kaskasia, Piankeshaw, Eel River, and Wea nations on August 3, 1795, the area opened for settlement. At the end of the War of 1812, and with the defeat of Indian chiefs Tecumseh and The Prophet in 1813, a second treaty was signed with the Indians August 20, 1814, by William Henry Harrison, who served as Wayne's aide in 1795.

The buildings that constitute the *Garst Museum* preserve and present this region's rich history. In 1852 George Coover built the Garst House as an inn for travelers on the Dayton and Union Railroad. John Hufnagle purchased the property in 1861 as a gift to his daughter Miranda Garst. It remained in the Garst family until 1946, when it was converted into a museum. It is on the National Register of Historic Sites.

Another son of Darke County is Lowell Thomas, one of the 20th century's most notable newsmen, known for his wondrous tales of exotic lands. Built in the 1880s, the Lowell Thomas birthplace, a two-story in Gothic Victorian style, was moved from Woodington to the Garst Museum grounds and completely restored.

The museum's Coppock Wing houses its Lowell Thomas and Annie Oakley collections, including the largest known collection of Annie Oakley memorabilia. The Village Wing features items from Buffalo Bill Cody, Anna Bier paintings, as well as an old schoolroom, a post office, a print shop, a barbershop, and a doctor's office, among others.

The Garst Museum is at 205 N. Broadway, Greenville; (937) 548-5250; garstmuseum.org. Open Tues through Sat, 10 a.m. to 4 p.m.; Sun, 1 to 4 p.m.; closed Mon, Easter, Independence Day, Thanksgiving, Christmas, and New Year's Eve and the month of Jan. Admission: adults $8; senior citizens $7: children (ages 6 to 17) $1.

annieoakley

A teenager with a gun? Today that phrase provokes anxiety, but it was a different story back in 1875. That's when 15-year-old Phoebe Ann Moses, born in a log cabin near North Star, challenged champion marksman and show-man Frank Butler to a shooting match and won. Annie, as she was called, prevailed over Butler at a place called Oakley near Cincinnati, and hence the legend of Annie Oakley was born.

Annie married Frank Butler a year later, and they began touring together and eventually were featured in Buffalo Bill's Wild West Show. Annie died on November 3, 1926, and she and Frank are still together, in North Star's Brock Cemetery.

Cedar Bog Nature Preserve has seen it all since its glacial upbringing—mastodons probably fed here and all of Ohio's Native American cultures lived in the area. The bog is the largest and best example of a boreal and prairie fen complex in the state, and as such it supports many rare plants as well as excellent orchid, prairie, and woodland wildflower displays. It is the artesian flow of cool water filtered through limestone gravel that makes this place environmentally unique. Spotted turtles and swamp rattlesnakes also call the bog home.

Cedar Bog Nature Preserve is at 980 Woodburn Rd., Urbana; (937) 484-3744, (800) 860-0147; cedarbognp.org. Open year-round. Cedar Bog Boardwalk is open daily, dawn to dusk; closed during deer gun-hunting season. The Education Center is open Wed through Sun, 10 a.m. to 4 p.m. Rates: adults $5; students $4. If the Education Center is closed, visitors may leave their admission money in the little blue box at the start of the boardwalk.

In 2000 the Westcott House Foundation was established to renovate a home designed by noted architect Frank Lloyd Wright. The **Westcott House,** the only prairie-style home in Ohio designed by Lloyd Wright, was fully restored and opened as a museum and educational center in 2005. Construction on the home began in 1904 and ended four years later. Wright designed the home for the Ohio manufacturer Burton J. Westcott and his wife, Orpha. The home was converted into an apartment building in the 1940s, so the effort to return it to its original configuration took a great deal of research, effort, and millions of dollars.

The house was quite a break from the traditional architecture of the time. Wright focused on the horizontal lines of the land on the American prairie and replicated the flat, horizontal plains in the lines of this and other prairie-style designs. Rather than following the rising, skyscraping designs popular in US cities prior to World War I, Wright created these low-rising structures, which gave a feeling of security and harmony with the land. To ground the home, he created a central hearth area. Surrounding benches create an inner room of sorts and a place of comfort. Rooms blend one into another, with a feeling of openness, and were designed as multipurpose areas.

The building materials and the design of the home reflect Wright's desire to blur the lines between interior and exterior, between nature and human construction. He built the home of wood and stucco, and he created connections with the surrounding landscape via a terrace, a pool, and gardens. Some have compared the home to a Shinto temple. A bank of divided windows stretches across an entire side of the house, creating an impressive vista, reminiscent of a shoji screen, perhaps inspired by Wright's trip to Japan shortly before he designed the home. These expanses of windows and skylights flood the entry and common areas with natural light. In addition, Japanese-inspired elements include sleeping porches, many restored lanterns, and a clay-tiled roof.

The Westcott House is at 1340 E. High St., Springfield; (937) 327-9291; westcotthouse.org. Tours: May through Oct, Wed through Sat at 11 a.m., noon, and 1, 2, 3, and 4 p.m.; Sun, 1, 2, 3, and 4 p.m. From Nov through April, Wed through Fri, 11 a.m., 1 and 3 p.m.; Sat, 11 a.m., noon, 1, 2, 3, and 4 p.m.; Sun, 1, 2, 3, and 4 p.m. Admission: adults $15; senior citizens and students $12. Reservations are strongly recommended.

To get a peek at what earned the Westcotts enough money to build this great home, head over to the center of the city of Springfield to the *Heritage Center.* The center has a rare Westcott automobile on display. The center has permanent exhibits highlighting Ohio and regional history in its 13,000 square feet of permanent gallery space and uses an additional 3,000 square feet for a variety of temporary and traveling exhibits.

The Heritage Center building itself is impressive. The massive 53,000-square-foot brick and stone edifice is an imposing structure in the middle of downtown and is listed on the National Register of Historic Sites. The structure was constructed in 1890 to house city offices and a farmers' market. Along with the Heritage Center, the history society maintains an archive and library resource center for students, researchers, or those attempting to hunt down their family history.

The Heritage Center is at 117 S. Fountain Ave., Springfield; (937) 324-0657; heritagecenter.us. The museum is open Tues through Fri, 9 a.m. to 5 p.m.; Sat, 9 a.m. to 3 p.m. The Research Library and Archives are open Wed through Fri, 10 a.m. to 5 p.m.; Sat, 10 a.m. to 3 p.m. Admission: free, but donations are accepted. Recommended donations are $5 for adults, $2 for children, and $10 for families. Fee for research is $5 per person per day for adults and $2 for students.

Ready to sail away to your own private island? *Oak Island at Indian Lake* could be the place to live out that fantasy. This cottage getaway is a solitary retreat on Oak Island. You'll have to take a boat to reach your private sanctuary.

Whether you are looking for a romantic vacation, family reunion, or family getaway, you can relax at the private beach or on the cottage's covered patios. The cottage has 1.5 baths and 3 bedrooms, each with a double bed; 2 roll-away beds are also available. The kitchen comes equipped with a range, oven, refrigerator, and freezer, as well as cooking and serving utensils.

Around the area of Indian Lake you'll find restaurants, sailing, water-skiing, golf, and plenty of natural areas for walks, hikes, and exploring. At the close of summer, generally in the first week of September, the residents around the lake set off flares around the rim of the lake to create a "Ring of Fire." This is a reenactment of a Native American tradition that welcomed the coming of autumn.

Oak Island at Indian Lake is accessible only by boat from Russells Point; (614) 560-3859; indianlake.com/island.htm. Open May through Sept. Rates vary by season, day of the week, and length of stay.

The 6,000-acre Indian Lake, with its shady islands, peninsulas, and lakefront homes, attracts recreation seekers for fishing, boating, and waterskiing.

Fifteen miles southeast of Indian Lake, a private park, **Zane Shawnee Caverns and Southwind Park,** offers a fascinating cavern, camping, and accommodations. A swift underground river eroded the 11 million-year-old cavern from the limestone, leaving a labyrinth of caves and tunnels and unusual crystal formations. Water seeping through the rock and dripping down on limestone boulders has created distinctive beehive crystals and, in one case, rare cave pearls. These pure white crystal balls formed in a small pool of water around tiny pieces of rock and dust. The only other set of similar pearls in existence is in a cave in Switzerland.

Zane Shawnee Caverns, with its many "rooms," splendid colors, and clear pools of 40-degree water, was discovered by a young boy in 1892 when his dog fell in a hole and dropped down into the cavern. Early visitors entered through that same hole (which is still visible from inside the cavern); they were lowered in a basket and given a kerosene lamp. In the early 1900s, these self-guided tours cost 10 cents. The Shawnee Nation United Remnant Band of Ohio purchased the caverns in 1996.

Today it takes about 40 minutes for guides to lead a group from one end of the cavern to the other. The tour reaches a depth of 132 feet below the surface, but various tunnels and crevasses shoot off from the main cavern to even greater depths. The caverns are open year-round. Tours are $11 for adults and $5 for children.

The park's 200 acres of woods, ridges, and ravines also offer camping and lodging for overnight guests at the Southwind Campground. If you're not a tent camper, Zane Shawnee Caverns and Southwind Park has 17 RV sites with electricity and 10 RV sites with electricity and water. The campground also has 12 permanent campsites for cold-weather camping, 8 with electricity and water and 4 with electricity only. Another delightful place to rest one's head is the Eagles' Nest. Set on stilts in a heavily wooded ravine, this screened sleeping shelter contains a double bed, with a picnic table and barbecue grill adjacent. Seven more summer cabins offer accommodations, each with electricity, a table and chairs, a screened porch, and a fire ring in front. Owl's Nest has bunked double beds; Hawk's Nest has one double bed and single bunk beds. Camping and lodging are $17 to $52 per night.

Other attractions at the caverns include the Shawnee Woodland Native American Museum (admission is $7 for adults and $4 for children) and the Zane/LaBelle Trading Post 1830s Pioneer Village and Historic Shawnee Village (admission is $6 for adults and $3 for children).

Zane Shawnee Caverns is on OH 540, 5 miles east of Bellefontaine; (937) 592-9592; zaneshawneecaverns.net Reservations and a deposit are required for accommodations.

america'sfirst concretestreet

Once the site of a Native American settlement, Bellefontaine (pronounced "bell-fountain") is most famous for something we take for granted today—paved roads. It was here in 1891 that the Buckeye Cement Company laid an 8-foot strip of concrete on Main Street, America's first concrete street. The company later paved around the courthouse, and this innovation attracted engineers from across the country. A section of the street was displayed at the 1893 Chicago World's Fair, winning a gold medal. We've been pouring concrete ever since.

Winter recreation in Logan County is centered at **Mad River Mountain** ski resort, with 20 slopes and trails for skiers and snowboarders, and 10 runs for snow tubing. The 144 hilly acres of the resort are open Dec through Mar. Ski instruction and rental equipment are offered. Mad River Mountain is on US 33 at 1000 Snow Valley Rd., 5 miles east of Bellefontaine; (937) 599-1015, (800) 231-7669; skimadriver.com.

Rural Logan County might seem an unusual place for two brothers to build a pair of castles, but that is precisely what Colonel Donn Piatt and General Abram Sanders Piatt did during the mid-1800s. Members of the Piatt family came to America in the 1670s from southeastern France. Donn and Abram's grandfather, Jacob Piatt, served on George Washington's staff during the Revolutionary War. Jacob's son Benjamin, after fighting in the War of 1812, acquired 1,700 acres in the Mac-A-Cheek Valley, named after a local Shawnee settlement. It was Benjamin's sons, Donn and Abram, who built the two stone castles a mile apart in what is today Logan County.

Abram Sanders Piatt built the first of the **Piatt Castles,** Castle Piatt Mac-A-Cheek, using an architectural style that blends Gothic revival and Second

Empire. The three-story home (with five-story watchtower) has walls 2 feet thick made of locally quarried limestone, which was hand-chiseled on the site.

The castle has remained in the Piatt family since its construction, and all furnishings in the castle are family originals. The first stop on self-guided tours of Castle Piatt Mac-A-Cheek is the spacious drawing room, with its intricate oak, walnut, and cherry floors and splendid ash, pine, and walnut walls. Fine woodwork graces the entire castle, as do frescoed ceilings painted by French artist Oliver Frey in 1880. These ceilings have survived a century surprisingly well, without so much as a touch-up.

The castle's furnishings include horsehair-stuffed couches and chairs, massive carved beds, and wardrobes—some dating as far back as the Revolutionary War period—plus a collection of Native American artifacts. The family's historic firearms collection and a private chapel, complete with altar and kneeler, are upstairs.

Down the road, Donn Piatt's Flemish-style *Mac-O-Chee Castle* (a variation of the name Mac-A-Cheek) contains impressive woodwork and ornately painted walls and ceilings throughout. The castle was completed in 1881, but the Piatt family lost ownership of this three-story, twin-spired structure in the mid-1890s, when Ella Piatt, Colonel Donn Piatt's widow, sold it. It served briefly as a health spa but eventually stood empty and even was used as a barn for more than a decade. Now it's back in the Piatt family and open to visitors. It is an excellent example of a late 19th-century estate.

The Piatt Castles are on OH 245, 1 and 2 miles east of West Liberty; (937) 465-2821; piattcastles.org. Mac-A-Cheek Castle is located at 10051

america'sfirst gasolinepowered automobile

It could have happened anywhere, but it happened here, in 1891. America's first gasoline-powered automobile chugged out of John Lambert's implement store and hit the roads in Ohio City, such as they were. No doubt this caused a stir, as the strange, noisy contraption tooled along, dodging trees and potholes. Lambert reportedly ran into a hitching post on one of his early forays, and this very first car was destroyed in a fire later that same year.

Lambert continued to tinker with automobiles and held 600 patents related to the invention.

Township Road 47. Mac-O-Chee Castle is at 2319 OH 287. Both castles are open mid-Apr through mid-May on weekends from 11 a.m. to 4 p.m.; May 25 through September 2: daily from 11 a.m. to 5 p.m. In Sept and Oct on weekends from 11 a.m. to 4 p.m. Admission: adults $12 for one castle, $20 for both; senior citizens $11 for one castle and $18 for both; children (ages 5 to 15) $7 for one castle and $12 for both.

Caves and caverns are scattered across (and under) Ohio, but the largest of such caverns open to the public are at **Ohio Caverns.** With a 54-degree temperature, a visit to Ohio Caverns can be enjoyed any time of year, no matter the weather on the "outside."

Inside, you'll discover exquisite crystal-white stalactite and stalagmite formations. Unique coloring and ever-changing shapes make this cave tour a treat. Like many such caverns, the more unusual formations have been named—the "Crystal King" and "Pathway through the Palace of the Gods." The real intrigue is not the clever designations, but rather the strange and natural beauty underground. Bring your camera and enjoy.

Ohio Caverns is at 2210 East OH 245, 4 miles east of West Liberty; (937) 465-4017; ohiocaverns.com. Open daily year-round: Apr through Oct, 9 a.m. to 5 p.m.; Nov through Mar, 9 a.m. to 4 p.m. Ohio Caverns offers 2 tours—Natural Wonders Tour, available year-round, and Historic Tour, available only Apr through Oct. The Natural Wonders Tour takes about 55 minutes and costs $15 for adults and $9 for children (ages 5 through 12). The Historic Tour lasts about 45 minutes and costs $14 for adults and $8 for children (ages 5 through 12). A combination fee for both tours, with a short break in between, is $25 for adults and $15 for children (ages 5 through 12).

On the afternoon of July 6, 1901, the town of Versailles suffered a disastrous fire. The epicenter of the blaze was the old Sheffel Mill, which had stood unused for many years and now burned like tinder as a fierce west wind pushed the flames into the heart of town. Six blocks of local businesses and 38 homes were destroyed.

The **Inn at Versailles** now occupies several of the structures built after the fire of 1901. The upstairs had been the Snyder Hotel, while the kitchen once housed the Beare's Coffee Shop. The lobby was the W.C. Beare Grocery Company, the Alsace Room was a drug store, and the Lorraine and Versailles rooms were a hardware store.

The inn's modern life began in 1992, when, after sitting vacant for years, it was completely renovated in the style of a French country inn. There are 23 rooms, including a master suite with fireplace, several two-bedroom suites and rooms with kitchenettes, and a full-service restaurant. Be sure to visit the nearby Winery at Versailles for tastings, events, and winery tours.

The Inn at Versailles is at 21 W. Main St., Versailles; (937) 526-3020; innatversailles.com. Rates: $89 to $159 per night.

At 10:56:20 Eastern Daylight Time on July 20, 1969, Neil Armstrong became the first man to step onto the lunar surface. "That's one small step for a man—one giant leap for mankind," crackled Armstrong's first radio transmission from Tranquility Base, as he accomplished the goal set by John Kennedy in the early 1960s. It was less than 70 years earlier that Dayton's Wright Brothers had conquered powered flight over the sands of Kitty Hawk—from the first successful aircraft to lunar exploration in a little more than six decades.

The *Neil Armstrong Air and Space Museum* in Wapakoneta celebrates the achievements of local boy Armstrong and other Ohioans who contributed to the field of aviation.

A NASA F5D Skylancer aircraft flown by Armstrong in the early 1960s greets visitors, and from the Skylancer you simply follow the runway lights to the entrance of the futuristic exhibit building.

Sketches, models, and photographs trace the history of manned flight, from the earliest use of balloons to powered aircraft and space travel. The bright yellow, single-engine Aeronca Champion propeller plane flown by Armstrong at age 16, and his Gemini 8 space capsule, span his accomplishments as an aviator. Other exhibits include spacesuits from the Gemini and Apollo missions, a Jupiter rocket engine, and not particularly tempting packets of astronaut

grandlake st.mary's

Stretching from Lake Erie to the Ohio River in western Ohio, the construction of the Miami & Erie Canal was a major catalyst in the state's development. For the canal to succeed, it needed a reliable water source at its high point, near Celina. Some 1,700 men, paid 30 cents a day, labored for years to create Grand Lake St. Mary's, the largest man-made lake in the world when it was completed in 1845. Today, with the canal long gone, the lake is a haven for recreation.

space food. One video projection room continuously shows marvelous footage of American astronauts from various Apollo missions walking, hopping, jumping, and driving on the lunar surface.

The Neil Armstrong Air and Space Museum is at I-75 and Bellefontaine Street at 500 Apollo Dr., Wapakoneta; (419) 738-8811, (800) 860-0142; ohiohistory.org/places/armstron. Open Tues through Sat, 9:30 a.m. to 5 p.m.; Sun noon to 5 p.m.; closed holidays. Admission: adults $8; senior citizens $7; children (ages 6 to 12) $4.

One location on the Wabash River was the site of both one of the worst defeats and one of the most important victories for American troops battling the Native Americans in the 1790s. Native warriors led by Little Turtle and Blue Jacket caught General Arthur St. Clair's forces in a surprise attack on November 4, 1791, killing or wounding three-quarters of the soldiers.

But two years after St. Clair's defeat, General "Mad" Anthony Wayne picked that spot on the Wabash to construct a fort consisting of 4 blockhouses connected by log stockade walls. Each blockhouse measured 20 feet square, and Wayne's troops finished **Fort Recovery** in less than a week. When the Native Americans attacked on the morning of June 30, 1794, Wayne's forces prevailed, setting the stage for the general's final victory over the natives at Fallen Timbers on August 20, 1794, and the signing of the Treaty of Greenville in 1795.

Visitors to Fort Recovery inspect the 2 reconstructed blockhouses and view artifacts from the original fort in the two-story stone museum. These artifacts include an army-issue felling ax, bottles, a skillet handle, and bone-handled knives and forks. The museum has other items used in battle here two centuries ago, such as howitzer shells, cannon balls, grapeshot, and parts of muskets and pistols.

One exhibit explains the construction of Fort Recovery, describing how 13-foot logs with one end axed to a point were placed on end in 3-foot-deep trenches to form the stockade walls. A gap approximately every 6 feet allowed the fort's defenders to point their rifles through the wall and fire on attackers. Other displays include mannequins of an army sergeant and a Native American brave clothed in their respective 1794 battle uniforms, a collection of muskets and military swords from the 1860s, plus Native American artifacts from Mercer County such as tomahawks, leather goods, and arrowheads.

Fort Recovery State Memorial is near the intersection of OH 49 and OH 119, Fort Recovery; (419) 375-4649, (800) 283-8920; ohiohistory.org/ museums-and-historic-sites/museum--historic-sites-by-name/fort-recovery. Open daily June through Aug, noon to 5 p.m., plus weekends in May and Sept, noon to 5 p.m. Admission: adults $5; children (ages 6 to 12) $2.

Lima residents boast of having one of the best county museums in the state—the **Allen County Museum**—and it is. Two floors in a modern brick building contain hundreds of items. Its pioneer kitchen contains old-fashioned butter stamps, molds, and churns, while the pioneer bedroom has a corn-husk mattress on a primitive wooden bed. The mother of the Haller twins (Kathern and Sophie) rocked her infants on the rare double cradle bench during their first year in 1852.

The museum has collected a variety of wagons and buggies, including a covered wagon and a hearse, as well as antique cars such as a magnificent 1909 Locomobile Sports Roadster. Downstairs features a number of muskets and pistols and all manner of Native American items including arrowheads, beads, ornate Hopi dolls and masks, pottery, blankets, and a large ribbed canoe. A 19th-century doctor's office and a general store are completely stocked with items typical of the era.

One unusual item is the 1903 Kodak "mugging" camera, used by the Lima police department at the turn of the 20th century (plus sample mug shots demonstrating the policemen's photographic abilities). Other collections include rocks, fossils, and minerals found in the county, and a group of antique farm implements.

Next to the museum is the Log House, furnished with primitive pioneer possessions, and the MacDonell House, a Victorian mansion renowned for its handsome woodwork, big game trophies, and period pieces.

treatyof greenville

In the summer of 1795, fresh from his victory at the Battle of Fallen Timbers, General "Mad" Anthony Wayne returned to Fort Greenville and waited. By July, 12 tribes with more than 1,300 braves arrived to hammer out a peace treaty with the whites.

On August 3, 1795, the Treaty of Greenville was signed, opening most of Ohio to white settlement. Outgunned, the Native Americans took cash and gave up two-thirds of what is today Ohio. For the native peoples, this was yet another sad chapter in their forced migration west.

The Allen County Museum is at 620 W. Market St., Lima; (419) 222-9426; allencountymuseum.org. Open Tues through Fri, 1 to 5 p.m.; Sat and Sun, 1 to 4 p.m. Admission is $3 for the MacDonell House, children (ages 8 and under) free. Admission to the museum is $5; children (ages 8 and under) free.

History Trail

In 1890 Warren G. Harding, then 25 years old, and his fiancée planned and had built the dark-green home at 380 Mount Vernon Ave., Marion. From the *Harding Home,* he conducted his famous "front porch" campaign in 1920 and won the presidency. The Harding years in the White House were turbulent ones—his administration was rocked by scandals, including the infamous Teapot Dome incident. Harding died in San Francisco in 1923, without completing his term of office.

The eldest son of a doctor, Harding was born in Blooming Grove, Ohio, on November 2, 1865. After working as a printer's apprentice, he bought the *Marion Daily Star* at the age of 19. In 1891 he married Florence Kling DeWolfe, daughter of one of Marion's wealthiest and most prominent Republicans, on the stairway of the home they had designed. Harding's election to the Ohio Senate in 1899, as lieutenant governor of Ohio in 1903, and to the US Senate in 1914 laid the groundwork for his successful presidential campaign in 1920. He used the large front porch of his home—the porch he had expanded in 1900—to speak to the 600,000 voters who traveled to Marion in the summer of 1920 to hear the acclaimed oratory of the Republican candidate.

Inside the entryway sits the small wooden desk where Harding sat on election night reading the latest telegraphed election returns. Nearly all the furnishings and accessories in the Harding home are exactly as the Hardings left them when they went to Washington in 1921. Many of the art objects collected by the Hardings on their three trips to Europe are there, and so is the hat worn by the 29th president at his inauguration. The small building behind the Harding residence, which served as the press headquarters during the 1920 campaign, now is a museum.

The Harding Home is at 380 Mount Vernon Ave., Marion; (740) 387-9630, (800) 600-6894; hardinghome.org. Open Memorial Day to Labor Day,

Thurs through Sun, noon to 5 p.m., plus weekends in Sept and Oct, noon to 5 p.m. Admission: adults $6; children (ages 6 to 12) $3.

Not far from the Harding Home are the 10-acre grounds containing the **Harding Tomb.** Constructed in 1927 of Georgia white marble, the 52-foot-tall memorial surrounds the graves of President and Mrs. Harding (she died in 1924, a year after her husband). Labrador granite tombstones cover the graves of the Hardings, who were buried here on December 21, 1927. The careful rows of maple trees on the grounds form the shape of a Latin cross.

The Harding Tomb is at the corner of OH 423 and Vernon Heights Boulevard, Marion; (740) 387-9630; ohiohistory.org/museums-and-historic-sites/museum--historic-sites-by-name/harding-memorial Open daylight hours; no admission charge.

Richard Hendricks purchased his dream in 1963—the 10,000-foot **Indian Trail Caverns** he had first visited as a child. Once called the Wyandot Indian Caverns, this bit of underground history first opened in 1927 but closed 10 years later. Hendricks, the postmaster in nearby Vanlue, worked nights and weekends whenever the weather would permit, clearing glacial debris from the floor of the caverns, and reopened them in 1973.

porkrind, anyone?

It may not be exactly a celebration of health food, but Harrod festivities honoring pork rinds reflect the local popularity of this legendary snack. Of course, the Pork Rind Heritage Festival features this lip-smacking treat, but it also includes a hog roast and a variety of other food fare. And no pork rind fan could leave without cheering on the Pork Rind Parade or staying to enjoy the live entertainment.

The festival is held on Main Street, Harrod, in mid-June; call (419) 648-5091 or visit the website, rudolphfoods.com, for more information.

The US government constructed a saw- and gristmill for Ohio's Wyandot Indians in 1820 in gratitude for their support during the War of 1812.

The mill was on the Sandusky River, and government-appointed millers ground flour and cornmeal for the Wyandot reservation until the Indians were relocated to Kansas in 1843, putting the mill out of operation.

A second mill was built 300 feet downstream from the first in 1861 and operated until 1941. This mill had a reputation for particularly good

TOP ANNUAL EVENTS

Columbus Arts Festival,
Columbus, June;
(614) 224-2606;
columbusarts.com

Peony Festival,
Van Wert, June;
(419) 771-8323;
vanwertpeony.com

Strawberry Festival,
Troy, June;
(937) 339-7714;
gostrawberries.com

Pork Rind Heritage Festival,
Harrod, June;
rudolphfoods.com

Rose Festival,
Columbus, June;
(614) 645-3300;
parks.columbus.gov

National Threshers Annual Reunion,
Fulton County Fairgrounds,
Wauseon, June;
(269) 962-2157;
nationalthreshers.com

London Strawberry Festival,
London, June;
londonstrawberryfestival.com

Miami Valley Steam Threshers Show,
Plain City, July;
(614) 270-0007;
miamivalleysteamshow.org

Wacky Boat Race,
Russells Point, Aug;
(937) 843-5392;
indianlakechamber.org

Bucyrus Bratwurst Festival,
Bucyrus, Aug;
(419) 562-2728;
bucyrusbratwurstfestival.com

stone-ground buckwheat and cornmeal, and has since become the country's first museum of milling—***Indian Mill State Memorial.***

The museum includes a detailed explanation of the four types of mill waterwheels: the overshot, undershot, breast, and horizontal wheels. Exhibits explain the history of gristmills and sawmills and their importance to early Ohio settlements. Perhaps the most intriguing feature of the museum is the working model of a water turbine mill. This model demonstrates the complex system of "flights" that transported grain and milled meal from floor to floor in the mill—from its entry down a chute to the grinding stones on the lower level to the upper floors for sifting, separating, and sacking. Outside

All Ohio Balloon Fest,
Marysville, Aug;
(937) 243-5833;
allohioballoonfest.com org

Dublin Irish Festival,
Dublin, Aug;
dublinirishfestival.org

Ohio State Fair,
Columbus, Aug;
(888) 646-3976;
ohiostatefair.com

Miami County Fair,
Troy, Aug;
(937) 335-7492;
miamicountyohiofair.com

Darke County Fair,
Greenville, Aug;
(937) 548-5044, (800) 736-3671;
darkecountyfair.com

Reynoldsburg Tomato Festival,
Reynoldsburg, Sept;
reynoldsburgtomatofestival.org

Marion Popcorn Festival,
Marion, Sept;
popcornfestival.com

Crestline Harvest–Antique Festival,
Crestline, Sept;
(419) 683-3800;
crestlineoh.com

Harvest and Herb Festival,
Ada, Sept;
(419) 634-0936;
www2.wcoil.com/~adanet/hhf.html

Ohio Heritage Days Festival,
Lucas, Sept;
(419) 892-2784;
malabarfarm.org

Ohio Gourd Show,
Greenville, late Sept, Oct;
(937) 547-0025;
americangourdsociety.org/Ohiochapter

the mill, a 3-acre park across the river bridge is a tranquil and picturesque spot for a picnic or just relaxing.

Indian Mill State Memorial is at 7417 CR 47, off OH 67 or US 23 northeast of Upper Sandusky; (419) 294-3857, (800) 600-7147; ohiohistory.org/museums-and-historic-sites/museum--historic-sites-by-name/indian-mill. Open May through Oct, Thurs through Sun, 1 to 4:30 p.m. Admission: adults $2; children (ages 4 to 12) $1.

Humphrey Bogart and Lauren Bacall married and honeymooned on a farm near Lucas, Ohio? Unlikely as that might seem, it did happen on May 21, 1945, at *Malabar Farm,* the 914-acre farm of Pulitzer Prize–winning novelist Louis Bromfield. Bromfield was born in nearby Mansfield in 1896 and graduated from Mansfield Senior High School. Though he studied agriculture at Cornell and journalism at Columbia, this prominent author and screenplay writer never received a college degree.

After driving ambulances in World War I, Bromfield remained in Europe and published his first novel, *The Green Bay Tree,* in 1925, launching a literary career that would produce 33 books over the next 33 years, as well as a number of screenplays. Although dedicated to his writing, Bromfield never lost his interest in agriculture. In 1939, when the outbreak of World War II forced Bromfield and his family to flee France, he began searching Ohio for suitable farm acreage to practice the conservation techniques he had learned from his grandfather and French farmers. He found Malabar—or, more accurately, created Malabar (which means "beautiful valley" in a Native American dialect) by purchasing 4 adjacent farms in the lush, rolling hills of Richland County. Saving only 4 rooms of the original farmhouse, Bromfield added 28 others, including 9 bedrooms, 6 full baths, and 4 half baths, producing the airy, rambling estate where he entertained family and friends.

thecrawford incident

Ohio was the site of many conflicts between white settlers and Native Americans. One of the most gruesome was the execution of Colonel William Crawford by Delaware and Wyandot Indians. In 1782 Crawford, a friend of George Washington, led a force of 480 men bent on attacking Native American villages along the Sandusky River.

Not only did his campaign fail, but Crawford was captured and held responsible for the atrocities committed by whites at Gnadenhutten. Crawford literally was burned alive at the stake after being beaten and tortured. Today Crawford County bears his name as a reminder of this incident.

Among the many visitors to Malabar were Hollywood celebrities such as William Powell, Errol Flynn, Dorothy Lamour, and Shirley Temple—all friends of Bromfield's from his work in motion pictures. Bromfield explained his innovative "grass farming" method of agriculture to them, a system of planting grasses in critical areas to arrest soil erosion and reinvigorate the earth. Bromfield distrusted the effects on the soil of using every available acre for grain production; instead he cultivated only enough acreage to support his dairy operation.

The Bromfield home is furnished exactly as it was when the family lived here, with many of the pieces brought back from France in 1939. Bromfield also imported the bright wallpapers from France, and all the oak floors and walnut doors are original. Two Grandma Moses paintings hang in the house, and, because of Bromfield's love of the outdoors, every room on the first floor has an outside door. Bromfield had the 29-drawer desk in his study custom built, only to discover he was unhappy with the way it "felt." He actually worked at a card table behind the desk.

The family's boxer dogs were important members of the household, and the doors of the house were equipped with special latches that the dogs could open, giving them free run of Malabar. In addition to guided tours of the house, self-guided tours of the barns, chicken coop, smokehouse, and the farm's active dairy operation are also offered. Cross-country skiing is popular at the farm in the winter, with rental equipment available.

Malabar Farm is at 4050 Bromfield Rd., west of OH 603 off Pleasant Valley Road, south of Lucas; (419) 892-2784; malabarfarm.org. Tours are conducted at noon, 2, and 4 p.m. on the following days through the year: Jan thru Apr, Sat and Sun; May, Tue through Sun; Memorial Day through Labor Day, daily; Sept through Dec, Tues through Sun; closed holidays.

Tours of the house are $4 per person. Wagon tours and hayrides of the farm are conducted at 1 and 3 p.m. on weekends May through Sept and on Sun in Oct; rides are $2 per person.

Just down the road from Malabar Farm is a former stagecoach stop on the old Cleveland-Marietta line called the ***Malabar Farm Restaurant.*** David Schrack and his sons, attracted to this location because of the rapidly flowing spring (later called Niman Spring), built the inn in 1820. The inn had deteriorated badly when Louis Bromfield acquired it in the late 1930s, but he renovated the structure and used it to house the overflow of guests visiting Malabar. Bromfield also took advantage

salesday

Talk about a tradition. London has held a livestock auction the first Tuesday of every month since 1856. In all those years, only four sales have been canceled: two in 1863, one in 1865, and one in 1868. Farmers bring their herds in for the 10 a.m. sale, and then spend the day "in town." Crowds often number 2,000 to 3,000 people on Public Square for a "sales day."

of the springhouse next to the inn, using the cold water flowing through the sandstone troughs to cool the organic produce sold at his roadside market.

The Malabar Farm Restaurant serves fine country fare in the brick two-story building, which has a large deck on three sides. Dinner selections include fish and chicken dishes, pasta, as well as steak and filet mignon. For lunch, there are salads, sandwiches, homemade soups, and specialty entrees. One dining room is elegantly paneled and trimmed in white; the other features bright wallpaper. Both have a Williamsburg flair, potted plants, and plenty of windows for enjoying the tall trees around the inn. The breads and desserts at Malabar are made from scratch, and the vanilla bean panna cotta with fresh berries is particularly good.

The Malabar Farm Restaurant is at 3645 Pleasant Valley Rd., just west of OH 603, south of Lucas; (419) 938-5205; malabarfarmrestaurant.com. Open Tues through Thurs, 11 a.m. to 8 p.m.; Fri and Sat, 11 a.m. to 9 p.m.; Sun, 11 a.m. to 7 p.m.

keene'sfireproof house

Fred Sharby was afraid of fire. Two of the theaters he owned burned flat, and he had a terror of dying in a fire. So he tore down his house on the north side of Roxbury Street in Keene and built a new one, all of fireproof materials. Steel girders, stucco, plaster, and fireproof floor tiles, doors of solid metal, and a furnace enclosed in cement walls have indeed lasted to this day without a fire.

Fred wasn't so lucky. He chose the night of November 28, 1942, to go to the Cocoanut Grove in Boston and died in that fire.

The late Charles Kelley King, chairman of the board of Mansfield's Ohio Brass Company, spent $400,000 building and furnishing his palatial French provincial estate in 1926—an estate now dedicated to the study and display of gardening, horticulture, birds, and related subjects, and called *Kingwood Center.*

King joined Ohio Brass in 1893, working his way through the ranks from chief engineer to sales manager, and later from vice president and president to chairman. After his death at age 84 in 1952, his will established an endowment for the development and perpetual maintenance of Kingwood.

Two of the three floors of the mansion are open to the public. Perhaps the most impressive room is the formal dining room, with its hand-painted

French wallpaper, delicate crystal chandelier, and antique chairs and table—a room that any monarch would proudly claim. The mansion also houses an extensive library on horticulture, landscaping, and related topics.

The grounds of the estate include 12 distinct gardens, each designed and arranged by the staff. The center plants 55,000 tulips each year, with the peak blooming season for these during the first two weeks in May. The tulips are replaced with 35,000 annuals to create a summer display. The paths also take you past Kingwood's collections of trees, shrubs, and ferns, and nature trails allow you to enjoy the abundant wildflowers. A variety of ducks and ornamental birds freely roam the grounds, and 130 species of native birds have been sighted on the premises. The greenhouse and orangery feature displays of seasonal flowering plants, cacti, orchids, and tropical plants.

Kingwood Center is at 900 Park Ave. West (OH 430), in Mansfield; (419) 522-0211; kingwoodcenter.org. Grounds and greenhouse are open daily, 8 a.m. to 5 p.m., Mar through Dec. Kingwood Hall is open May through Sept, with tours every Sat at 11 a.m. and 2 p.m. Kingwood Hall admission is $1 per person, children (ages 12 and under) free.

The modern carousel emerged in the 1870s, when an English engineer-manufacturer named Frederick Savage applied steam power to these marvelous devices. Within a few years of this enhancement, Robert Tidman,

ALSO WORTH SEEING

Franklin Park Conservatory and Botanical Gardens,
Columbus

German Village,
Columbus

Short North arts and entertainment district,
Columbus

Columbus Zoo

Columbus Museum of Art

COSI, Center of Science and Industry,
Columbus

Ohio Historical Society and Ohio Village,
Columbus

Wexner Center for the Arts,
Columbus

Wyandot Lake,
Columbus

an amusement ride manufacturer from England, designed one of the first up-and-down cranking devices that gave the horses their now-familiar galloping motion. Machines could now support two and three (eventually up to five) concentric rows of elaborately carved wooden horses and various other menagerie figures, as well as the many decorative panels and trimmings that were used to give the carousel a grand appearance by hiding its mechanicals. Musical accompaniment also evolved, from the simplicity of a drum or set of bells to the rich sounds of a band organ.

Consequently, public demand for carousels reached new heights in much of Europe and America, rising steadily in the years approaching the turn of the century and then truly booming in the two decades following 1900. This demand was further driven by the increased number of amusement parks built on both continents. Wherever it was, the carousel became a central part of a magnificent social event, as crowds of people in their Sunday best would climb aboard a favorite steed or just sit and listen to the lively music while enjoying the breeze generated by the machine.

Unique carving styles emerged from each of three separate regions producing carousels. English carousel figures were the easiest to identify because their "romance" side (the side that faced out and thus received more detailed carving) was on the left, unlike most other European and all American figures, whose outer side was on the right. This difference stemmed from the clockwise direction of English carousels, which encouraged riders to mount their horse properly from the left and was a result of the fact that the ring-catching game so popular in continental Europe and America never caught on in England. Conversely, carousels in the US and the rest of Europe rotated counterclockwise to leave the right hand free to reach for the ring.

With tools in hand, gifted craftsmen gave us what has come to be known as the "golden age" of the wooden carousel in America, which extended from around 1880 to the early 1930s. During this time, carousels became evermore artistically grand and technologically advanced, with electricity replacing steam and the development of an overhead cranking mechanism, still in use today, that produced a smoother galloping motion.

Mansfield is home to the first new hand-carved wooden carousel built since the 1930s. Reminiscent of a turn-of-the-20th-century Philadelphia-style carousel, the main attraction at **_Richland Carrousel Park_** features 52 distinctive wooden animals and 2 chariots. The carousel has 30 horses and 22 menagerie figures including 4 bears, 4 ostriches, 4 cats, 4 rabbits, a goat, a giraffe, a lion, a tiger, a zebra, and a mythical hippocampus. The carousel is one the few which is wheelchair accessible. The horse in front of the chariot swivels and the chariot seat lifts up to accommodate a wheelchair.

These colorful figures were hand carved and painted in Mansfield. Guarding the entrance to the carousel are 2 large bronze horses, cast from antique molds.

Lincoln's Last Journey

Abraham Lincoln journeyed across Ohio in life and death, and some say the slain president still travels Ohio's railways. Between the time of the popular vote and the formal vote of the Electoral College in 1860, Lincoln visited Ohio. It was, we are told, in the office of Ohio governor William Dennison that Lincoln actually heard he had won the presidency. Visitors to the Ohio Statehouse can see the very desk at which the governor and President-elect Lincoln sat that day. The desk has been preserved and the current governor uses it as part of his working office. The rest of the rooms and chambers have also been restored to the style, color, and furnishings that Mr. Lincoln saw during that happy visit.

Lincoln journeyed back across Ohio on the trip that marked the close of his presidency and the end of his life. The funeral train for the slain president stopped in Columbus, and the body of Lincoln lay in state in the statehouse rotunda. The educational center in the lower level of the building documents that sad event, describing the crowds that packed the statehouse and grounds to pay their respects to the fallen leader.

The Lincoln funeral train also gave people in farming and rural regions the chance of a glimpse of their assassinated president. A special lead engine, or pilot car, steamed down the rails in advance of the funeral train. People came to the tracks to wait in sad tribute. As the train, draped in black, passed by, some could see the ornate coffin and the men on guard around it.

The image of that somber journey burned itself into the memories of the adults and children who stood in a final tribute along the rail line. But some say that moment was also somehow burned into the fabric of time. Each April 27, legend has it that Lincoln's train again rolls down the track. The muffled sound of the steam locomotive passes through the quiet Ohio countryside. Those who tell the tale of the recurring trip say that the dim light from the funeral train illuminates the ever-vigilant guards who will forever stand over the last journey of their fallen leader.

Music is provided by a Stinson organ, which helps conjure up childhood memories for many of the carousel's riders. Eighteen hand-painted scenery panels adorn the top of the carousel, depicting Mansfield past and present.

Richland Carrousel Park is at 75 N. Main St., Mansfield; (419) 522-4223; richlandcarrousel.com. Open Memorial Day through Labor Day, Mon through Thurs, 10 a.m. to 5 p.m.; Fri, 10 a.m. to 8 p.m.; Sat, 10 a.m. to 5 p.m.; and Sun, 11 a.m. to 5 p.m. Every Fri from 5 to 8 p.m. is family night, with 5 rides for $2. Open the day after Labor Day until the day before Memorial Day daily 11 a.m. to 5 p.m. and the first Friday 11 a.m. to 8 p.m.; closed on holidays. No admission charge; rides are $1.

A walk through the Bible? That's what you'll find at the ***Living Bible Museum,*** dedicated to "bringing God's word to life." The vision for this unique museum—Ohio's only wax museum—dates back to the early 1970s, when pastor Richard Diamond and his wife, Alwilda, toured a museum in Georgia that depicted the Ascension of Christ. Moved by the exhibit, the

The Lady in Gray

If you take a moment to stroll through the historic Camp Chase Confederate Cemetery in Columbus, some say the Lady in Gray may join you. A grieving young woman with her hair tied back in a bun and dressed in an 1860s-style gray traveling suit is fabled to walk among the gravestones there. Visitors to the site, which rests on what was Camp Chase Union Military Camp during the Civil War, have reported seeing this sad woman, always looking down and weeping.

Adding to the legend, flowers have been placed on the grave of the Unknown Soldier and on the grave of Benjamin Allen, a Confederate soldier in the 50th Tennessee regiment. Since the site is also home to Civil War reenactments and commemorations, the legend grows. Those participating in the reenactments and dressed in period garb or uniform have reported either being joined by the Lady in Gray, hearing an otherworldly weeping, or having their commemorations disrupted by violent gusts of wind.

So as you stroll among the tombstones, the Lady in Gray could be lingering nearby, still grieving for a loved one lost in the great Civil War. The annual Camp Chase Memorial Service for fallen Confederate Soldiers is held at the cemetery at 2900 Sullivant Ave., Columbus. This commemoration has been held at this site since 1895.

Diamonds started planning for a Bible museum. After years of work, the museum opened its doors for the first time on August 15, 1987.

The Living Bible Museum has 70 scenes and over 300 wax figures for vivid life-size re-creations of favorite Old and New Testament stories, including a wax re-creation of the Last Supper. From the Creation of Man to the Judgment of Man, these scenes are complete with narrative and special effects. The Living Bible Museum now has 4 museums—Life of Christ, Miracles of the Old Testament, Museum of Christian Martyrs, and Heart of the Reformation.

The Living Bible Museum is at 500 Tingley Ave., Mansfield; (419) 524-0139, (800) 222-0139; livingbiblemuseum.org. Open Apr through Oct, Mon through Sat, 9 a.m. to 5 p.m.; Sun, 3 to 7 p.m.; Nov through Mar, Mon through Sat, 10 a.m. to 5 p.m. Admission for each museum: adults $5.50; senior citizens $5.25; children (ages 6 to 18) $4.50; family $27; age 5 and under free. A package rate for all 4 tours is adults $20; senior citizens $19; children (ages 6 to 18) $16; and families $75.

During the Civil War, the grounds were used as a Union army training facility because of a healthy spring located near the site. In the 1880s, Mansfield donated the land to the State of Ohio for a reformatory. Work began on the **Ohio State Reformatory** in 1885.

"Mansfield's Greatest Day," proclaimed the *Richland Shield* with a banner headline on November 4, 1886. The cornerstone laid that day evolved into a magnificent chateauesque structure. Noted architect Levi T. Scofield designed the Ohio State Reformatory to resemble medieval chateaus and castles. Spiritual and uplifting architecture was intended to provide a transcendent religious experience to help reform the behavior of young male prisoners. The East Cell Block houses the world's largest freestanding steel cell block, rising six tiers. After numerous delays, the first prisoners arrived at this turn-of-the-20th-century prison in 1896, and inmates passed time there for nearly 100 years, until its closing in 1990.

The Ohio State Reformatory is listed on the National Register of Historic Places and today welcomes visitors. It also welcomes film crews. *The Shawshank Redemption* with Tim Robbins and Morgan Freeman was shot here, and so were scenes from *Air Force One* with Harrison Ford, *Tango and Cash,* and *Harry and Walter Go to New York.* Special events at the reformatory include the always popular Ghost Hunts and the Haunted Prison Experience around Halloween.

The Ohio State Reformatory is at 100 Reformatory Rd., Mansfield; (419) 522-2644; mrps.org. The facility is open May through Aug with self-guided tours daily from 11 a.m. to 4 p.m. Guided tours are offered Sat and Sun at 11 a.m. and 12:30, 2, 3, and 3:30 p.m. Admission for self-guided tours: adults $9; senior citizens $7; children (ages 6 to 17) $7. Guided tours are an additional $5 per person. Audio wands are an additional $5 per person on self-guided tours.

The popular Haunted Prison Experience takes place in late Sept through Halloween. Cost is $17.

On select Saturdays and Sundays throughout the year, the Ohio State Reformatory also offers Ghost Hunts, which are different from the Halloween Haunted Prison Experience. The hunts are informal attempts to document paranormal activity. Admission is $70 per person and includes access to the facility from 8 p.m until 5 a.m. with a late dinner of pizza and soda. Ghost Hunts are limited to ages 18 and over and are not sleepovers.

If you are hungry for a superb meal in an elegant setting, **Doc Henderson's** may be just the prescription. This upscale restaurant is located in a lovely, historic home. The former residence of a local doctor—hence the name—was built around 1884 and is on the National Register of Historic Places. An extensive remodeling project has created a bistro-style main dining room with a creative menu and a good, if not extensive, wine list. Appetizers, main dishes, and desserts range from the traditional to the exotic. There are fish and chips for the mainstream palate, but look for the specials that may feature calamari with a Thai curry mayonnaise, or try the chicken saltimbocca. Make sure to leave a little room for the special Tuxedo Cake to top off your meal. It's a delightful concoction of a layer of moist chocolate cake and moist white cake with Bavarian crème filling drenched with a chocolate ganache.

Doc Henderson's restaurant is located at 318 E. Fifth St. in Marysville; (937) 642-6661; dochendersonsrestaurant.com. Open Mon through Thurs, 11 a.m. to 9 p.m.; Fri and Sat, 11 a.m. to 10 p.m.

Between 1839 and 1861, Ohio inmates constructed the foundation and ground floor of the **Ohio Statehouse.** Built in the Greek revival style, the statehouse is situated on a 10-acre site donated by four prominent Columbus landowners. Greek revival was the architecture of choice in 19th-century America, with Greece representing one of the world's earliest democracies.

The statehouse, with its center rotunda and cupola, mimics the stature of the Greek Parthenon. The large Doric colonnades are typical of Greek revival structures.

Construction of this significant building did not happen easily; it took 7 architects more than 22 years, encompassing a cholera epidemic and an 8-year work stoppage. One of the most important architects on the project was Nathan B. Kelly. He added many flourishes to the building, though his thanks was to be fired because the commissioners overseeing the project viewed these same flourishes as both too expensive and too lavish. To Kelly's credit, it was he who realized that the design contained no heating or ventilation system, an oversight he corrected.

During the 20th century, growth in state government resulted in the building being continuously remodeled, with its magnificent high-ceilinged rooms slowly chopped up and subdivided with new walls and drop ceiling after drop ceiling. Heating and cooling systems produced a ground floor most notable for its exposed (and occasionally leaking) steam pipes and wiring.

A comprehensive restoration of the statehouse and adjoining Senate Building in the 1990s was long overdue. This massive project, which required the Ohio house and senate to meet outside the statehouse complex for two years, restored Ohio's most significant government buildings to their earlier grandeur. The Capitol Atrium, which connects the two buildings, was added as well. It was on this site in 1859 that Abraham Lincoln spoke to a small group of Ohioans about the just-completed Lincoln-Douglas debates. The ground floor today hosts a museum and visitor center, with guided tours available.

Free guided tours are offered on the hour, Mon through Fri, from 10 a.m. to 3 p.m.; Sat, noon to 3 p.m. Tours last about an hour. Self-guided tours can be taken anytime during statehouse hours. Self-guided tour brochures and tour wands are available at the Statehouse Museum Shop. Use of the prerecorded wands is free but visitors must leave an ID with the museum clerk until the wand is returned.

The Ohio Statehouse is at the corner of Broad and High Streets at 1 Capitol Sq., Columbus; (614) 752-6350, (614) 728-2695, (888) 644-6123; ohio-statehouse.org. Open Mon through Fri, 7 a.m. to 6 p.m.; Sat and Sun, 11 a.m. to 5 p.m.; closed holidays. No admission charge.

Moored in the Scioto River downtown in Ohio's capital city is a unique attraction, the **Columbus Santa Maria**. Built to commemorate the 500th anniversary of Christopher Columbus's historic voyage, this is the world's most authentic representation of Columbus's flagship. Tours of this historic vessel give one a new appreciation for the hardships endured by early mariners who spent months at sea on crafts such as these.

The *Santa Maria* was constructed from plans provided by the King of Spain in 1990. She measures 98 feet in length, and her 65-foot mainmast was

The Ohio State Fair

Perhaps the carnival rides on the midway aren't your idea of getting away from the crowds and onto the road less traveled. But visitors to the Ohio State Fair, as well as many of Ohio's county fairs, can find the simple pleasures of yesteryear if they look beyond the glare of the midway.

Visiting the animal exhibits takes you back to the time when fairs were truly a celebration of rural life. Here's an example: One of the most charming and whimsical animal competitions is found in the rabbit barn. There is something comical about a judge walking down a row of fluffy bunnies, noses wiggling, whiskers twitching, and tall rabbit ears standing up on alert. You may be amazed at just how many kinds of rabbits are shown at the fairs, from tiny dwarfs to those the size of the average dog, and some with ears that droop like those of a basset hound.

The more traditional farm animals also are a treat for all members of the family to observe. Check the daily schedule for the children's competitions. You'll be charmed by the spunk of a 3-foot-tall girl or boy showing a cow, goat, or pig that has to be twice the child's weight.

Just a trip through the barns can bring a smile to your face. The goats will greet you with grumpy bleats, and the sheep are forever being groomed and fluffed by their owners. To keep the animals clean and fresh looking, some owners will wrap them in blankets, often with a signature color and the name of the family farm. It looks, to the city dweller, as if they are uniformed and suited up for some kind of sheep football game.

The modern fair is awash with food wagons featuring fried just about anything. But if you want something that will keep you in that bygone, farm feeling, just keep walking past the wagons to the Dairy Barn. Not only can you see a huge sculpture of something (it changes every year) made out of pounds and pounds of butter, but you can get a scoop or a cone of some dairy-fresh ice cream, or a cheese sandwich that doesn't taste like it came out of a plastic wrapper.

carved from a single Douglas fir tree. Her sails cover 2,700 square feet and her rigging requires 4,000 feet of line.

The Columbus *Santa Maria* is moored just north of West Broad Street at Marconi Boulevard, Columbus; (614) 645-8760; santamaria.org. Open June through Aug, Wed through Fri, 10 a.m. to 5 p.m.; Sat and Sun, noon to 6 p.m.; Apr through May and Sept through Oct, Wed through Fri, 10 a.m. to 3 p.m.; Sat and Sun, noon to 5 p.m.; extended hours during the summer. Admission: adults $4.50; senior citizens $4; children (ages 5 through 17) $3.50.

Looking for fresh food or just a fresh shopping experience? Try the **North Market** in Columbus. In operation since 1876, the market is a celebration of food and fun. During the summer months, there is an outdoor market showcasing the best from neighboring farms, as well as entertainment and children's activities. Gourmet cooks can find the freshest eggs, poultry, meats, seafood, cheeses, vegetables, and fruits. A Touch of Earth offers a large assortment of spices and herbs. Fresh herbs are also available at North Market Spices.

If you want to add specialty baked goods to your table, or just nibble on a delicious snack while you shop, stop in at Pastaria, Omega Artisan Baking, or Curds & Whey. You can even complete your table with fresh flowers from Market Blooms or a bottle of that special wine from The Barrel & The Bottle.

International specialties are also within easy reach at the North Market. Flavors of India stocks a full line of Indian foods and spices. Firdous Express serves Mediterranean foods, including a line of fresh-baked goods. Sushi and Japanese groceries can be found at Nida's Sushi. Hubert's Polish Kitchen serves delish pierogi, cabbage rolls, kielbasa, and more from authentic Polish recipes handed down for generations. CalJohn's Flavor & Fire will light your taste buds with spicy soups, chili, jambalaya, and other peppery provisions.

The North Market is located at 59 Spruce St., Columbus; (614) 463-9664; northmarket.com. Open Mon, 9 a.m. to 5 p.m. (optional merchant day; not all businesses are open); Tues to Fri, 9 a.m. to 7 p.m.; Sat, 8 a.m. to 5 p.m.; Sun, noon to 5 p.m.

The North Market sits in the midst of two of Columbus's best entertainment areas, the Arena District (named for Nationwide Arena, home of the Columbus Blue Jackets NFL hockey team) and the Short North. These commercial areas and residential neighborhoods just north of the heart of downtown are loaded with great restaurants, bars, clubs, and other entertainment venues. Similarly, if you take High Street south of downtown, visitors find two other popular gathering areas, the Brewery District and German Village.

wherethe
tomatoisking

Tomato juice, tomato soup, tomato sauce—they all are standard fare at the annual Tomato Festival in Reynoldsburg. But you'll find some surprising and different tomato dishes, too, from fried-green tomatoes to tomato brownies.

Reynoldsburg takes special pride in the red fruit—or vegetable, depending on your point of view. You'll see the lovely red round tomato on city signs proclaiming Reynoldsburg "The Tomato Capital."

It's certain that the tomato is king during the yearly celebration as the city welcomes farmers, cooks, and tomato lovers to town to eat and compete.

The festival is generally held in the early part of September. Visit reynoldsburgtomatofestival.org for a tomato festival update.

One of the city's most storied restaurants is located in the heart of Grandview. Serving delicious cuisine for more than three decades, Spagio was opened by Chef Hubert Seifert. The name itself is a salute to the chef's delectable dishes. "Spa" refers to good health food and "gio" describes the touches from around the world. Menu favorites include Mama Seifert's Meatloaf, Spagio seafood stew, and lobster-filled ravioli.

Spagio also has a lounge with a wide array of wines and small plates for a comfortable retreat. If you want to try the food at home, Spagio also offers cooking classes throughout the year in a state-of-the-art kitchen. Fee is $75 per person. Check the website for listings. Two tantalizing classes are Dinner in Paris and Cooking with Wine and Spirits.

Spagio is located at 1295 Grandview Ave., Grandview; (614) 486-1114; spagio.com. Open Tues through Thurs, 11 a.m. to 11 p.m.; Fri and Sat, 11 a.m. to midnight; Sun, 10:30 a.m. to 10:30 p.m.

Columbus has more than its share of quirky and unusual museums. Offerings include the *Early Television Museum,* which features hundreds of pre–World War II American and British TVs, including mechanical

Kelton House

Your tours in the Columbus area may take you to the lovely Kelton House. This grand and charming mansion was built in 1852 and is a fine example of Greek revival architecture. The home and its lovely Victorian garden at 586 E. Town St. are now a favorite spot, not just for tours, but for special events such as wedding and anniversary celebrations.

The Junior League operates the mansion, but legend has it that the home still feels the touch of the Kelton family. Fernando Kelton built the home in the mid-1800s, and it remained in the family until 1975. The last of the Keltons to occupy the home was Fernando Kelton's granddaughter, Grace Bird Kelton. She was nationally known in her own right as an interior designer. She preserved the lovely old home's furnishing in the graceful style of her grandfather's era.

The legend surrounding Kelton House is that though Ms. Kelton passed from this world on Christmas Eve 1975, she just couldn't leave the care of the family manse to outsiders. Tales tell of the former owner returning to rearrange the furniture or move objects or just walk through the house to make sure that the current caretakers don't forget who is really in charge of this piece of Kelton family history.

televisions from the 1920s and 1930s. Other displays include a collection of antique picture tubes and early television studio production equipment and a 60-line flying spot TV scanner camera from the 1930s. Visitors can see themselves as they would have appeared on a 1930s mechanical television system.

The Early Television Museum is at 5396 Franklin St., Hilliard (a suburb northwest of Columbus); (614) 771-0510; earlytelevision.org. Open Sat, 10 a.m. to 6 p.m., and Sun, noon to 5 p.m. No admission charge, but donations welcome.

Another intriguing small museum is the *Motts Military Museum* in suburban Groveport, which is dedicated to preserving the memory of all who have served in the US military. Exhibits and artifacts span from the Revolutionary War to modern times, many associated with a particular soldier or group of soldiers. For example, the Civil War Union Coat on display was worn by a Major Thomas Henry at Gettysburg in 1863. And the Civil War Colt .44 revolver was donated to the museum by a relative of the soldier who carried it in 1860. Other exhibits include one of Columbus native Eddie Rickenbacker's medals, a World War II Landing Craft, and a corncob pipe owned by General Douglas MacArthur.

The Motts Military Museum is at 5075 S. Hamilton Rd., Groveport; (614) 836-1500; mottsmilitarymuseum.org. Open Tues through Sat, 9 a.m. to 5 p.m.; Sun, 1 to 5 p.m. Adults $5; senior citizens $4; students $3.

Gahanna has become part of the Columbus metropolitan area, but the city also has been able to preserve some of its historic structures and with them, a unique identity. Original log homes and Victorian-influenced homes and shops still grace this city core. One way to enjoy this history on a nice day is to take a walking tour around the ***historic district of Gahanna.*** The area was settled just after the Revolutionary War. The federal government gave away plots of land as payment to Union soldiers. John Clark formally founded the city in 1849.

You could start your tour at the ***Lily Stone Bed & Breakfast*** at 106 S. High St. This building began its life as the Stone family home and was built around the year 1900. The Stone family that settled here were descendents of Thomas Stone, one of the signers of the Declaration of Independence. The Gahanna Historical Association owns the B&B, and volunteers keep the 4-guest-room operation going. Rates are $65 per night. Call (614) 475-1976; gahannahistory.org.

Almost directly across the street is the home of the city's founder, John Clark. Just to the north of the John Clark House is one of the original log homes build in the Gahanna area. This house was originally built in 1840 and was relocated to this spot by the Historical Society in 1968.

If you head farther north on High Street, you will find the Sanctuary. This late Gothic revival–style building is on the National Register of Historic Places. Built as a Lutheran church in 1895, the impressive brick structure has become a popular place for wedding receptions. If you do not see a bride and groom posing for wedding photos there, you may see them at Creekside Park.

Walk west on Town Street toward the river and turn south or left on Mill Street. Town Street and Granville Street bound the park, where an old mill once labored. Now a waterfall graces the former millrace. This park is one of the centerpieces of an effort to preserve and rejuvenate the historic district.

Along your walk through the historic district you will find shops offering handicrafts, antiques, and other collectibles.

Roses Are for Romance

Romance off the beaten path could mean treating your special someone to—not a dozen roses—but hundreds of dozens! You can't pick them and take them home, but the two of you can share the sweet smell of romance as you stroll through the rose gardens of Whetstone Park in Columbus.

The park is home to ball fields and to wooded paths and ponds, but the highlight of the area is the impressive display of rosebushes, especially during the month of June, when the park hosts the rose festival. Rose fanciers love to walk among the varieties and see their favorite flowers. The casual gardener will appreciate the rows and rows of roses just for their broad spectrum of colors and light, inviting fragrance.

If you wander the Park of Roses on summer weekends, don't be surprised to see a wedding party using this as a floral background for their most romantic day. The park also hosts many concerts and poetry readings in the spring and summer months.

The poet Robert Burns wrote, "My love is like a red, red, rose . . ." The park can't guarantee love, but a romantic ramble through the roses could be a good beginning.

The rose festival is held in early to mid-June at Whetstone Park, 3293 N. High St., Columbus. Call (614) 645-3300 or visit the Columbus Parks and Recreation website at parks.columbus.gov for information.

If you are still hankering for a little more Gahanna history, take a little drive down Johnstown road to what the locals call the "Moosesonian." While scarcely displaying the wealth or breadth of collections of the Smithsonian, the ***Ohio State Moose Association Museum*** will be of special interest if you, or a family member, belong to the Loyal Order of Moose or the Women of the Moose. While modest, this collection of pictures, documents, and moose memorabilia is one of only two such collections in the country.

The Ohio State Moose Association Museum is at 335 W. Johnstown Rd., Gahanna; (614) 476-9103; gahannamoose.org. Open Mon through Thurs, 3:30 to 11 p.m.; Fri and Sat, noon to midnight; Sun 12:30 to 8:30 p.m. Admission: free.

The Hanby family and the work done at the ***Hanby House*** touched the lives of many Americans during the mid-1800s. This house, built in 1846, served as a stop on the Underground Railroad, helping slaves in their flight from the South to freedom. Benjamin Hanby was a minister, teacher, and an abolitionist.

Hanby also was famous as a composer. Among his works are "Darling Nellie Gray" and "Up on the Housetop." The Hanby House contains many family belongings, including the original printing plates for "Darling Nellie Gray" and the composer's flute.

Bishop William Hanby, Benjamin Hanby's father, was a United Brethren minister and cofounder of Otterbein College. Hanby House has been designated a United Methodist shrine.

The Hanby House is located at 160 W. Main St., Westerville; (614) 891-6289, (800) 600-6834; hanbyhouse.org. Open May through Sept, Sat and Sun, 1 to 4 p.m. Admission: adults $3; senior citizens $2.50; children (ages 5 to 17) $1.

Gentlemen, start your engines. That's what visitors to the **Motorcycle Hall of Fame Museum** no doubt would like to do . . . start up the many powerful and exotic bikes on display. Enshrined in the Hall of Fame are more than 200 motorcyclists who have made major contributions to the sport—from early 20th-century racing champ Ralph Hepburn to modern-day enthusiast Jay Leno. In addition to the Hall of Fame, the museum consists of 3 large exhibit areas.

One favorite exhibit is the *Heroes of Harley-Davidson,* which features many great Harley bikes. But the focus of this exhibit is the people who have built Harley-Davidson into one of the world's great commercial brands.

For example, you will see a painstaking re-creation of the famous Milwaukee backyard shed where William Harley and Arthur Davidson created their first motorcycle in 1903. And you'll learn about Bessie Stringfield, the 1940s African-American "Motorcycle Queen of Miami" who broke color and gender barriers as a competitive rider. Whether your interest is racing or cruising, any motorcycle enthusiast will be in hog heaven here.

The Motorcycle Hall of Fame Museum is at 13515 Yarmouth Dr., Pickerington; (614) 856-2222; motorcylemuseum.org. Open daily 9 a.m. to 5 p.m.; closed holidays. Admission: adults $10; senior citizens $8; children (ages 12 to 17) $3.

Places to Stay in West Central Ohio

COLUMBUS

German Village Guest House
748 Jaeger St.
(866) 587-2738
gvguesthouse.com

RUSSELLS POINT

Oak Island at Indian Lake
accessible only by boat
from Russells Point
(614) 560-3859
indianlake.com/island.htm

VERSAILLES

Inn at Versailles
21 W. Main St.
(937) 526-3020
innatversailles.com

Places to Eat in West Central Ohio

BELLVILLE

Der Dutchman Restaurant
720 OH 97
(419) 886-7070
dhgroup.com/en/bv/bv-restaurant.php

COLUMBUS

Figlio
1369 Grandview Ave.
(614) 481-8850
figliopizza.com

Rigby's Kitchen
698 High St.
(614) 461-7888
rigsbyskitchen.com

Spagio
1295 Grandview Ave.
(614) 486-1114
spagio.com

LUCAS

Malabar Farm Restaurant
3645 Pleasant Valley Rd.
(419) 938-5205
malabarfarmrestaurant.com

HELPFUL WEBSITES

Ohio Division of Travel and Tourism:
discoverohio.com

Columbus Convention and Visitors Bureau:
experiencecolumbus.com

Columbus Dispatch:
dispatch.com

Historic Plain

Surrounded by cornfields in the plains of northwest Ohio is a unique historical village—***AuGlaize Village.*** Seventeen reconstructed or restored buildings (ca. 1860 to 1920) have been gathered from the surrounding area and provide visitors with a glimpse of life a century ago in this flat farming region of the state. Self-guided tours of AuGlaize allow you to explore at your own pace.

In Dr. Cameron's office, built in 1874 in Jewell, there are old medical journals and catalogs advertising medical products such as foot and ankle braces and the "Harvard Physician's Chair" that rural doctors used for surgery, adjusting it to one of dozens of positions depending on the particular procedure to be performed. Dr. Cameron owned one of these chairs, and it is in the back room of his office.

The Chapel of Crosses Church, which the congregation of Saint John's Lutheran Church in Sherwood built in 1875, is a one-room frame structure containing an antique wooden pump organ. The Story and Clark Company of Chicago manufactured this ornately carved instrument in 1892.

NORTHWEST OHIO

The Sherry School has textbooks from the mid-1800s, including *McGuffey's Eclectic Spelling Book*, teacher Mable Carroll's attendance records from the 1882 school year, and a student's certificate of promotion from 1896. The mailboxes in the front room of the old post office from Mark Centre still have mail in them—a 1906 copy of the *Saturday Evening Post* and a postcard dated 1899 notifying a Defiance man that he owes the Farmer Mutual Fire Protection Association another 25 cents on his insurance policy.

Other restored buildings include a completely equipped 1903 dentist's office (containing some grisly-looking instruments), the Ayersville Telephone Company with its old-fashioned switchboard and telephones, a blacksmith's

BEST ATTRACTIONS

AuGlaize Village

Fort Defiance

Independence Dam State Park

Historic Sauder Village

Barn Restaurant

Toledo Museum of Art

Tony Packo's Cafe

Wildwood Preserve Metropark

Fallen Timbers State Memorial

Isaac Ludwig Mill

LaRoe's Restaurant

Fort Meigs

Schedel Arboretum and Gardens

Heineman's Winery and Crystal Cave

Perry's Cave

Mon Ami Winery

Marblehead Lighthouse

Glacial Grooves

Cedar Point

Merry-Go-Round Museum

Wagner's 1844 Inn

Captain Montague's

Edison Birthplace Museum

Old Prague Restaurant

Rutherford B. Hayes Presidential Center

Crystal Traditions of Tiffin

Firelands Museum

Historic Lyme Village

Mad River & NKP Railroad Society Museum

Seneca Caverns

shop, the Minsel Barber Shop, a sawmill, a gas station, a railroad station, an operating smokehouse, and a broom factory.

AuGlaize Village's 2 museums hold a varied collection of pioneer items. One building has an extensive assortment of antique farm implements, such as an elaborate, horse-drawn straw baler, and numerous fruit and tobacco presses.

Also in the museum is a 1936 farm tractor, a 1937 four-wheel-drive tractor, and a rare 1919 Defiance Motor Company truck. This local auto and truck manufacturer assembled vehicles for six years until the company failed in 1925. For military buffs, a separate building contains military equipment and hardware, including Civil War uniforms, cannons and mortars, and a variety of pistols and muskets (including a 1763 "Brown Bess" flintlock). Model railroad enthusiasts will enjoy the building filled with small trains.

Throughout its season, AuGlaize Village hosts special events days, such as the annual Harvest Demonstration and the Johnny Appleseed Festival. Craft experts show the old-fashioned way to dip candles and weave rugs, and demonstrate other pioneer skills.

AuGlaize Village is south of US 24 on Krouse Road, 3 miles west of Defiance at 12296 Krouse Rd.; (419) 782-7255; auglaizevillage.com. The village is open for about 7 event weekends May through Oct, 11 a.m. to 4 p.m. Check the website for list of events. Admission: adults $3; senior citizens $2; children (ages 12 to 18) $1.

A quiet residential neighborhood in nearby Defiance is the site of a former fortification that played a significant role in this region's history. The bluff at the confluence of the

fountaincity

Bryan was known as "Fountain City" because of its artesian wells. It all started in 1841 when Daniel Wyatt was digging a well next to his log cabin. He stopped digging at the end of one day; when he awoke the next morning, water was pouring out of the hole. Water would flow from just about any hole dug in the area, and this liquid abundance attracted settlers to Bryan.

But the spouting water was not completely a blessing. In the 1880s a New Yorker claimed the fountains violated a patent he held, and he demanded $10 from each well owner, a claim described locally as the "Great Swindle." And some of the fountains resulted in litigation, as neighbors were flooded out by the spewing discharge. The flow gradually subsided, with the last fountain petering out in 1971.

Maumee and Auglaize Rivers was where General "Mad" Anthony Wayne's American troops built **Fort Defiance** in 1794. Wayne launched his campaign against the Native Americans and British in the area from this fort, which consisted of 4 blockhouses and a tall stockade fence around the perimeter. It was erected in five weeks, and General Wayne, admiring the completed fortification, is reported to have said, "I defy the British, the Indians, and all the devils in hell to take it!" Upon hearing that, a fellow officer suggested, "Then call it Fort Defiance."

It was from here that Wayne's forces marched against the Native Americans, defeating them at the Battle of Fallen Timbers. Two cannons, one facing each river, are all that remain of the fort today. When you stand on that hill, however, at the junction of these great rivers, the strategic importance of this spot is readily apparent.

The Fort Defiance Memorial is at the end of Washington Avenue in Defiance. It is open daylight hours, and no admission is charged.

East of Defiance in nearby Independence is another historic site. **Independence Dam State Park** is a long, narrow green space between the swift Maumee River and a now-idle section of the old Miami and Erie Canal. This canal, which was built between the 1820s and the 1840s, connected Toledo (and Lake Erie) with Cincinnati (and the Ohio River). As part of the canal construction boom in Ohio early in the 19th century, the Miami and Erie provided cheap transportation for goods and new settlers, stimulating the economic development of the region. Nevertheless, by as early as the 1850s, the speed and flexibility of the railroad signaled the beginning of the end of the canal era.

Independence Dam was built to divert water from the river to the canal, and this section of the Miami and Erie holds water to this day. The massive wooden gates of Lock 13 at the entrance to the park are the only such gates still in existence on this canal. In sharp contrast to the boom years, today the banks are overgrown, and the former towpaths have been erased by time.

Visitors to the park can take advantage of the hiking trails, picnic areas, and primitive campsites. Fishing and boating are popular on the wide Maumee River, and the park has boat-launching ramps.

Independence Dam State Park is at 27722 OH 424, 3 miles east of Defiance; (419) 237-2593; dnr.state.oh.us/indpndam/tabid/747/Default.aspx. Open year-round; no admission charge.

Erie J. Sauder always had an interest in the history of northwest Ohio. First he collected antique woodworking tools to display for his customers at the Sauder Woodworking Company. From woodworking equipment, his collection expanded to include farm tools and household items used in this section of the state in the late 1800s. These were the humble beginnings of the *Historic Sauder Village* near Archbold. This part of the state was one of the last to be settled because of the 2,000-square-mile Black Swamp. Only after massive drainage and land reclamation in the 1850s was this unhealthy muck transformed into fertile farmland.

Historic Sauder Village is a well-organized, carefully presented living museum. The village actually consists of 3 major areas: the restored farmstead, the pioneer craft village, and the museum.

Period pieces furnish the farmhouse, which was built in 1860. Wood cooking and heating stoves, rope-spring beds, and a wooden pump organ are typical of the items found in the two-story home. Costumed guides in each room explain the history and demonstrate the utility of the furnishings and equipment—how to use a hand-crank apple peeler, for instance. The last stop on the farmhouse tour is the root cellar, where the farm family stored its fruits and vegetables during the winter months. Horses, sheep, turkeys, ducks, geese, and chickens roam the farmyard.

The craft village consists of a cluster of rustic buildings set in a circle, each housing an expert in a particular craft. Brooms are made the old-fashioned way in the broom shop and are available for purchase, while the blacksmith busily forges candleholders, ladles, gates, and railings. One of the most popular shops belongs to Mark Matthews, the village glassblower. Taking 2,000°F glass from the bottom of the furnace, Mark adds color chips to the clear glass, then blows and hand shapes the soft, hot glass into beautiful spheres and paperweights. As with the other craftspeople in the village, Mark explains each step of the process. Other craft demonstrations at Sauder include woodworking and pottery. The village also has a copper, a spinner, a weaver, a tinsmith, and a basket maker who demonstrate their crafts.

The village museum contains an impressive collection of tools, machinery, and household items used by early settlers in this region. A large number of old farm wagons, buggies, and carts are on display, as are farm craft tools, such as woodworking tools, and farm implements, including an 1886 potato digger and an 1860 cultivator. The museum's Conestoga wagon, first designed in 1755 in Conestoga Valley, Pennsylvania, once transported new-comers to the area. Countless meat grinders, butter churns, wood-burning stoves, and foot-powered sewing machines fill this vast exhibit space. A quilting demonstration also takes place there. If you need more time to see it all, spend the night at the 98-room Sauder Heritage Inn, or in the 48-site campground, and make it a two-day visit.

Historic Sauder Village is located at 22611 OH 2, northeast of Archbold; (419) 446-2541, (800) 590-9755; saudervillage.org. Open Late Apr through May, Tues through Fri, 10 a.m. to 3:30 p.m.; Sat, 10 a.m. to 5 p.m.; Sun, noon to 4 p.m.; June through Labor Day, Tues through Sat, 10 a.m. to 5 p.m.; Sun, noon to 4 p.m.; Sept and Oct, Tues through Fri, 10 a.m. to 3:30 p.m.; Sat, 10 a.m. to 5 p.m.; Sun, noon to 4 p.m. Closed November through late April. Admission: adults $15; senior citizens $13.50; children (ages 6 to 16) $8.

florida, in ohio?

The town of Florida may or may not be on the site of a Native American village named Sna-ketown. The tribe of Shawnee Chief Captain Snake did occupy a village in this part of the state from about 1786 until 1794, when confronted by the army of General "Mad" Anthony Wayne. But was it where Florida stands today? An archaeological dig in 1984 sponsored by the Ohio Humani-ties Council attempted to answer this question, with mixed results. Although the dig did uncover arrowheads, animal bones, and a 40-foot canal boat, no conclu-sive evidence of Snaketown was discovered. One thing is certain: jokes about the name Florida, especially during an Ohio winter, are guaranteed.

If you have worked up an appe-tite touring the Historic Sauder Vil-lage, stop in next door at the *Barn Restaurant.* This restaurant is housed in an actual poplar barn, which was originally built 2 miles northeast of its present location in 1861. Sauder saved the barn from being razed and had it moved in 1974. Country cooking is the order of the day here, where you can find family-style dinners of chicken, ham, and beef. Other menu items include a selection of steaks, shrimp, and perch. The menu also offers a variety of sandwiches and sal-ads. There are always two fresh soups warming in the large pots, includ-ing unusual ones such as Kneppley soup—a ham broth with dough drops. A generous salad bar is loaded with just about every type of salad imagin-able, plus a myriad of salad fixings.

The exposed rough beams of this structure, the antique farm implements mounted on the walls, and the period costumes worn by the waitresses all enhance the rustic atmosphere of the Barn Restaurant. All breads and pastries at the restaurant are made fresh daily at the Doughbox Bakery, which is next door.

The Barn Restaurant is at Sauder Village on OH 2, northeast of Archbold; (419) 445-2231, (800) 590-9755; saudervillage.org. Open year-round Mon through Sat, 11 a.m. to 8 p.m.; Sunday buffet, 11 a.m. to 2 p.m. (The Doughbox Bakery is open Mon through Fri, 7 a.m. to 5 p.m., and Sat, 7 a.m. to 3 p.m. The drive-up window opens a half hour earlier for those who can't wait.)

A walk along the trails in *Goll Woods State Nature Preserve* takes you through the best living example of the Great Black Swamp forest that covered much of this region of postglacial lake plains, located to the south and west of Lake Erie. Native American people and settlers tended to avoid this swampy area, as the old-growth forest combined with the swampy floor imbued the area with a certain eerie and foreboding atmosphere. The Great Black Swamp is one of the few remaining virgin, old-growth forests in the state, with some trees estimated to be 400 years old. This area of swamp forest and wetlands was part of the Goll family farm from the early 1800s. The state purchased the land from the family in the 1960s to preserve this rare and well-preserved piece of Ohio's natural history and the preserve was opened to the public in 1975. The pioneer-era cemetery of the Goll family remains as part of the park.

In the approximately 40-acre forest, white oaks, chinquapin oaks, burr oaks, and cottonwoods create a magnificent canopy in the warmer months, and some have trunks more than 4 feet in diameter. Ohio Department of Natural Resource officials estimated that one crusty burr oak might be 500 years old. You can also find specimens of big tooth aspen, rock elm, black gum, black maple, dogwood, ironwood, bitternut, and pignut hickory trees. Though many of these giant trees remain in this 321-acre preserve, gone are the population of wolves, beaver, bobcats, cougars, black bear, and elk that once found a home in the preserve. Along with the forest, this natural area also has swamp meadows. This forest and wetland provides a refuge for many animals, including deer, red-tailed fox, and squirrels, and many species of birds, including the red-headed woodpecker, barred owl, scarlet tanager, and the rose-breasted grosbeak. Besides being a popular haunt for birders, the preserve attracts wildflower enthusiasts who visit each spring looking for a glimpse of spotted coralroot or three-bird orchids.

The preserve also boasts a wide array of amphibians, such as salamanders, turtles, and frogs, and is a bit too well known for mosquitoes. While summer brings warmer weather and the magnificent tree canopy, it also brings swarms of mosquitoes. If you are interested in hiking and exploring the preserve, consider an early spring visit, before the mosquitoes hatch. If you come later, be warned to slather on a good coating of strong repellent.

There are roughly 3 miles of trails through the preserve. Trailheads can be found off the main parking lot. The Burr Oak trail is the most popular and is about 1 mile long.

Goll Woods State Nature Preserve is north and west of the city of Archbold; ohiodnr.com/location/dnap/goll_woods/tabid/942/Default.aspx. From Archbold, go north on OH 66 for 1.5 miles to Township Road F, go west for 3 miles to the junction with Township Road 26, then go south about 0.25 mile to the preserve parking lot located on the east side of the road. Open sunrise to sunset daily.

If you are traveling in northwest Ohio from the spring to early fall, a visit to the ***Butterfly House in Whitehouse*** could provide a colorful addition to the day's travels. More than 1,000 butterflies waft around this indoor environment to the delight of the visitor. The broad range of North and South American and Asian butterflies and moths appear like little flying jewels, with colors ranging from a striking cobalt blue to sunny yellows. Generally around 100 species play hide-and-seek with the visitors to the butterfly house.

ALSO WORTH SEEING

Toledo Zoo

Toledo Museum of Art

COSI, Center of Science and Industry,
Toledo

Maumee Bay State Park,
Oregon

The indoor greenhouse provides an enjoyable environment for people as well as these showy insects. Feeders, filled with sugar water, are a popular gathering point for the colorful insects. A variety of plants and an indoor water feature provide a relaxing setting as you try to spot as many of the species as you can.

There are special programs, presentations, and events that highlight the life cycle, migration, and other facets of butterfly life, so you might want to check the website for dates and times. One very special event takes place in September when hundreds of locally raised monarch butterflies are released into the wild to begin their fall migration to Mexico.

The Butterfly House in Whitehouse is located at 11455 Obee Rd., Whitehouse; (419) 877-2733; butterfly-house.com. Open May through Aug, Mon through Sat, 10 a.m. to 5 p.m.; Sun, noon to 5 p.m.; Sept, Thurs through Sat, 10 a.m. to 5 p.m.; Sun, noon to 5 p.m. Open weekends in Oct from noon to 5 p.m. Admission: adults $9; senior citizens $8; children (ages 4 to 11) $7.

One of the finest art museums in the US is in Toledo—the **Toledo Museum of Art.** Founded in 1901, the museum is a privately endowed nonprofit arts institution with extensive collections of glass, American and European paintings, sculpture, decorative arts, and graphic arts.

In an hour or a day, browse and discover treasures from ancient Egypt, Greece, and Rome; riches within a medieval cloister; and the splendors of a room from a French château. Marvel at great works by such masters as El Greco, Rubens, Rembrandt, Gainsborough, Turner, van Gogh, Degas, Monet, Matisse, Picasso, Remington, Hopper, and Nevelson.

The Toledo Museum of Art is at 2445 Monroe St., Toledo; (419) 255-8000, (800) 644-6862; toledomuseum.org. Open Tues through Thurs, 10 a.m. to 4 p.m.; Fri, 10 a.m. to 10 p.m.; Sat, 10 a.m. to 6 p.m.; Sun, noon to 6 p.m. No admission charge.

The first Libbey Glass factory was founded in Cambridge, Massachusetts, in 1818, a long way from Toledo. But abundant natural gas lured the factory to Toledo 70 years later, helping to make Toledo the "glass capital of the world." Long a pioneer in the development of modern glassmaking, Libbey Glass made its mark internationally in 1893, when the company constructed a house completely built of glass for the World's Columbian Exhibition in Chicago. Many of the other pieces created specifically for the exhibition are now displayed at the Toledo Museum of Art.

But it's not art that draws crowds to the **Libbey Glass Outlet;** rather it's bargains. Here you will find stemware, fountain ware, tumblers and mugs, plates and bowls, canisters and ashtrays, plus L.E. Smith handcrafted glassware, all at factory outlet prices.

The Libbey Glass Outlet is at 205 S. Erie St., Toledo; (419) 254-5000. Open Mon through Fri, 9:30 a.m. to 5:30 p.m.; Sat, 8 a.m. to 5 p.m.; Sun, 10 a.m. to 5 p.m.

Tony Packo's Hungarian hot dogs have been scarfed down by Toledoans for more than 80 years. Billing itself as the place "where man bites dog," **Tony Packo's Cafe** was made famous outside Toledo by Jamie Farr, who, as *M*A*S*H*'s Corporal Klinger, yearned for the spicy food of his favorite hometown eatery.

Farr and other celebrity visitors to Tony Packo's engage in a local tradition—signing a hot dog bun, which is then mounted and displayed for all to enjoy. In addition to hot dogs, diners find spicy pickles and peppers, steaming hand-rolled stuffed cabbage, spicy chili, Hungarian hamburgers, and homemade chicken soup with Hungarian dumplings.

Tony Packo's Cafe is at 1902 Front St., Toledo; (419) 691-6054; tony-packo.com. Open Mon through Thurs, 11 a.m. to 10 p.m.; Fri and Sat, 11 a.m. to 11 p.m.; Sun, noon to 9 p.m.

Lucas County also is the location of one of the state's most scenic parks—**Wildwood Preserve Metropark.** These 500-plus acres of lush natural beauty, with hardwood forests, ravines, meadows, and the serene Ottawa River, contain wildlife such as deer, fox, mink, muskrat, opossum, and raccoon. Owls, hawks, and pheasant nest here, and wildflowers such as bittercress, buttercups, and wild hyacinth are abundant.

The 5 primary hiking trails allow visitors to explore the high ridge and the cottonwood and sycamore trees in the river floodplain. The prairie trail leads hikers through one of the last tallgrass prairie remnants in the state, where some of the grasses reach a height of 10 feet. The newest area features a boardwalk trail, a covered bridge, and a historic one-room schoolhouse.

The elegant Manor House, a Georgian colonial brick mansion, is nestled in a clearing and surrounded by deep, cool woods. This stately former residence has 22 rooms, with tours offered Apr and May, Thurs through Fri and Sun, noon to 5 p.m.; June through Aug, Tues, Thurs, Fri, and Sun, noon to

5 p.m. The Manor House will be closed until January 5, 2014. Other facilities in the park include picnic tables, barbecue grills, shelter houses, and playground equipment.

Wildwood Preserve Metropark is at 5100 W. Central Ave. (OH 120), east of I-475 and west of downtown Toledo 43615; (419) 407-9720, (419) 407-9701, (419) 407-9700; metroparkstoledo.com/metro/parksandplaces/index.asp?page_id=513. Open daily, 7 a.m. to dark; no admission charge.

The desire to preserve and honor the traditions and memorabilia from a century and a half of service in a proud profession led to the creation of the ***Toledo Firefighters Museum.*** This museum is only open on Saturday afternoons, so plan ahead if you want to visit the 1920s-vintage firehouse, Old Station Number 18. The impetus for starting this historical center was to have a permanent home for "Neptune." Neptune is the nickname for a wooden hand pumper that was shipped to the city of Toledo via the Erie Canal. The museum also displays a range of historic firefighting equipment from equipment used by the first bucket brigades to an 1895 Ahrens Steamer, a 1929 Pirch Pumper, a 1936 Schecht ladder track, and a 1948 Buffalo Pumper. One particularly striking and romantic vehicle is the horse-drawn steamer, a shiny red, black, and brass wagon. Also red, and quite rare, is the more modern and utilitarian-looking 1969 Willey's Fire Jeep. The story of more than 150 years of Toledo firefighting also is told in timelines, newspaper stories, pictures, toys, vintage uniforms, and historic documents. The center also helps to educate children about fire emergencies. One display replicates a child's bedroom. Fire prevention bureau staff uses this area to help children role play and learn how to react if a fire were to break out.

The Toledo Firefighters Museum is at 918 W. Sylvania Ave., Toledo; (419) 478-3473; toledofiremuseum.com. Open Sat, noon to 4 p.m. Admission: free, but donations are welcomed

Part of the Toledo area Metropark system, ***Oak Openings Preserve*** encompasses nearly 4,000 acres. The preserve has been hailed by the Nature Conservancy as one of the "200 last great places on earth." Oak Openings is basically a huge beach that once bordered a lake, but a lake that has long since receded into history. As the huge glaciers moved across Ohio, they created these glacial lakes and thick sandy beaches along their shores. This thick sand now creates an unusual natural area that provides a home to many plant and animal species.

The preserve area is so large that it is a good idea to start off your explorations at the Buehner Nature Center, where you can get an overview of the history of the area through interactive displays. After learning about the formation and current importance of this region for wildlife, you can use the center's maps and information to plot your strategy for exploring the preserve. The park offers more than 50 miles of trails ranging in length from about 0.5 mile to more than 17 miles. Many trailheads are easy to access from the nature center, and their names suggest the varied habitats you can experience. Enjoy a hike on the Ridge Trail (2.5 miles), the Horseshoe Lake Trail (1.5 miles), the Sand Dunes Trail (1.7 miles), the Ferns and Lakes Trail (blue) (2.9 miles), the Lake Circuit Trail (0.6 mile), or the Evergreen Trail (1.9 miles). Some trails are designated for bikes, and there are 26 miles of horse trails too. Cross-county skiing is also permitted on all trails in the winter.

Throughout much of the preserve, it is easy to see the sandy beaches and sand dunes. There are also other types of habitats, such as wetland areas, savannahs, and prairie. Between the sand and the wetland conditions, it is difficult for large trees to take root. Settlers nicknamed the region "Oak Openings" because the soil conditions were such that trees grew far apart here so it was easy to find openings through which to drive wagons.

The preserve provides a haven for many rare and endangered species. Moths and butterflies, such as Edward's hairstreak—brown with touches of blue and orange—and the brown Persius dusky wing have been spotted here. Exotic plant species found in the dunes and oak savannah areas include the strange-looking and rain-loving earth star (fungi) as well as sand cherry bushes, prickly pear cactus, and goat's rue, which was once employed as a medicine to fight the plague. As you walk the dune, you might spot a glimpse of red as a scarlet tanager flies by. Bluebirds, indigo buntings, and whippoorwills make the preserve their home and migrating songbirds use the wetlands as a refueling stop on their annual journeys north and south. In the wetlands and prairie areas, look for spotted turtles as well as a host of interesting plant species. In late summer the yellow sneezeweed, with yellow petals surrounded a huge center, will be in bloom. Always worth the hunt for the enthusiast of the exotic are the bug-digesting sundews. The grass pink orchids and the fringed orchids are delicate additions to this landscape, but the wildflower photographer will find plenty

Bowling Green Ghost

Those attending a theater production at Bowling Green State University may, according to university legend, meet the theater department's resident ghost—Alice.

This ghost is Ohio's version of Phantom of the Opera, for Alice must, according to the superstitious, be invited to every theater performance. This must be a formal invitation issued by the stage manager, who must be alone on stage. If Alice is not consulted or not thanked after the performance, actors report that Alice is given to shows of temper, such as knocking over set pieces.

Just who Alice is—or was—also is a matter of legend. According to one of the most popular stories, Alice was a Bowling Green student and a budding actress. She was on her way to the theater to receive an honor as "Actress of the Year," but was killed in a car crash before collecting her prize. Another tale is that she actually was killed in the theater when a falling object cut short her performance as Desdemona in Shakespeare's *Othello*.

Those students and staff who have communed with Alice say she sometimes appears as a shadowy figure with long, flowing hair. She also has returned in full costume when *Othello* is being performed, perhaps to finish the performance that she began so many years ago. So, if you attend a Bowling Green State University theater production, just be warned—there is always the possibility of a very special guest appearance by the famous Alice!

of other subjects with coneflowers, asters, and a host of others dotting the somewhat soggy ground.

Oak Openings Preserve is located at 4139 Girdham Rd., Swanton; (419) 407-9747; metroparkstoledo.com/metro/parksandplaces/index.asp?page_id=510. Open daily, 7 a.m. until dark. Admission is free.

On August 20, 1794, General "Mad" Anthony Wayne's army engaged a Native American war party led by Chief Little Turtle at the battleground known as Fallen Timbers, so called because a tornado felled a grove of trees here. Today, more than two centuries after the battle, ***Fallen Timbers State Memorial*** is a peaceful reminder of that pivotal conflict—one that shaped the future of Ohio's settlement by whites from the East. Wayne's defeat of the natives here, on a bluff above the north bank of the Maumee River, led to the signing of the Treaty of Greenville in 1795, under which the Native Americans surrendered their claims to most of Ohio.

Turkey Foot Rock, a large boulder at Fallen Timbers, is the subject of native lore. According to legend, Chief Turkey Foot of the Ottawa tribe stood at this rock to rally his warriors against General Wayne's troops. The chief was later killed on this spot, and for years after the battle, Ottawa braves would come to Turkey Foot Rock and offer tobacco to the Great Spirit for their deceased leader.

Fallen Timbers State Memorial is on US 24, west of Maumee; (419) 535-3050, (800) 860-0149; ohiohistory.org/museums-and-historic-sites/museum--historic-sites-by-name/fallen-timbers. Open daylight hours; no admission charge.

A friendly rivalry between Gilead (now Grand Rapids) and Providence—just across the Maumee River—lasted for generations. The Howard family settled at the site of Grand Rapids in 1822, attracted to the location by its great natural beauty and the potential for commerce, thanks to the river.

On the other side of the Maumee, Peter Manor constructed a sawmill in 1822, and Providence took an early lead as the center of development for the area. That original sawmill was razed to make room for the Miami and Erie Canal.

In 1865 a much larger mill went up, and almost 150 years later, the **Isaac Ludwig Mill** still operates, if only for demonstration purposes. Most of the mill's equipment is more than 75 years old, and some dates back to pre–Civil War days. River water diverted to a canal falls through 2 turbines, creating a combined force of 230 horsepower.

The canal era in this part of Ohio peaked in the 1850s, and when the railroad arrived here, it arrived in Gilead, renamed Grand Rapids, shifting commerce back across the river. An 1848 fire nearly wiped out Providence, and the great cholera epidemic of 1854 took a particularly heavy toll on the town, which today consists of only the mill, a church a building that once served as a hotel for canal travelers, and a lone home.

Although the Isaac Ludwig Mill survived the fire of 1848, a blaze a century later, in 1940, destroyed the top floors of this historic structure. The mill bears the name of its second owner, who acquired it in 1865. Isaac Ludwig died in 1906 and is buried in the township cemetery at Mount Pleasant.

Carefully restored and listed on the National Register of Historic Places, Isaac Ludwig Mill today offers a glimpse of Ohio's past. The mill produced flour, meal, and livestock feed commercially until the 1940 fire, and it

TOP ANNUAL EVENTS

Maple Sugaring Festival,
Toledo, Apr;
(419) 841-1007;
toledoohio.com/events.html

International Migratory Bird Day,
Oak Harbor, May;
(419) 898-0960;
friendsofmageemarsh.org/imbdnews
.html

Historic Port Clinton Walleye Fest,
Port Clinton, May;
walleyefestival.com

Put-in-Bay Pooch Parade,
Put-in-Bay, June;
putinbay.com

Annual Founder's Day Celebration,
Put-in-Bay, June;
put-in-bay.com

Crosby Festival of the Arts,
Toledo, June;
(419) 536-5566;
toledogarden.org

Lagrange Street Polish Festival,
Toledo, July;
polishfestival.org

Oak Ridge Festival,
Attica, July and Oct;
oakridgefestival.com

Key West Days at Put-in-Bay,
Put-in-Bay, Aug;
(419) 625-5009;
shoresandislands.com

Maumee Summer Fair,
Maumee, Aug;
(419) 893-5805;
maumeesummerfair.com

**National Tractor Pulling
Championships,**
Bowling Green, Aug;
(888) 385-7855;
pulltown.com

Milan Melon Festival,
Milan, Sept, Labor Day Weekend;
milanmelonfestival.org

Hancock Heritage Days,
Finley, Sept;
(800) 424-3315;
visitfindlay.com

**Tiffin Seneca County Living History
Festival,**
Tiffin, Sept;
(419) 447-4141;
tiffinfestival.com

Johnny Appleseed Festival,
Defiance, Oct;
(419) 782-0739;
visitdefianceohio.com/pages/calendar
.html

continues to grind corn into cornmeal and wheat into flour as it has for decades. Visitors not only observe the art of water-powered milling, but also may purchase the results. Water power also drives drills and saws and demonstrations of lumber being cut. The canal boat the *Volunteer* transports visitors through a restored 1-mile stretch of the original canal, including Lock 44.

Isaac Ludwig Mill is on US 24 at OH 578, across the Maumee River from Grand Rapids; (419) 407-9741; metroparkstoledo.com/metro/parksand-places/index.asp?page_id=517. Open May through Oct, Wed through Fri, 10 a.m. to 2 p.m. (5 p.m. in the summer); weekends, noon to 5 p.m. No admission charge to the mill. Canal boat rides: adults $6; senior citizens $5; children (ages 3 to 12) $4.

After your mill tour, come across the river to charming Grand Rapids, a town that has overcome considerable adversity. Fire has destroyed nearly every building at one time or another during its century-and-a-half history, and spring flooding has done serious damage, especially the floods of 1903 and 1913. As recently as 1957, floodwaters filled downtown in a mere five minutes, sending residents scrambling to rooftops.

Serious restoration of Grand Rapids began in 1975, and what started slowly has picked up momentum, with most structures now in pristine condition. Special events throughout the year, from the spring flood watch, which attracts thousands to view the surging power of the scenic Maumee, to the October Applebutter Fest, add to the town's interest. Intriguing shops line both sides of Front Street.

LaRoe's Restaurant serves hearty food and relaxing drinks in its restaurant and tavern year-round. Housed in a building dating from the 1890s, this eye- and appetite-pleasing establishment is a local favorite. Tiffany lamps, hanging plants, bentwood chairs, and exposed brick walls create a nostalgic atmosphere. The works of artist Bill Kuhlman, who grew up here and now lives in Whitehouse, Ohio, adorn the walls of the restaurant and tavern. Kuhlman uses oil, pencil, chalk, and watercolor to produce his renderings of past and current residents of the area. And in a town so dominated by a river and its many floods, we suppose it's not surprising to find that the tavern features water-level indicators from some of the floods that have filled the place—water was 4 feet deep in here in 1959 and up to 2 feet in 1982. Even the abrupt entrance of a Chevrolet Astro van inside the tavern in 2010 couldn't stop LaRoe's. With the addition of the Riverside Patio in 2009, LaRoe's Restaurant is thriving. Owner David LaRoe presents casual dining and straightforward recipes at his eatery. A wide selection of soups, sandwiches, and salads awaits hungry explorers, as do dinners ranging from country ribs and steaks to fettuccine Alfredo and blackened redfish.

LaRoe's is at 24138 Front St., Grand Rapids; laroesrestaurant.com; (419) 832-3082. Open for lunch and dinner 7 days a week, plus Sunday brunch.

Standing in the Grand Battery of **Fort Meigs,** with its 3 twelve-pounder cannons aimed across the Maumee River, you can almost hear the blast of cannon fire and feel the rain of falling earth and timber from shells exploding nearby. The fort was under siege for nine days and nights in May 1813, but the American forces in the fort held off the British attack and repelled them again when the British launched a second invasion three months later.

Ohio's role in the War of 1812 is not given much space in the history books, but the American forces, commanded by General William Henry Harrison, twice turned back British offensives at the fort that Harrison named for Ohio's governor at the time, Return Jonathan Meigs. Harrison's forces constructed the fort in early February 1813, and this fortification became the base for 3,000 troops. On April 28, British forces began to construct a camp and gun batteries opposite Fort Meigs; 4 batteries across the river and 2 east of the fort. The British siege began May 1, 1813, and lasted until May 9.

The entire Fort Meigs fortification has been carefully reconstructed, including the 7 blockhouses and the 2,000-yard stockade wall. A flat-topped mound of earth built against the inside of the wall forms a banquette (or firing step), where the soldiers stood to fire musket rounds at the invaders attacking the 10-acre fort. Some of the blockhouses contain museums describing the history of the battles here, while others contain twelve-pounder cannons as they did in May 1813. Signs aid visitors taking a self-guided tour of the fort by explaining the significance of various locations inside the stockade. On weekends, costumed soldiers set up camp at Fort Meigs, further enhancing the sensation that one has stepped back in time to the early 19th century. Just outside the stockade walls are picnic tables and barbecue grills.

Fort Meigs is at 29100 W. River Rd., on OH 65 west of the intersection with OH 25, in Perrysburg; (419) 874-4121, (800) 283-8916; fortmeigs.org. Open Apr through Oct, Wed through Sat, 9:30 a.m. to 5 p.m.; Sun, noon to 5 p.m. The visitor center and museum are open year-round with those same hours. Admission: adults $8; senior citizens $7; children $4; children (under age 5) free.

blanchardriver inspiration

"Down by the Old Mill Stream," Tell Taylor's famous song, was inspired by the Blanchard River. Taylor was born in nearby Vanlue and grew up in Findlay.

He moved to New York City in 1897, opening one of Tin Pan Alley's first music publishing houses. During a visit home in 1908, Taylor spent some time along the Blanchard at the Misamore mill. It was this visit that inspired the song, published in 1910.

Taylor returned to Findlay for good in 1922 and is buried along the river he made famous.

You can step back into the early 1800s as you visit the *Wolcott House Museum Complex.* James Wolcott and his wife, Mary, a Miami Indian, boarded a dugout canoe and followed the Maumee River down to the foot of the rapids at Maumee City. This part of Ohio was becoming an important shipping point and offered entrepreneurs like Wolcott an opportunity to build a business. Wolcott built warehouses and steamships to transport merchandise during an era of bustling lake and canal trade.

James and Mary also purchased 300 acres of land to build their impressive home, which is a blend of classic and federal architecture. As you stroll through the museum complex, you can visit this home and also a 1840s saltbox-style farmhouse, a log home, a country church, a Greek revival–style home from the mid-1800s, and a railroad depot complete with caboose and boxcar.

If you have a chance to call ahead, ask about special events. Throughout the year the complex plans craft classes for children and festivals to tempt all members of the family out on the lawns for some old-fashioned fun.

The Wolcott House Museum Complex is at 1035 River Rd., Maumee; (419) 893-9602; wolcotthouse.org. Open Apr through Dec, Thurs through Sun; guided tours at 12:30 and 2:30 p.m. Admission: adults $6; senior citizens $5; students $2.50.

As you are driving around Wood County, you just might pass part of the *Snook's Dream Cars Automobile Museum* out on the open road. Bill Snook and his son Jeff are the curators of the museum and since they keep all the "exhibits" in working condition, they just can't help occasionally taking one of the vintage cars for a spin.

This is a living museum where vintage cars are not only displayed but also repaired. The Snooks have re-created a 1940s-era Texaco station, complete with service bays and a variety of the pieces and parts you would have seen on display in a pre-war filling station. There is also an interesting collection of promotional items that would have delighted customers asking for a fill-up some 70 years ago. A collection of coin-operated games will please the children (and the adult children as well).

The cars in the collection cover the 1930s to the 1960s. You will see coupes, convertibles, sedans, roadsters and race cars. American carmakers from the past and present are represented, such as Cadillac, Ford, Chevrolet, Buick, Pontiac, Packard, Kaiser, as well as some foreign dream cars, among them models from Jaguar, Triumph, MG, and Lotus.

Snook's Dream Cars Automobile Museum is at 13920 County Home Rd., Bowling Green; (419) 353-8338; snooksdreamcars.com. Open Mon through Fri, 9 a.m. to 4 p.m.; Sat and Sun, "by appointment or by chance." Admission: adults $6; senior citizens $5; children $4.

Island Adventure

Gardens, especially traditional Japanese gardens, are havens for contemplation and peace. The **Schedel Arboretum and Gardens** welcomes guests into such a quiet place. An extensive 17-acre arboretum surrounds a gracious home that was formerly the residence of Joseph and Marie Schedel.

The home, built in 1882, and the gardens were the beneficiary of the Schedels' loving attention and now serve as their living memorial. They created a foundation to support the home and grounds after their deaths in the 1980s. The home features many unusual items purchased by the couple on their world travels. These include Japanese silk embroideries, Persian rugs, and a Hereke silk prayer rug, as well as carved antique jade and bronze pieces that are more than 3,000 years old.

The grounds are home to a wide variety of native and exotic plant life. The Japanese garden tends to draw the visitor's attention to its stone lanterns, bridges, and a stupa—a stone memorial tower shaped like a pagoda. The landscaped grounds also host 16 species of pine trees, including the bristlecone pine, which is believed to be the oldest living tree species on earth.

Waterfalls, pools, and 2 lakes add the relaxing sounds of water to the landscape. They also provide a home for fish, ducks, blue herons, and white egrets. The gardens also host an annual outdoor sculpture exhibit featuring the work of nationally prominent sculptors.

The Schedel Arboretum and Gardens is located at 19255 W. Portage River South Rd., Elmore; (419) 862-3182; schedel-gardens.org. Open May through Oct, Tues through Sat, 10 a.m. to 4 p.m.; Sun, noon to 4 p.m. (Must enter by 3 p.m.) Admission: adults $10; senior citizens $9; children (ages 6 to 12) $6.

The *Magee Marsh Wildlife Area,* adjoining Crane Creek State Park, is a 2,000-acre wildlife area. This wetland is both home to a wide variety of birds and animals, and a resting and feeding place for migratory water-fowl, making it a particular favorite with birders. Bring binoculars and look for warblers and waterfowl, and maybe one of Ohio's small but growing number of bald eagles. More than 300 bird species have been sighted at the marsh, and 143 species are known to nest there. Turtles, frogs, and toads are also residents of the marsh, along with muskrats, mink, raccoons, rabbits, and white-tailed deer.

Visitors can enjoy 3 walking trails, each about a mile long. You can also take a drive down the road to the beach to get a flavor of the marsh environment. The Crane Creek State Park beach is open for swimming and picnicking in the summer months.

The Magee Marsh Wildlife Area is at 13229 West OH 2, Oak Har-bor; (419) 898-0960; dnr.state.oh.us/Home/wild_resourcessubhomepage/ WildlifeAreaMaps/NorthwestOhioWildlifeAreaMaps/MageeMarshWildlifeArea/ tabid/19778/Default.aspx. Open dawn to dusk. The Sportsmen's Migratory Bird Center is open year-round, Mon through Fri, 8 a.m. to 5 p.m. Open from 11 a.m. to 5 p.m. on weekends in the summer.

A half dozen islands are sprinkled in Lake Erie just north of Catawba and Marblehead peninsulas. Easily accessible by air or ferry, Put-in-Bay is the center of activity on South Bass Island. A large protected harbor attracts boaters, who often dock their vessels overnight.

This safe harbor also attracted Commodore Oliver Hazard Perry in 1813. His fleet lay at anchor here before defeating the British fleet commanded by Captain Robert H. Barclay in the Battle of Lake Erie on September 10, 1813. To commemorate Perry's triumph and pay tribute to the subsequent decades of peaceful relations between the US and Canada along their lengthy, unfortified border, a monument was constructed at Put-in-Bay. This 352-foot-tall column, built of pink granite from Milford, Massachusetts, has a 45-foot-diameter base. It was built between 1912 and 1915 and is the world's largest Doric column. The *Perry Victory and International Peace Memorial's* observation deck is open to the public daily from late Apr to late Oct. Admission to the memorial is $3 for adults (ages 16 and up). All special events and admission to the visitor center are free. Check the website for more information, nps.gov/pevi/index.htm.

First-class nautical memorabilia abound at Robert Stone's and William Timmerman's *Cargo Net.* You can find (and purchase) everything from authentic ships' wheels and massive brass bells to pottery and nautical art in this fabulous shop, which does its own antique nautical-item restoration. Many antique pieces are available—a World War II navy submarine periscope mounted on a custom mahogany base at $19,500 during our last visit. Also displayed was a spectacular 1870s telescope ($6,200), and a 135-pound ship's bell ($950), plus 2 magnificent original English pub bars. For those who hear the call of the sea, a visit to the Cargo Net is a must.

The Cargo Net is at 1961 Langram Rd., Put-in-Bay; (419) 285-4231; the-cargonet.com. Open noon to 5 p.m. daily from Memorial Day to mid-Sept.

After a walking tour of the town of Put-in-Bay, it's time to explore other points on this small, wooded island. Bicycles and golf carts are two of the most enjoyable ways to survey South Bass, and rentals are available. Trams, buses, and taxis also transport visitors around the island.

About halfway across the island from Put-in-Bay (10 minutes by bicycle) on Catawba Road is *Heineman's Winery and Crystal Cave.* Heineman's offers tours of both a unique geode cave and its winery and sells wine by the glass, bottle, or case. The cave, 40 feet beneath the surface, is actually an unusually large geode. Geodes (stones with a cavity lined with crystal) are relatively common in nature, but they are normally no larger than a baseball or softball. The Crystal Cave geode is large enough to hold 30 people. It was created under pressure over 4.5 million years. The cave remains a cool 52 degrees year round, and guides explain the history and geology of this unique formation.

After the cave tour, join another guide for a tour of the winery. Heineman's grows approximately 50 percent of the grapes they need, purchasing the rest from other island vineyards. From 12 kinds of grapes, Heineman's produces almost 20 wines, plus fresh grape juice, with an output of 30,000 gallons of wine and juice annually. The Lake Erie islands are ideally suited for vineyards because of the soil's high limestone content and a relatively late frost, thanks to the warming influence of Lake Erie.

On the winery tour, visitors can see large presses that squeeze 180 gallons of juice from each ton of grapes. The grapes ferment in oak barrels, some holding as much as 1,680 gallons, or in stainless-steel tanks. Other stops on the winery tour include the bottling, labeling, and packing areas.

After your tour, enjoy a glass of Heineman's wine in the wine garden, which has picnic tables and nicely kept gardens. Cheese plates are also served.

Heineman's Winery and Crystal Cave tours are given from May through Sept, 11 a.m. to 5 p.m. daily. The winery is open daily from mid-Apr to late Oct, 11 a.m. to 7 p.m.; Sun, noon to 7 p.m. The winery and cave are at 978 Catawba Ave., Put-in-Bay; (419) 285-2811; heinemanswinery.com. Admission for the combined tour is $7 for adults and $3 for children (ages 6 to 11), and it includes a complimentary glass of wine or grape juice.

Across the street from Heineman's is another cave—a much larger one—known as **Perry's Cave.** Commodore Oliver Hazard Perry is credited with the discovery of this limestone cavern, which measures 208 feet by 165 feet and is 52 feet below the surface. Perry used water from the cave to fill the water kegs for his ships prior to the Battle of Lake Erie in 1813.

Along the north wall of the cave is a large lake of crystal-clear water, which rises and falls with the level of Lake Erie. The luxurious Victory Hotel, once the largest hotel in the world, pumped water from this lake for its drinking water. The hotel burned down in 1919, and its ruins are on the south side of the island on the grounds of South Bass Island State Park. Also on the park's grounds are gemstone mining areas where you can sift for semiprecious gemstones, an antique car museum, butterfly house, human maze race, 25-foot-tall climbing wall, and a miniature golf course.

Perry's Cave is open weekends in spring and fall, daily during summer months, 10:30 a.m. to 6 p.m. The cave is located near Put-in-Bay; (419) 285-2405; perryscave.com. Admission for 3 of the attractions is $19 for adults and $11 for children (ages 6 to 12). A super combo packet for all 5 attractions is $26 for adults and $18 for children (ages 6 to 12).

The Lake Erie islands bustle with modern-day visitors during the summer season, but the ***Stonehenge Estate Tour*** on South Bass Island allows you a quiet retreat to life on the island more than 100 years ago.

The estate is an example of the type of family farm and winery that was common on the island in the late 1800s. Both the historic stone farmhouse and the winepress cottage are on the National Register of Historic Places. Antiques, photographs, and island memorabilia in the house and the cottage help you catch the spirit of turn-of-the-20th-century island life.

The estate covers 7 acres. Visitors tour the landscaped grounds, as well as search for souvenirs in the gift shop. A self-guided audio tour also is available.

Stonehenge Estate Tour is located on South Bass Island, 808 Langram Rd., Put-in-Bay; (419) 285-6134; stonehenge-put-in-bay.com. Open daily during the summer, 11 a.m. to 5 p.m. Admission: adults (ages 16 and up) $7; children (ages 6 to 15) $4.

English Pines Bed and Breakfast provides quality overnight lodging for visitors not ready to ferry back to the mainland. This home, within walking distance of "downtown," dates from the island's early settlement in the mid-1800s and features ornate flourishes. The inn's 12 guest rooms each can accommodate up to four people and have private baths. A continental breakfast is included.

English Pines Bed and Breakfast is at 182 Concord Ave., Put-in-Bay; (419) 285-2521; englishpines.com. Rates: $85 to $200 per night.

Traveling to South Bass Island is relatively easy most of the year, with Miller Boat Line, providing ferry service from the Catawba peninsula to the south end of the island; (800) 500-2421; millerferry.com. The company ferries both autos and passengers, though reservations are sometimes required for automobiles. Ferry service to the island is available only from March through November, because the island is iced-in during winter months.

The fastest boats from Port Clinton to downtown Put-in-Bay are Jet Express's hydrojet catamarans, which make the trip in 22 minutes. These 3,500-horsepower, super-modern vessels run circles around the older ferry boats as they zip you to and from South Bass Island. For more information call Jet Express at (800) 245-1538; jet-express.com.

Are you dreaming of a walk along a beach, away from cars and the bustle of life? Rather than hop a plane to the Caribbean you can hop on a ferry and spend some relaxing days at **St. Hazards on the Beach** on Middle Bass Island. The resort has villas, cabins, and campsites. Cabins sleep up to four people, and the villas can sleep up to six. Both have refrigerators and microwaves; the villas have a full kitchen. You will have to bring your own towels and linens. For water enthusiasts there is a heated pool and Jacuzzi, along with 200 feet of private beach. The complex also features an on-site store, restaurant, and bike rentals. Call in advance for reservations and ferry information.

St. Hazards is at 1223 Fox Rd., Middle Bass; (800) 837-5211; sthazards .com. Campground rates: $45 to $75 per night; lodging rates: $85 to $200.

The Lake Erie islands and nearby coastal towns were once the center of champagne production in the US, and that tradition continues at the historic **Mon Ami Winery,** which also houses a pleasant restaurant. This winery has been in continuous operation since 1870, producing champagne by the old-fashioned "method *champenoise*," the French technique of fermenting in the bottle.

Constructed of native stone and walnut, the restaurant and winery are surrounded by tall trees and lovely gardens. Old aging barrels are stacked behind the building and are available for sale. Natural woods, exposed stone, classy murals, and intimate spaces dominate the main dining room.

The dinner menu at Mon Ami has presented delights such as slow-roasted garlic prime rib, poultry, veal, and fresh pastas. For seafood lovers, a half dozen entrees have been offered, including scampi a la pesto; swordfish, salmon, and halibut with black bean sauce; and fresh Lake Erie walleye and perch. After your dinner, the dessert cart will tempt you with sweets, such as cheesecake topped with chocolate, Amaretto pie, and fresh fruit, to name a few. For lunch at Mon Ami, your choices include homemade soups, fresh salads, a number of sandwiches, and entrees, such as salmon patties, seafood pasta, and chicken Parmesan.

Mon Ami offers a complete selection of wines and champagnes, made from Lake Erie island grapes, and a large wine store sells bottles and cases of these wines, as well as the popular champagne–celery seed salad dressing. Tours of the winery are given daily at 2 and 4 p.m. (times may change, so call ahead).

Mon Ami Restaurant and Winery is on Catawba Island (which used to be an island but is now a peninsula) at 3845 E. Wine Cellar Rd., just off OH

53, east of Port Clinton; (419) 797-4445; monamiwinery.com. Open Mon through Sat, 11:30 a.m. to 10 p.m.; Sun, 11:30 a.m. to 8 p.m.

The *Five Bells Inn* is an interesting Dutch colonial structure built in 1907. Located on 2.5 acres, this bed-and-breakfast offers a grassy lawn that leads down to the beach on Lake Erie. From the back porch guests have a good view of the lake—and you can enjoy that view while soaking in the inn's hot tub. The inn does have beach access as well as porches and decks for relaxing in the great outdoors.

Rooms are decorated in light and airy colors—giving the guest that summer cottage feeling. Each of the rooms has a private bath. Rooms 4 and 7 have a whirlpool tub (but no shower). Rooms 1 through 5 are in the main house. Rooms 6 through 8 are in a cottage behind the main house. Breakfast is included with the inn rooms.

Besides the inn rooms, there is also a two-bedroom cottage for rent during the off-season. Breakfast is not included with the cottage rental, but it is equipped with a full kitchen, linens, and tableware. Guests in the cottage also have access to the hot tub and the beach. The cottage rents for $200 per night.

The Five Bells Inn is located at 2766 Sand Rd., Port Clinton; (888) 734-1555; 5bellsinn.com. Rates: May 15 through September 30 on weekends, $139 to $200 per night; the rest of the year, $119 to $200.

The *Scenic Rock Ledge Inn and Cabins* offers two options for the vacationer: You can stay in one of the freestanding cabins or enjoy a bed-and-breakfast experience while staying at the historic inn. The inn was built around 1900 and has lovely views of the lake. Guests in the 5 rooms and 1 suite have private baths and queen-size beds and are treated to breakfast in the morning. The suite also has a whirlpool tub, a lake view, and a fireplace.

The cabins afford a different experience. Some have lake views, and all have fully equipped kitchens, including a microwave, coffeemaker, and tableware. For that outdoor cooking experience, cabin guests also have outdoor grills and picnic tables. The cabins are more rustic than the romantic inn rooms. Cabins, like inn rooms, do have air-conditioning, and they vary in size and floor plans. Some cabins have one bedroom; others have two. All can sleep four people (but some on a sleeper sofa). Two bathrooms are also available in some units.

Scenic Rock Ledge Inn and Cabins is located at 2772 E. Sand Rd., Port Clinton; (419) 734-3265, (877) 994-7625; scenicrockledgeinn.com. Rates start at $115 per night, double occupancy. Check the website for cabin rentals. During the summer months, there may be minimum stays for some accommodations.

Not far away is one of the most popular public beaches on Lake Erie—the lengthy stretch of sand at *East Harbor State Park.* Lifeguards watch swimmers during summer months, and there are snack bars and bathhouses (with showers).

In addition to the lakefront beach, the park contains 800 acres of water in 3 protected harbors. Middle Harbor, with its restriction on motorboats, offers an ideal environment for the thousands of resident and migratory waterfowl attracted to the lush acreage, making bird-watching a favorite pastime. East Harbor State Park is the home of many black-crowned night herons, and a large great blue heron nesting ground is nearby.

Boat launching ramps are in the park, and a park naturalist conducts nature programs during the summer. Winter sports at East Harbor include ice fishing, iceboating, skating, sledding, and snowmobiling.

East Harbor State Park is at 1169 N. Buck Rd. off OH 269, near the junction of OH 269 and OH 163, Marblehead; (419) 734-4424; dnr.state.oh.us/parks/eastharbor/tabid/733/Default.aspx.

Standing guard at what is known as the "roughest point in Lake Erie," the *Marblehead Lighthouse* is the oldest continuously operating light-house on the Great Lakes. The shallow water in this part of the lake, along with 200 miles of open water between Buffalo and Marblehead, allows howling northeasters to generate waves 10 to 15 feet tall.

The crash of those waves against the rocks around the lighthouse often shoots spray all the way up to the beacon 67 feet above the water. The Marblehead Lighthouse, built of native limestone in 1821, originally used candles for its light. The candles were replaced by oil-burning lamps, which in turn were replaced by an electric light and a 300-millimeter glass lens, which make the beacon visible for 7 miles.

Although rough water often bashes this peninsula in the spring and fall, peaceful days prevail in the summer. Picnic tables near the lighthouse make this an excellent place to stop and relax as you explore the Lake Erie shoreline. The Keepers House contains displays relating to the lighthouse and the peninsula's history, plus a small gift shop.

The Marblehead Lighthouse is off OH 163 in Marblehead. Open for tours weekdays, 1 to 5 p.m.; no admission charge. Tours are offered in the afternoon during the summer at a charge of $2 per person.

One man's love of model trains multiplied by more than 40 years' work has produced the ***Train-O-Rama.*** Max Timmons took up model railroading in 1952, and his family carried on his dream of creating a model-train world that would exhilarate model train enthusiasts and charm everyone.

The miniature world created at Train-O-Rama is alive with two dozen operating model trains and some remarkable landscape features—12,000 pieces of train equipment in all. The display features O, O-27 gauges, S-gauge, and HO gauge. Within a few feet you can pass by a whole range of mountains, see rivers and waterfalls, drop by a drive-in movie theater, and go to the circus. The display has more than 1,000 lightbulbs flickering on miniature street lamps or in windows. Along with the trains there are many moving pieces that help the scenes come alive, whether it is a farm field, a ski lodge, or the airport.

Judging from the visitor map that the Train-O-Rama keeps, people from around the world share Max's fascination for model trains. Guests from all 50 states and 74 foreign countries have all documented their visit to the tiny world of Train-O-Rama.

Visitors can begin or add to their own train sets at the gift shop. Model trains, train supplies, and train-related gift items are for sale.

Train-O-Rama is located at 6732 E. Harbor Rd. (OH 163), Marblehead; (419) 734-5856; trainorama.net. Open Mon through Sat, 11 a.m. to 5 p.m.; Sun, 1 to 5 p.m. Extended summer hours: Mon through Sat, 10 a.m. to 5 p.m.; Sun, 1 to 5 p.m. Admission: adults $8; senior citizens $7; children (ages 4 to 11) $6

Four miles north of Marblehead and 9 miles northwest of Sandusky is ***Kelleys Island.*** It was originally called Cunningham Island, named for the island's first white inhabitant, who lived here from 1800 to 1812. But Native Americans visited the island sometime between AD 1200 and 1600 and created the inscriptions (or pictographs) pecked into the 32-by-21-foot flat-topped slab of limestone known as ***Inscription Rock.*** The rock rests on the water's edge on the south side of the island, and its pictographs have nearly been erased by erosion. Fortunately, a visitor here in 1850, US Army Captain Seth Eastman, made a permanent record of the inscriptions. He carefully measured and drew in detail the pictographs, and from his drawings, reliefs have been made of the inscriptions. These reliefs, including the one exhibited at Inscription Rock, clearly reveal at least eight human figures wearing headdresses etched in the rock, plus bird and animal figures.

Inscription Rock is near the intersection of Water Street and Addison Road on the south side of Kelleys Island; (419) 797-4530; ohiohistory.org/museums-and-historic-sites/museum--historic-sites-by-name/inscription-rock. Open daylight hours; no admission charge.

The quarries on 2,800-acre Kelleys Island once supplied 500 one thousand-ton boatloads of limestone annually, and vineyards, wineries, and fruit and vegetable farms flourished. At the turn of the 20th century, the island had a year-round population of 1,700. Today the quarries have closed and farming activity has declined, but the island, with a year-round population of approximately 300, offers restaurants, lodging, bicycle and boat rentals, and tram tours to visitors.

The site of the ***Glacial Grooves*** is on the north side of Kelleys Island. A glacier moving down from Labrador, Canada, scoured these grooves into the limestone bedrock. The grooved limestone is a trough 400 feet long, 25 to 35 feet wide, and 10 to 15 feet deep, and it's one of the most accessible examples of such grooves in the world.

These grooves were formed at a time when this part of the earth was much colder and wetter than today. Snow and ice would not completely melt during the short summers 30,000 years ago, so an ever-deeper mass of frozen snow accumulated. As the weight of this mass increased, the glacier crept southward at the rate of an inch or two per day, taking 5,000 years to arrive at the site of the Glacial Grooves. The pressure of that mass, which was up to a mile deep, carved the grooves still visible in the island's limestone. Even more spectacular grooves once existed in this area, but they were destroyed by a nearby quarrying operation.

The Glacial Grooves are at the north end of Division Street, Kelleys Island; (419) 797-4530; ohiohistory.org/museums-and-historic-sites/museum--historic-sites-by-name/glacial-grooves. Open daylight hours; no admission charge.

Just across the road from the Glacial Grooves is Kelleys Island State Park. The park offers campsites (rented on a first-come, first-served basis), a sandy swimming beach, and boat ramps; (419) 746-2546; dnr.state.oh.us/parks/parks/lakeerie/kelleys/tabid/18980/default.aspx.

The *Kelleys Island Ferry Boat Line* provides daily ferry service between Kelleys Island and Marblehead from Apr through Dec; (419) 798-9763, (888) 225-4325; kelleyislandferry.com. The Griffing Flying Service provides air transport to the island from the Griffing-Sandusky Airport; (419) 626-5161; griffingflyingservice.com.

If you aren't ready to take the last ferry back to the mainland, stay over-night on Kelleys at the *Eagle's Nest Bed & Breakfast.* Three rooms are available in the guest house, which is separate from the residence of own-ers Mark and Robin Volz. The upper unit is a one-bedroom apartment with a living room (and queen-size sofa bed), bedroom, small kitchen, private bath, and sundeck. The two downstairs units each have a microwave and refrigerator, a private bath, and plenty of country charm.

Eagle's Nest Bed & Breakfast is at 216 Cameron Rd., Kelleys Island; (419) 746-2708 (summer), (winter); eaglesnestbnb.com. Rates: $95 to $179 per night.

Back on the mainland, amusement park aficionados will definitely want to visit one of Ohio's most popular parks, *Cedar Point.* Situated at the tip of a long, narrow peninsula jutting out into Lake Erie, this 364-acre park delights guests with a wide assortment of rides, more than 100 entertainers performing in live shows, and a huge 18-acre waterpark. However, it is the park's unmatched collection of roller coasters that attracts visitors from all over the country. Sixteen in all, they range from junior coasters to the Millen-nium Force, which drops 300 feet at 93 miles per hour, and the 420-foot-tall, 120-miles-per-hour Top Thrill Dragster, the tallest and fastest roller coaster in the world. New in 2013, the GateKeeper is said to be the longest winged roller coaster, boasting a mammoth drop. Riders say it takes your breath away. Check the website at cedarpoint.com for more information.

For those needing accommodations at Cedar Point, the park has its own 650-room lakeside hotel, an all-suites hotel, RV campground, and the Light-house Point upscale camping complex with cabins, cottages, and luxury RV sites. Hotels rooms range from $120 to $650 per night, while standard six-person suites at Sandcastle Suites range from $200 to $450 per night. The cottages and cabins accommodate six people and range from $150 to $295 per night. Only a short drive away is the Breakers Express, a 350-room value-priced hotel. Prices at Breakers Express range from $75 to $190 per night. Accommodations are available early May through the end of Oct.

Two-night packages are available throughout the summer. For reservations, call (419) 627-2106. Cedar Point also has 2 marinas with slips available for day rental.

Cedar Point is on the Cedar Point Causeway, north of Sandusky; (419) 627-2350; cedarpoint.com. Open early May through Aug plus weekends in Sept and Oct.

On the square in the heart of downtown Sandusky, in a magnificent 1920s neoclassical building that once housed the city's post office, is the unique *Merry-Go-Round Museum*. The centerpiece of the museum is a fully restored and operational Allen Herschell carousel; a ride on this indoor gem is an absolute must. But there is much more to discover in this fabulous structure, now listed on the National Register of Historic Places.

Stop by and watch carousel carvers at work. They will explain and show you what it takes to restore neglected pieces, returning them to their full beauty. The museum includes a series of restoration workshops. Also on display are many examples of classic carousel animals, including those of Gustav Dentzel. A replica of his Philadelphia Caroussell Builder shop, which opened in 1867, is authentic down to the sign over the door, the tools on the wall, the workbenches, and the partially carved animals.

The Merry-Go-Round Museum is at the corner of West Washington and Jackson Streets at 301 Jackson, Sandusky; (419) 626-6111; merrygoround museum.org. Open Memorial Day through Labor Day, Mon through Sat, 10 a.m. to 5 p.m.; Sun, noon to 5 p.m. Open Oct through Dec, Wed through Sat, 11 a.m. to 5 p.m.; Sun noon to 5 p.m. Admission: adults $6; senior citizens $5; children (ages 4 to 14) $4 . Admission includes one ride token.

For tranquil accommodations in the heart of Lake Erie vacation coun-try, try a comfortable Sandusky bed-and-breakfast, *Wagner's 1844 Inn.* This fine old structure features 3 guest rooms, each with a private bath, a Victorian parlor with an antique Steinway piano, a living room with a wood-burning fireplace, and a screened porch and enclosed courtyard.

Innkeeper Barbara Wagner decided the time was right for a bed-and-breakfast after her child moved away from home. Barbara gave up her full-time nursing career to operate her own business. As she puts it, "Since I love to cook, entertain, and decorate, a bed-and-breakfast was a logical choice."

Breakfast is served in the formal dining room in the winter and on the porch in summer. A typical morning meal includes fresh fruit and juice, baked rolls or muffins (perhaps the popular pecan rolls), muesli cereal, or a German pancake. Once the home of grocer and dry goods store owner William Simpson, one of the founders of Sandusky, the 1844 Inn is today loaded with antiques. Its style is Italianate, and it is listed on the National Register of Historic Places.

Wagner's 1844 Inn is at 230 E. Washington St., Sandusky; (419) 626-1726; lrbcg.com/wagnersinn. Rates: $75 to $130 per night, double occupancy, including continental breakfast. Reservations recommended.

A bed-and-breakfast with an in-ground swimming pool is hardly typical; **Captain Montague's** offers that and more. A lakefront park, beach, boat basin, amphitheater, and pier are just 2 blocks away. And visitors enjoy murder mystery weekends throughout the year; this bed-and-breakfast has earned top honors for its creative murder mystery series.

Judy and Mike Tann offer accommodations in their southern colonial–style home, which is a generous 6,200 square feet. Built in 1876, the home has 4 Victorian guest bedrooms, each with a private bath, and 1 suite.

Captain Montague's is named for ship captain Charles Montague, who made the house famous for its grand parties at the turn of the 20th century. Four of the guest rooms are named in honor of the Captain, his wife, Sarah, son Newton, and daughter Edith.

The intricately carved solid black walnut front staircase, and the parlor and dining room mantles, are exquisite. The large gazebo, once a carriage house, offers a relaxing place to enjoy the inviting pool surrounded by begonia-filled hanging baskets and an ivy-covered white lattice fence; the Amish-built, adult-size swing set; and the well-manicured gardens, which have garnered numerous awards.

Captain Montague's is at 229 Center St., Huron; (419) 433-4756,

huron's shipbuildingera

Lake Erie's coastal communities boomed during the early 19th century as trade along the lake expanded. Villages located at the mouths of rivers feeding the lake often had natural harbors, and Huron was no exception.

Here shipbuilding flourished, including the construction of the mighty steamships—the royalty of lake vessels. The steamer *Walk-in-the-Water* kicked off the steamship era on Lake Erie in 1818, but met a tragic end when it went down off Buffalo. Huron's shipbuilding dominance ended with the construction of the canal at nearby Milan.

(800) 276-4756; captainmontagues.com. Rates: $135 to $225 per night, double occupancy, including breakfast. Reservations and a deposit required.

The achievements of Ohio-born Thomas Edison are staggering—he invented the phonograph, the incandescent light, the motion picture camera, the fluoroscope, and the nickel-iron-alkaline battery. In fact, at the time of his death Edison held 1,093 different American patents.

The *Edison Birthplace Museum* in Milan provides an opportunity for visitors to learn more about this prolific inventor. Edison's father, Samuel, was involved in the Papineau-Mackenzie Rebellion, an unsuccessful Canadian counterpart to the American Revolution. Samuel migrated to Milan in 1839, attracted by the boom in shipping created there by the canal linking Milan, an inland community, with Lake Erie. In fact, in the 1840s, Milan was one of the world's major grain ports and shipbuilding centers. For example, in 1847, 918,000 bushels of grain were shipped from Milan, and 14 warehouses loaded as many as 20 schooners per day—amazing statistics for a town 8 miles from the lakefront! Milan's boom was short-lived, however, for the coming of the railroad and the flood of 1868 ended the town's brief heyday as a port.

The small, redbrick house where Thomas Edison was born on February 11, 1847, is just up the hill from the former location of Milan's warehouses and port. The Edison home and adjacent small museum contain a number of his inventions—an early mimeograph machine (which Edison sold to the A.B. Dick Company in 1887), phonographs, telegraph equipment, dictating machines, motion picture cameras—and a model of Edison's 1893 movie studio, called the "Black Maria," which rotated and had an adjustable opening in the roof to allow sunlight to illuminate the stage.

Pictures of Edison with family and friends like Henry Ford adorn the walls of the home, and Edison's hat, cape, cane, and slippers are displayed, as is an unusual pig-shaped footstool. Edison bought his birthplace from his sister's family in 1906 and was shocked to find on a visit here in 1923 that this house did not yet have electric lights, a situation he quickly remedied.

The Edison Birthplace Museum is north of OH 113 at 9 N. Edison Dr., Milan; (419) 499-2135; tomedison.org. Open Feb on weekends, 1 to 4 p.m.; March, Wed through Sun, 1 to 4 p.m.; Apr and May, Tues through Sun, 1 to 4 p.m.; June through Aug, Tues through Sat, 10 a.m. to 5 p.m.; Sun 1 to 5 p.m.; Sept and Oct, Tues through Sun, 1 to 5 p.m.; Nov, Wed through Sun,

1 to 4 p.m.; Dec weekends, 1 to 4 p.m. Admission: adults $7; senior citizens $6; children (ages 6 to 12) $4.

Two blocks from Edison's birthplace is Milan's central business district, which was built around a 1-square-block park. Hundred-year-old buildings house many of the town's shops, and the shady park makes Milan a pleasant stop.

Vermilion is perhaps Ohio's most picturesque Lake Erie coastal town, with quaint homes set on meandering lagoons, sumptuous sail and power pleasure craft, and fine dining. Vermilion exudes an atmosphere of peacefulness and prosperity, and attracts visitors with sun, seafood, and recreation.

One Vermilion restaurant warrants special attention—*Old Prague Restaurant.* Set in a delightful cedar structure in the center of Vermilion's shopping district, this distinctive establishment serves both Old World recipes and American favorites. The large, open dining area offers a homey, comfortable setting, and the friendly people at Old Prague make guests feel almost like family.

The specialties at Old Prague are "Nationality Favorites," which include Bohemian goulash, chicken paprikash (farm-fresh chicken in zesty sour cream sauce), and wiener schnitzel. Two other popular entrees are roast duck and roast pork, which are served with sauerkraut. All meals come with traditional egg dumplings or spaetzles.

American dinner entrees include Boston strip steak, ham steak, grilled chicken breast, and roast chicken with stuffing. Those who favor fish can choose from a half dozen dinners such as fresh Lake Erie perch, scallops, broiled salmon, or a fisherman's platter. Lighter fare includes sandwiches, vegetarian risotto, cabbage rolls, salads, and appetizers. Two homemade soups are served daily.

The Old Prague Restaurant is at 5586 Liberty Ave. (US 6), Vermilion; (440) 967-7182; oldprague.com. Open daily June through Oct. Hours vary the rest of the year. Check the website for times.

Presidential Path

Rutherford B. Hayes (or "Ruddy," as he was known to his friends) was president of the US exactly 100 years before Jimmy Carter. For a glimpse at the politics and lifestyle of that era, visit the *Rutherford B. Hayes*

Presidential Center in Fremont. The center, on a lush 25 acres known as Spiegel Grove, consists of a stately Victorian mansion, the expansive Hayes museum, and a presidential library with more than 70,000 volumes.

The museum contains exhibits from Hayes's early career as a lawyer, first in Fremont (which was then known as Lower Sandusky) and later in Cincinnati. Hayes, in fact, was instrumental in having the name of Lower Sandusky changed to Fremont. With nearby towns named Sandusky, and Upper Sandusky, the residents of Fremont gratefully accepted the change, as did the US Post Office.

It was in Cincinnati that Hayes became involved in politics, and old party tickets indicate his first race was in 1859 for city solicitor. At the outbreak of the Civil War, Hayes enlisted in the Union army, and a letter from his wife, Lucy Webb Hayes, written to him while he was in the army, is on display. Hayes was wounded several times during the war, seriously at the Battle of South Mountain.

Nominated for a seat in Congress before the war's conclusion, Hayes refused to leave active duty to campaign. After his four years in Congress, he was elected governor of Ohio in 1867 and 1869, and again in 1875. The museum's campaign relics include political cartoons, newspaper clippings, hats, and banners. Hayes's favorite chair, which he used while governor, is also there.

Hayes's election to the presidency took place in 1876, but a dispute over 20 electoral votes was not resolved until March 2, 1877—three days before the inauguration! By an electoral vote count of 185 to 184, Hayes became the 19th president of the US, defeating New York governor Samuel Tilden. Photographs of Hayes's inauguration are in the museum, as is the Haviland china used by the Hayes White House. A magnificent sideboard carved by Cincinnatian Henry L. Fry for use in the private White House dining room, and the presidential glassware used by presidents from Andrew Jackson through Hayes, are also displayed.

A short walk from the museum across the shady lawn brings you to the elegant Hayes Mansion. This enormous home has 31 rooms, and a large front porch faces the towering trees of Spiegel Grove. Members of the Hayes family lived in the mansion until 1965, when it was opened to the public for guided tours.

President and Mrs. Hayes used many of the furnishings now in the home when they returned to Fremont from Washington in 1881. Many of the pieces were gifts from around the world that they received while in the White House. Although each room has lavish appointments, the dining room, with its massive table for 24 guests, is exceptional. Fourteen fireplaces warmed the spacious residence, some with mantels of Italian marble, others of hand-carved hardwoods with tile insets. The 13-foot ceilings in the drawing room are just tall enough to accommodate the life-size portrait of Hayes and its ornate frame. Throughout the home are the original gas lighting fixtures, which have been converted to electricity.

The Rutherford B. Hayes Presidential Center is at the corner of Buckland and Hayes Avenues in Fremont; (419) 332-2081; rbhayes.org. The museum and residence are open Mon through Sat, 9 a.m. to 5 p.m.; Sun and holidays, noon to 5 p.m. Admission for museum or residence: adults $7.50; senior citizens $6.50; children (ages 6 to 12) $3. A combination ticket to tour both the museum and the home is adults $13; senior citizens $12; children (ages 6 to 12) $5. The library is open Mon through Sat, 9 a.m. to 5 p.m.; no admission charge.

For collectors, the city of Tiffin is well known for its distinctive glass. That legacy continues at *Crystal Traditions of Tiffin.* This glass manufacturing company welcomes visitors to observe glassblowing and handwheel engraving. Sand carving and crystal repair are other services offered. The showroom sells both the company's best and crystal giftware and quality art glass from throughout the world. The outlet offers seconds, closeouts, and discontinued items.

Crystal Traditions of Tiffin is at 145 Madison St., Tiffin; (888) 298-7236; crystaltraditions.com. Open Mon through Fri, 10 a.m. to 5 p.m.; Sat, 10 a.m. to 2 p.m. No admission charge for tours, offered Mon through Fri, 10 a.m. to 5 p.m.

The Firelands region of Ohio takes its name from the Revolutionary War period. While the British held New York City, they made frequent raids against the coastal towns in Connecticut, burning homes, barns, and stores. After the conflict, the citizens petitioned the new state of Connecticut for compensation for their losses, and in 1792 the "fire-sufferers" were awarded land on the western edge of Connecticut's Western Reserve lands in Ohio— the Firelands.

The *Firelands Museum* is operated by the Firelands Historical Society, the second-oldest such society in the state. The museum was described by the society's first members as merely a "cabinet of curios," but today hundreds of items are on display in the two-story Preston-Wickham House, which local newspaper editor Samuel Preston built in 1835 as a wedding present for his daughter, Lucy, and her husband, Frederick Wickham. The extensive gun collection includes dozens of weapons: pistols, rifles, and muskets, some made before the American Revolution, plus military swords and knives. In the Native American exhibit, moccasins, beads, baskets, and tomahawks, as well as ancient points, gouges, and hatchets are displayed.

The basement is filled with an impressive group of pioneer tools, such as a 6-foot blacksmith's bellows, a yarn winder and spinning wheel, butter churns, farm implements, and game traps. On the second floor is a marvelous wooden Indian (ca. 1860) that once stood in front of a local tobacco shop, and the bell clapper from the old Norwalk courthouse that burned down in 1913 (the bell melted in the heat). Period clothing and personal items from early residents of the region are exhibited, as is the first organ manufactured by Norwalk's A.B. Chase Company in the 1870s.

The Firelands Museum is at 4 Case Ave., Norwalk; (419) 668-6038; firelandsmuseum.org. From June through Aug, the museum is open Tues through Sat, 10 a.m. to 3 p.m.; Sun, noon to 4 p.m. Open weekends in May, Sept, and Oct, Sat, 10 a.m. to 3 p.m.; Sun, noon to 4 p.m. Admission: adults $5; senior citizens $4; children (ages 12 to 18) $3.

The elegant exterior of the *Georgian Manor Inn* reflects the civility and elegance of another era. The Georgian revival home, built in 1906 by a local dentist, is now an elegant bed-and-breakfast nicely located on 1.4 acres and surrounded by a number of large historic homes and estates. Each of the 4 guest rooms in the 27-room mansion is decorated with antiques and reproductions. The sunroom, the library, the living room with its oak-manteled fireplace, and the parlor offer comfortable indoor surroundings, but guests are often drawn to the tranquility of the gardens and 2 porches. A patio looks out over a 3-foot waterfall and small stream that flows into a lovely pond. In spring and summer, the gardens are filled with the color and scent of a variety of herbs and flowers.

The Georgian Manor Inn is at 123 W. Main St., Norwalk; (419) 663-8132, (800) 668-1644; georgianmanorinn.com. Lodging rates: $140 to $210 per night.

When John Wright arrived in America in 1843, a young man of 20, he dreamed of one day building a vast estate similar to those in his native England. Forty years later, after acquiring 2,400 acres, he established a sawmill and kiln to prepare lumber and brick for what is today known as *Wright Mansion.*

When listed on the National Register of Historic Places in 1974, the Wright family home was declared significant as "an unusually substantial and stately example of the Second Empire–style mansion found as a relatively isolated farmhouse rather than an urban residence." But for a "farmhouse," Wright's home was constructed with many surprisingly modern conveniences, thanks to his ingenuity. For example, he installed two bathrooms with running water and flush toilets that were supplied with water pumped by a windmill to a large tank on the third floor. This at a time—the 1880s—when most rural residences still used water pitchers and chamber pots.

Piped natural gas was unheard of in this country setting before 1900, but Wright developed his own gas system, making acetylene in a small brick building at a corner of his front yard and routing it to chandeliers on all three floors of his home. And a central heating plant in the basement sent hot steam to radiators throughout the house.

The Wright Mansion is the centerpiece of *Historic Lyme Village,* a 16-structure collection of historic buildings. Tours of Wright Mansion take visitors past magnificent woodwork used throughout this expansive residence: beams and rafters of oak, and intricate interior trim of walnut, curly maple, and cherry.

After walking past the huge parlor doors, visitors find room after room of period furnishings, including Wright's piano. A graceful staircase ascends to the second floor, which has 8 bedrooms. Most of the third floor is a huge ballroom, with a stage set directly under the central tower at the front of the home.

More rustic structures make up the rest of Lyme Village. Ohio settler pieces, such as a rope bed, spinning wheel, and wood cooking stove, furnish Annie Brown's log home, built in 1851 in Seneca County. Ms. Brown occupied this modest house from 1869 to 1951.

Spinning and weaving exhibits (and occasional demonstrations) can be found in the Schriner Log House, an 1870-vintage structure that was used as a residence until 1947. Other occasional Lyme Village demonstrations include blacksmithing and woodworking at the North Adams Barn, built more than a century ago.

Antique farm implements fill the Biebricher Centennial Barn (erected in 1876), a Gothic board-and-batten building with unusual louvered windows. The Seymour House, moved to Lyme Village in 1976 to save it from demolition, is one of the oldest homes in this part of Ohio, and it served as the Seymour family home for more than a century (1836–1948). It likely was a stop on the Underground Railroad. Today it houses country furnishings typical of the early 19th century, including a fabulous old pump organ. Other structures of note include the Merry School House, built in the 1860s and used as a school until 1935; the Detterman Church, built in 1848 and believed to be one of only two known remaining original log churches in Ohio; and Schug Hardware, the hardware collection from Bellevue's C.W. Schug Hardware, which was in business from 1927 until the 1980s. Visitors may also explore the Cooper-Fries General Store, filled with displays and merchandise, and the Greenslade Cobbler's Shop.

Lyme Village also includes a unique museum—the Postmark Collectors Club Museum. Formerly housed in private homes, a converted school bus, and in a building that twice served as the Lyme, Ohio, post office, the museum has found a permanent home in the Groton Township Hall. Millions of postmarks—the "cancels" used by postal authorities to show where mail originated and to void stamps—fill the museum, the most extensive such collection in the world.

Historic Lyme Village is at 5001 OH 4, just east of Bellevue; (419) 483-4949; lymevillage.com. Tours are given June through Aug, Tues through Sat, 11 a.m. to 4 p.m., and Sun, noon to 4 p.m.; Sept Sun, noon to 4 p.m. Admission: adults $9; senior citizens $8; children (ages 6 to 12) $5.

Railroad buffs, youngsters, and anyone who has ever dreamed of being the engineer on a fast-moving freight train as it streaks across the countryside will want to climb aboard the many trains displayed at the *Mad River & NKP Railroad Society Museum.* On self-guided tours of the rail yard, you'll discover a number of intriguing locomotives, passenger cars, and even cabooses. Many of these are open, permitting you to virtually walk through railroad history.

Those who are knowledgeable about trains especially appreciate some of the Nickel Plate Road additions to the museum's collection, including

Alco RSD-12 Diesel and Dynamometer Car X50041. But anyone will enjoy visiting the RPO Post Office Car, complete with mail sacks, sorting bins, and mail crane. Inside the Nickel Plate Box Car and Fruit Growers Refrigerator Car are extensive displays of railroad models, lanterns, locks, timetables, signs, photos, badges, and the like.

And when you climb into the cab of the museum's Wabash F Diesel, you can't help but imagine yourself racing along the main line from New York to Chicago or crossing the Rockies on your way to deliver freight to the West Coast. From the cupola of a caboose, you get a feel for the working environment at the other end of a long freight train, while tours of America's first dome car demonstrate how trains treated their passengers in days gone by.

An old section house serves as the welcome center for the museum. It's staffed by volunteers, many of them current and former railroad workers who enjoy answering questions and explaining life on the rails. Be sure to ask about upcoming railroad excursions on Ohio tracks.

The Mad River & NKP Railroad Society Museum is on Southwest Street, just south of US 20, Bellevue; (419) 483-2222; madrivermuseum.org. Open daily, noon to 4 p.m., Memorial Day to Labor Day; weekends only in May, Sept, and Oct. Admission: adults $7; senior citizens $6; children (ages 3 to 12) $4.

Widely known as the "Earth Crack," **Seneca Caverns** was designated a Registered Natural Landmark in 1997. Discovered in 1872, the cave was opened to the public by the Bell family in 1933.

A one-hour tour takes visitors through 7 rooms or levels, the deepest 110 feet below the surface to the Ole Mist'ry River. Fossilized fish, shells, and corals are visible throughout the limestone cavern, which remains a cool 54 degrees year-round. Comfortable walking shoes are a must. Visitors also may pan for gemstones and minerals at the cavern or browse the gift shop.

Seneca Caverns is off OH 269, 4 miles south of Bellevue; (419) 483-6711; senecacavernsohio.com. Open daily Memorial Day to Labor Day, 9 a.m. to 7 p.m.; weekends only in May and from Sept to mid-Oct, 10 a.m. to 5 p.m. Rates: adults $15; senior citizens $13; children (ages 13 to 17) $13; children (ages 5 to 12) $8.

Places to Stay in Northwest Ohio

HURON

Captain Montague's
229 Center St.
(419) 433-4756
captainmontagues.com

KELLEYS ISLAND

Eagle's Nest Bed & Breakfast
216 Cameron Rd.
(419) 746-2708 (summer),
(419) 625-9635 (winter)
eaglesnestbnb.com

MIDDLE BASS ISLAND

St. Hazards on the Beach
(800) 837-5211
sthazards.com

NORWALK

Georgian Manor Inn
123 W. Main St.
(419) 663-8132,
(800) 668-1644
georgianmanorinn.com

PORT CLINTON

Five Bells Inn
2766 Sand Rd.
(888) 734-1555
fivebellsinn.com

Scenic Rock Ledge Inn and Cabins
2772 E. Sand Rd.
(419) 734-3265,
(877) 994-7625
scenicrockledgeinn.com

PUT-IN-BAY

English Pines Bed and Breakfast
182 Concord Ave.
(419) 285-2521
englishpines.com

SANDUSKY

Wagner's 1844 Inn
230 E. Washington St.
(419) 626-1726
lrbcg.com/wagnersinn

Places to Eat in Northwest Ohio

ARCHBOLD

Barn Restaurant
North of Archbold,
¼ mile east of OH 66
(419) 445-2231
saudervillage.org

CATAWBA ISLAND

Mon Ami Restaurant and Winery
3845 E. Wine Cellar Rd.
(419) 797-4445
monamiwinery.com

HELPFUL WEBSITES

Ohio Division of Travel and Tourism:
discoverohio.com

Toledo Convention and Visitors Bureau:
dotoledo.org

Toledo Blade:
toledoblade.com

Ottawa County Visitors Bureau:
shoreandislands.com

Cedar Point:
cedarpoint.com

GRAND RAPIDS

LaRoe's Restaurant
24138 Front Street
(419) 832-3082
laroesrestaurant.com

TOLEDO

Tony Packo's Cafe
1902 Front St.
(419) 691-6054
tonypacko.com

VERMILION

Old Prague Restaurant
5586 Liberty Ave.
(440) 967-7182
oldprague.com

Index